Nkrumah & the Chiefs

The Politics of Chieftaincy in Ghana 1951–60

RICHARD RATHBONE

*Professor of Modern History of Africa
in the University of London*

F. Reimmer
ACCRA

Ohio University Press
ATHENS

James Currey
OXFORD

James Currey
73 Botley Road
Oxford OX2 0BS

F. Reimmer Book Services
20 Abebresem St.
PO Box CT 3499
Cantonments Accra, Ghana

Ohio University Press
Scott Quadrangle
Athens, Ohio 45701

British Library Cataloguing in Publication Data
Rathbone, R. J. A. R. (Richard John Alex Ruben), 1942-
Nkrumah & the chiefs : the politics of chieftaincy in
Ghana, 1951-1960. - (West African Studies)
1. Nkrumah, Kwame, 1909-1972 2. Chiefdoms 3. Ghana - Politics
and government - To 1957 4. Ghana - Politics and government
- 1957-1979
I. Title
966.7'05
     ISBN 0-85255-771-X (James Currey paper)
     ISBN 0-85255-770-1 (James Currey cloth)

Library of Congress Cataloging-in-Publication Data
Rathbone, Richard.
Nkrumah and the chiefs : the politics of chieftancy in Ghana, 1951–1960/Richard Rathbone.
  p. cm. -- (West African series)
Includes bibliographical references and index.
ISBN 0-8214-1305-8 (cloth : alk. paper) — ISBN 0-8214-1306-6 (paper : alk. paper)
  1. Ghana--Politics and government. 2. Ghana--Politics and government--1957-1979. 3. Local government--Ghana--History--20th century. 4. Nkrumah, Kwame, 1909-1972. 5. Chiefdoms--Ghana--History--20th century. 6. Tribal government--Ghana--History--20th century. 6. Tribal government--Ghana--History--20th century. 7. Convention People's Party (Ghana)--History. I. Title. II. West African series (Oxford, England).

DT511.R28 1999
320.9667'09'045--dc21

                          99-046031

Typeset in 10.6/11.6 pt Monotype Ehrhardt
by Long House Publishing Services, Cumbria, UK
Printed in Great Britain
by Villiers Publications, London N3

Nkrumah & the Chiefs

Western African Studies

Contents

List of Maps & Photographs

Preface

All books are difficult to write, a matter sometimes overlooked by overenthusiastic reviewers who have yet to see themselves in print rather than typescript. In purely artisanal terms, the research effort which underpins this volume was simple enough. It is a direct result of several years immersion in the archives of both Ghana and the United Kingdom, the reading of as much of Ghana's press as remains and treasured conversations with veteran Ghanaian politicians and chiefs. Most of this was a labour of love; as it is for most professional historians, research is high on my list of earthly delights. But this research has been especially enjoyable as it involved two further extended research periods in Ghana. For over 30 years Ghana and Ghanaians have been kind to me and research there has always been an ideal combination of hard labour and the pleasure of the company of friends seen all too infrequently. All researchers encounter problems on an almost daily basis, but the thrill of the chase, the joy of finding the evidence which solves this or that problem and a fine research environment all conspired to make this research unusually rewarding.

So the reasons why this was hard to write were not the usual technical problems of frustrated access to sources or inadequate research funding. They had much more to do with the uncomfortable things the evidence seemed to be saying. That discomfort can only be explained by a fragment of biography. Like many of my generation of historians of Africa, I was a refugee from the better-trodden paths of English and European history. The intellectual attractions of African history and its challenges were considerable. But for a young scholar in the 1960s, Africa's allure was also a personal and emotional matter. Africa was seductive because of its radical rejection of oppression and most particularly its increasingly successful combat with colonialism, which are achievements I continue to celebrate.

That enthusiasm had a great deal to do with Ghana which I first came to know as a blissfully happy undergraduate exchange student at the University in Legon in 1963. That experience entirely persuaded me that if Africa was the continent of

Preface

the future, then Ghana was in the vanguard of positive change. This involved hero worship which is always forgivable in the young. The hero was of course Kwame Nkrumah. My return to Ghana in 1966 coincided with Ghana's first military intervention and the deposition of Nkrumah which I regarded as a tragedy. In the wake of that drama, however, I encountered for the first time numbers of Ghanaians who did not share my enthusiasm for this great figure of 20th-century history. For some Ghanaians Nkrumah and his governments had seemed excessively oppressive. The numerous commissions of enquiry which raked over the proximate past after the coup in 1966 certainly produced evidence of corruption and misgovernment. But I retained an essentially heroic view of the by then exiled ex-president, whose past achievements had, I believed, been undermined by the misgovernment and peculation of his lieutenants, and by international developments over which he had no control. Broadly that remained my position. I knew too much to share the full hagiographical intensity of those whose writings came close to canonizing Nkrumah. But I also knew far too much not to recognize his singular greatness.

Much of my earlier work had concerned the history of government in Ghana. But the research for my last book, *Murder and politics in colonial Ghana*, took me away from events in Accra and into the past of country-dwellers. Here for the first time I encountered what I believe to be a somewhat under-acknowledged problematic in recent Ghanaian historical writing, namely chieftaincy. Before this, my view of chieftaincy was patronizing at best and dismissive at worst. As I come from a culture in which the peripheral tags of the past – kings and queens, palaces and processions – also haunt the present, Ghana seemed to be familiar territory. Chieftaincy was, I felt, harmless, romantic flummery which had precious little to do with the brave new world for which *real* Ghanaians strove.

But several years spent in the company of the shade of one of Ghana's greatest kings of the 20th century, Nana Sir Ofori Atta, and those living witnesses who knew him, taught me that chieftaincy mattered very greatly. As I learnt more, it was clear that the domestic political history of Ghana in the 1930s and 1940s was incomprehensible without an active consideration of the fate of chieftaincy. Its central significance is less apparent in the extensive secondary literature, including some of my own work, largely because we were all, quite understandably, more fascinated by the central epic of Ghana's recent history, namely the rise of nationalism and the ending of colonial rule. My concern with the recent history of a great pre-colonial African kingdom, Akyem Abuakwa, and its royal family suggested that there was more to Ghana's recent history than nationalist triumph. There was another story, that of the ways in which nationalists and nationalist governments sought to control the countryside. At the centre of those struggles lay the chiefs and their institutions.

The great collection of evidence on the ending of colonial rule to be found in the Public Record Office at Kew, some of which I published in *Ghana; British documents on the end of Empire*, reinforces the idea that the history of nationalism should dominate our vision of Ghanaian history in the 1940s and 1950s. It is scarcely surprising that this *colonial* record documents the struggles of a colonial power with its local opponents. But the records in the National Archives of Ghana for the same period and beyond tell a rather different story. This is essentially a rich collection on the history and politics of governance *in* Ghana. By 1951 those records have a great deal to say about how Kwame Nkrumah and his Convention Peoples' Party sought to govern and direct Ghanaians. It has surprisingly little to tell us about the CPP's struggle with the government of the United Kingdom. It has, rather, a great deal to say about establishing control over Ghana. A central feature of that story was those governments' attempts to break, co-opt and coerce chieftaincy. Had chieftaincy been the attractive, decaying anachronism I once believed it to have been, it would never have warranted the enormous amount of government time, and consequently the enormous quantity of records, devoted to these processes.

As a result of my research I came to understand and even sympathize with some of the impatient perceptions of chieftaincy demonstrated by Kwame Nkrumah's governments. But that same research produced a much grimmer, more equivocal narrative than I had expected. The assault upon chieftaincy in southern Ghana, which is the central concern of this book, was a much rougher story than I had expected to encounter. Despite that, I stand by what I have previously said in print; criticisms of Nkrumah and the CPP governments of 1951–66 must be qualified by an informed awareness of their limited choices. But in what follows, some readers might share my sense that the CPP's drive for its own brand of progress was at times cynical and even brutal. What was personally upsetting was learning that what was being ground down in these processes was far from being marginal. Chieftaincy, the evidence insists, was and is part of Ghana's long history and part of what makes Ghana distinctive and remarkable.

This book will anger those for whom Nkrumah must always be a saint rather than a hugely important national and international politician. It will also anger those in Ghana who consider the years during which Nkrumah dominated Ghana as the first act of a much longer nightmare, as I do not go nearly far enough for them either. But as I have suggested, learning this history has been a painful experience for a middle-aged scholar forced by the evidence to recognize that the hero of his adolescence was a ruthless as well as a great politician. This is accordingly a book written with some sadness; it is a book in which there are very few jokes.

I acknowledge with sincere gratitude the generosity of the British Academy whose funding allowed me to work extensively in Ghana on two separate occasions in the 1990s. The School of Oriental and African Studies was also generous in giving me two periods of study leave in the same decade; my greatest debt is to my colleagues in an outstanding History Department who support the research effort of individuals by bearing, without complaint, heavier teaching loads during absences. In Ghana my much-loved fictive kinswoman, my Auntie, Emily Asiedu, made me feel happy as well as comfortable by opening her home to me and by her unfailing kindness. My dear, much respected friend Professor Robert Addo-Fening again spared me time and shared his great command of his country's history. In Kyebi I enjoyed the kindness of Guggisberg Ofori-Atta and A.K. Amoako-Atta and I wish to record my thanks to the late Okyenhene Osagyefo

Preface

Kuntunkununku II for permission to use the State Archives. In the National Archives I was greatly helped once more by Cletus Anzeogwu and Joseph Anim-Asante and the rest of the helpful but terribly underpaid staff. At the university I was made welcome by the late Professor Kofi Agovi whose premature death is a great loss to African studies. Still at Legon I offer thanks to my colleagues Drs Akosua Perbi and Kojo Amanor and the staff in the Institute of African Studies and Balme Libraries. As I finished this book I learnt of the death of Isaac Tufuo, 'Sir Isaac', a fine historian and a wonderful friend for over 30 years. Professors Nana Arhin Brempong (Kwame Arhin) and A. Adu Boahen made time for me, again, in busy schedules. Lastly I am deeply grateful for the time and memory given so freely over many years by a number of veterans, some now sadly dead. Over the years I have learnt much from Ako Adjei, Bafour Akoto, R.R. Amponsah, Modesto Apaloo, Kojo Botsio and Komla Gbedemah. The guidance and kindness of the scholar and chief, Nana Agyeman Badu, Dormaahene, whose tragic death also occurred while I was finishing this book, are a happy memory.

In Europe and the USA I am grateful to many friends and colleagues who have helped me in various ways, most especially Emmanuel Akyeampong, Jean Allman, Moses and Ernie Anafu, Fusao Ariga, Stefano Boni, Alistair Chisholm, Natasha Gray, Ann Hugon, John Lonsdale, Tom McCaskie, John Parker, J.D.Y. Peel and Ivor Wilks. Being edited by a publisher who is also a fine historian, Douglas Johnson, was exciting as well as always supportive; his appointment of an inspired but anonymous manuscript reader provided me with invaluable pages by an outstandingly perceptive critic of an earlier draft. Above all, my sincere thanks go to my wife Frances, for everything. None of these fine people is responsible for the errors and misperceptions; these remain mine and mine alone.

Note on Orthography & Titles

For those who are new to Ghanaian history, place names and personal names pose problems because of the shifting orthography of Twi, the language of the Akan people with whom this book is concerned. Although there are standard forms today, many people still use older orthography as does much of the archival and other material used in this book. I have tried to use the current orthography when using my own words but have also tried to honour the original sources by using their exact words. Thus readers will find that the great city of the Asante, Kumase, is usually given as 'Kumasi' in the sources. The same is true for a number of other place names such as Kyebi, whose older form is Kibi, Akyem Abuakwa which has replaced Akim Abuakwa, Kwawu for Kwahu, Akuapem for Akwapim, Fante for Fanti and so on. You will soon get the hang of it.

Confusingly, Twi-speakers use the word *oman* to denote both a town and a state – testimony to the importance of towns in Akan state formation. A chief or king of a town or state is denoted by the suffix '-hene'. Thus the king of the *oman* of Mampong is known as the Mamponghene or the Omanhene of Mampong. The other chiefly titles are explained as they emerge in the text. There is a prefix shift from 'o' to 'a' to denote plurals, e.g. *oman/aman*.

A final problem concerns the frequent confusion between Asante and Ashanti. I have used Asante throughout to denote the people of that great Twi-speaking confederation and Ashanti to denote the administrative region of that name. Not everyone who lived in the Ashanti region was Asante; many Asante lived outside the Ashanti Region.

A paramount chief greets Prime Minister Nkrumah (*West Africa*)

Above. The Okyenhene addresses a gathering including prime minister Nkrumah at the opening of a new road in Akyem Abuakwa in 1952 (*West Africa*)
Below. The prime minister opens a new post office at Coaltar-Kraboa in Akyem Abuakwa. The Okyenhene is on the left of the photograph (*West Africa*)

The Ghanaian cabinet at independence, March 1957. *Seated left to right:* the Hon A. E. Inkumsah (Housing); the Hon Kojo Botsio (Trade and Labour); the Hon Kwame Nkrumah (Prime Minister); the Hon K. A. Gbedemah (Finance); the Hon A. Casely Hayford (Communications); *Standing left to right,* are the Hon A. Ofori-Atta (Local Government) the Hon N. A. Welbeck (Works); the Hon B. Yeboah-Afari (Agriculture); the Hon J. H. Allassan (Health); the Hon J. B. Erzuah (Education); the Hon L. R. Abavana (Minister without Portfolio); the Hon Ako Adjei, (Interior); the Hon Krobo Edusei (Minister without Portfolio) (*Ghana Information Services*)

The Asantehene in 1960 (*Ivor Wilks*)

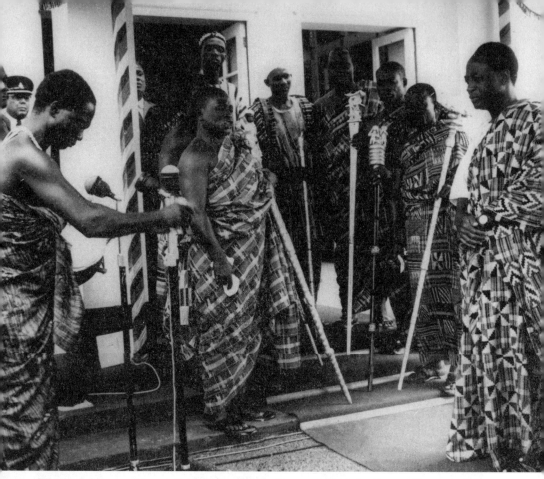

Nkrumah is greeted by traditional linguists at the opening of the first parliament of the first Republic in 1960 (*West Africa*)

1

Introduction

On an overcast day in 1995, an extraordinary event was held in the main football stadium in Kumase, central Ghana. The late king of the great west African forest kingdom of Asante, Asantehene Otumfuo Opoku Ware II, celebrated the 25th anniversary of his accession, his enstoolment, in a dignified dazzle of gold which compensated for the lack of sun. It was a rare occasion not least because Ghana is a poor country. Sumptuous spectacles of this sort are very costly and this was to prove a very sumptuous spectacle indeed; and, unusually for a Ghanaian occasion, it was one that was shared by millions of television viewers throughout the world, for the event was covered by the world's press and most especially by CNN. Showing the video of this event to students who have never been to West Africa is, for me, always like looking at it for the first time. What they mostly want to know is utterly reasonable. Quite what is that we were watching?

On the surface the event was pure *National Geographic Magazine* or The Discovery Channel. It was a day-long ceremony involving praise-singing, drumming and the state parade of all this great king's sub-chiefs paying him respect and offering him their obedience. Each chief or queen-mother was arrayed in distinctive locally woven, dyed or appliqué cloth. Each was weighed down quite literally by numerous rings, necklaces and crowns, the products of the ancient arts of the region's goldsmiths and all made from the distinctively coloured, locally mined gold. For those who have read some of the considerable body of pre-colonial writing on the kingdom of Asante and especially the work of Thomas Bowdich,[1] it all seems comfortably familiar. The Asantehene holding court in public, captured forever on state-of-the-art video-recording technology, looks remarkably like the wonderful, justly famous coloured illustration in Bowdich's book of a similar festival held in that excited foreigner's presence nearly two centuries before.

There is a great romantic temptation to see this as evidence of timelessness, or of age-old tradition unchanged save for the odd chief wearing Ray Bans or a

[1] *Mission from Cape Coast Castle to Ashantee.*

1

digital watch. But that simply will not do. Ghana is a modern state and its citizens are people whose world-view is more informed by the Internet and MTV than by the shadows of the forgotten ancestors. The majority of the chiefs we see are, unlike their ancestors pictured in the sketch in Bowdich, men and women with modern professional qualifications. Of those I recognized, there were several university teachers, a gynaecologist, lawyers, accountants, and so on. They drive cars, own credit cards and know their way around Hamburg and Manhattan. Was it therefore just a pageant, just a bunch of enthusiasts who enjoy recreational dressing-up, like those stalwarts who re-fight the English or the American civil wars with such extraordinary gravity? More cynically, was it perhaps a well-judged show, just a means of bringing large numbers of tourists and their hard currency to Ghana?

Analogies and materialist suggestions are at best rather weak explanations. This great event was about celebrating a great king and an ancient state. Although every Ghanaian present on that day, and there were hundreds of thousands of them as well as the press corps in the stadium that day, would have seen the events in a variety of ways, nuanced by their own experiences and feelings. It was a mighty affirmation of Ghana, of Asante and rather remarkably, for reasons which will become apparent, of chieftaincy itself. It is remarkable because the decade of Ghanaian politics with which this book is primarily concerned looked very like the attentuated death-throes of chieftaincy at the time. For many Asante, that day in 1995 was also a celebration of the survival of chieftaincy against very heavy odds.

For outsiders, the persistence of chieftaincy in Ghana is bewildering. And it is very persistent. Any casual reader of Ghana's numerous daily and Sunday newspapers would be struck first of all by their very direct, robust, even vitriolic political style. No less arresting is the earnestness with which intimate personal matters like the toils of discordant marriages, those unlovable in-laws from hell or the fearful, fumbling discoveries of adolescence are discussed. Lastly there are the seemingly endless enthusiastic pages devoted to the Ghanaian love affair with sport and especially football. A more dedicated content-analysis would suggest something which looks like a paradox in a very modern state like Ghana. There are innumerable stories about major and minor chiefs and the contests for chieftaincy, some of which occasionally have violent and even bloody repercussions.[2] The considerable frequency of such accounts suggests that Ghana's experienced journalists[3] and the market-sensitive men and women who own these newspapers, regard stories about chieftaincy as the kind of eye-catching material, 'good copy', that their numerous readers relish; in a very competitive market one must assume that proprietors and editors know or at least believe that these stories help to sell

[2] The density of these stories is considerable. For example on a very few days the following stories appeared: '4 elevated Techiman chiefs welcome probe', *Ghanaian Times*, 2 March 1996; 'Mpraeso chieftaincy dispute', *The Statesman*, 3 March 1996; 'Chiefs and politics', *The Ghanaian Chronicle*, 7 March 1996; 'Chiefs and moral responsibility', *Ghanaian Times*, 7 March 1996; 'Chiraa-Wenchi lands', *Ghanaian Chronicle*, 14 March 1996; 'Boy 15 killed in stool dispute', *Ghanaian Times*, 21 March 1996 and so on.

[3] A Ghanaian career which had its beginnings in the early 19th century and for which many train today in the well-respected School of Journalism in Accra.

newspapers. While this is a set of impressionistic comments by a frequent visitor to Ghana who tries to read every newspaper each day, it is not merely my observation. Paul Nugent has also noted that 'ordinary Ghanaians take chieftaincy very seriously' and that 'chieftaincy is seldom far from the centre of the frame'.[4] Chiefs, chieftaincy wrangles and the behaviour of royal families are big news in Ghana.

My earlier suggestion that this might seem to be a paradox is made for good reasons. For the last 50 years at the very least it has been frequently stated by Ghanaian and non-Ghanaian observers that chieftaincy in Ghana, and in the rest of Africa for that matter, would wither and eventually die a natural death. Modernization in its many forms was, the argument went, creating an entirely new kind of citizenry in Africa for whom these ancient forms of government would have less and less relevance; thus, chieftaincy would enjoy declining appeal and would eventually die with precious few mourners at the collective graveside. In the case of Ghana, a highly literate and increasingly much travelled, sophisticated, internationalist elite and an ever increasing number of urbanized people involved in modern occupations surely had little time for the arbitrary rule of men and, very much less frequently women, whose major qualification for office, power and respect was the happy accident of high birth.

This has always seemed to be an entirely logical argument to me. It seems, after all, to be supported by the lessons of universal history. The great outburst of radical and popular nationalism in Africa which followed the ending of the Second World War was both a clamour for independence from overseas domination, from colonialism, and for modern representative democracy of the sort colonialism explicitly and implicitly denied to its subjects. Chieftaincy and democracy appeared to be definitionally antithetical even if some chiefs, like autocrats everywhere, claimed that they exercised power democratically.

African nationalism after 1945 was undoubtedly revolutionary; colonial rule and chieftaincy were widely perceived to be unheavenly twins linked by mutual support, an unholy alliance, and they were thus jointly destined to enjoy the fate of all doomed *anciens régimes*. Moreover nationalist ideology, and its translation into policy throughout Africa, was very insistent about the imperatives of material modernization and economic transformation. Chiefs were widely regarded as barriers to the achievement of either of these goals; they stood for the past, for other-worldly values, and were opposed to both individualism and modernizing corporatism. The processes by which chiefs ruled, the rituals and ideas which maintained their authority, were, it was widely claimed, the enemies of rapid transformation. Africa's and Africans' besetting problems were broadly those of 'underdevelopment'; chieftaincy was seen as a significant aspect of the problem rather than as part of the solution.

Nationalists as well as history argued that chieftaincy would wither and they had, as we shall see, good instrumental as well as intellectual grounds for insisting upon this. Many first-rate scholars, both African and non-African, wrote

[4] In 'An abandoned project', *Journal of Legal Pluralism and Unofficial Law*, p. 204.

extensively about the remarkable changes which were taking place in Africa after the Second World War. But it is instructive to pause and consider what informed their predictions about chieftaincy in the midst of all this ferment. Without exception these scholars had cut their intellectual teeth on the apparently ineluctable world-historical processes which had destroyed the power of aristocracies from Paris to Peking and accordingly, without compromising their intellectual integrity, they could and would happily agree with the nationalists. Just like the nationalists, they too were convinced that chieftaincy was every bit as anachronistic as colonialism. Chieftaincy would die just as religion was supposed to fade as material progress and scientific endeavour made for its social and emotional redundancy.

Not everyone felt that chieftaincy was doomed to disappear. David Apter, one of the most perceptive analysts of Ghana's politics in the 1950s, believed in mutation rather than outright extinction. The functional significance of chieftaincy was, he argued by the mid-1950s, being 'transposed in kind via charisma to the larger social membership around the symbol of nationhood' and especially around the particularly alluring personality of Kwame Nkrumah.[5] But Apter was very much in a minority. In Africa, as elsewhere, nationalism was the offspring of material progress; material progress demanded rational, legal and bureaucratic systems and not the arbitrary day-to-day management by individuals qualified by little more than descent. Chieftaincy, rooted in custom and sustained by its mediation with and sometimes control of the supernatural, could not cohabit happily for long with capitalism, the internal combustion engine, literacy, the telephone and international travel.

These calculations were not entirely false. But part of the concern of this book is with the disconcerting tenacity of chieftaincy in southern Ghana. It focuses in particular on a decade in which chieftaincy was undermined and then re-configured by hostile governments bent on its subjugation. It certainly does not argue that what survives is merely the most recent recension of an unchanging tradition; that would be silly as well as utterly wrong. Chieftaincy today in Ghana and more widely in Africa is very precisely the result of historical processes which have changed much of its essence over time; modern chieftaincy is very definitely not an unaltered relic of the past even if most chieftaincy is, as is high office anywhere, quite literally decorated with the peripheral if often eye-catching emblems of the past. Nor does this book claim to have discovered what chieftaincy either was or is. Even in so small a state as Ghana, chieftaincy can never be more than a neat way of expressing considerable variety. Chieftaincy has been shaped by values of strikingly different cultural traditions and consequently carries sharply differing meanings from area to area. Even more importantly, each chiefdom has its own particular contingent history dating from the depths of the largely unknowable past to the present. What unites them all is their experience of an assault upon them which altered them in ways which went far beyond the shifts and adaptations which inhere in less traumatic historical change.

---

5 *The Gold Coast in Transition*, p. 305.

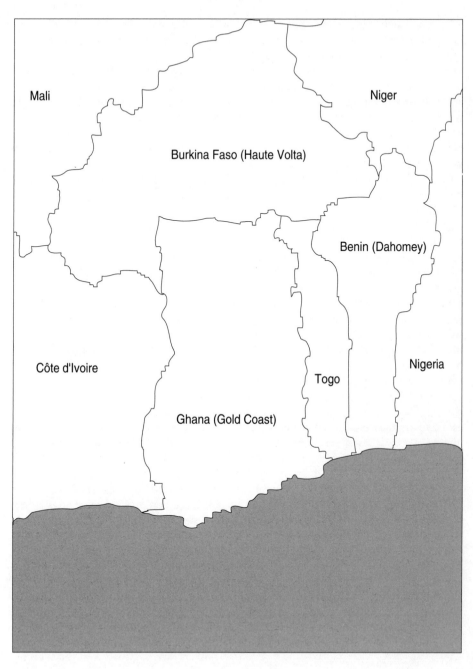

Map 1.1 The Gold Coast (Ghana)

Introduction

The implicit argument of this book is that the nature of Ghana's historiography has tended to obscure the absolute importance of chieftaincy in its recent history. This is relatively simply explained. For scholars of my generation who began working on Africa in the 1960s, and for many of those who taught us, the *terminus ad quem* of African history was that continent's liberation from colonial rule. That exciting process, those exhilarating moments when the past visibly, tangibly and thrillingly gave way to the future, was what drew many of us to the field. Our enthusiasm and idealism needs no apology even if it might now seem very dated, probably romantic and even quaint with hindsight. But its intellectual consequence was the construction of a linear, even evolutionary historical approach which stressed the importance of the scholarly generation of an affirmative narrative history of resistance and modernization over the *longue durée*.

The most sympathetic heroes of these narratives were the founding fathers and mothers of what became the varied nationalist elites and the liberation movements they built. Such people were courageously to defy colonial power and to lead their countries towards the radical reassertion of the sovereignty temporarily denied to them by colonial rule. Those with different agendas, a cohort which included many chiefs, were widely perceived as essentially conservative, even reactionary obstacles to progress. At worst they were denigrated as 'collaborators' with colonial regimes and at best doomed to be regarded as pathetic archaic forces whose days were numbered.[6] Being unfashionable, their political ideas, and they did have interesting political ideas, have been largely ignored and their struggles with the political forces that came to dominate in the years following independence have been marginalized in the better known master narratives.[7]

In the case of Ghana this has led to a scholarly concentration upon the extremely stimulating history of nationalism whose roots were quite accurately ascribed to the mid-19th century. For many scholars, nationalism and modern history were almost interchangeable ideas. It is worth remembering that despite Ghana's physical and demographic smallness, more had been written about the political party led by Nkrumah, the Convention Peoples' Party, which took Ghana into independence, than on any African political party until South Africa's African National Congress came to the fore in the 1970s.[8] And more had been written on Nkrumah than on any other individual African until the memorable release from detention of Nelson Mandela.

Of course not all of that literature was enthusiastic about the CPP or Nkrumah; but that is scarcely the point. Whether the CPP was regarded positively as the vanguard party of assertive, progressive, left-wing anti-colonialism in Africa or negatively as authoritarian and corrupt, or even the cat's paw of Moscow's imperial

---

[6] An example is provided by a reviewer of D. Austin's *Politics in Ghana* who wrote them off for 'their reactionary ideas and their dedication to tribalistic and ritualistic oligarchy'. See *African Affairs*, Vol. 64, No. 255, January 1965.

[7] I try to argue this case at greater length in *Nana Sir Ofori Atta and the conservative nationalist tradition in Ghana*, p. 13.

[8] Although there is still a great deal we do not know about the history of the party.

pretensions, it was still the cynosure of Africanists' gaze. That owed a very great deal to the huge significance of the pioneering role of Ghana's nationalist movement for Africa as a whole and to the considerable personal attraction of its leading figure, Nkrumah. But almost without exception, the CPP's battles with the British dominate these accounts. Its domestic policy, its internal wars, most significantly those fought with some of the country's 'traditional rulers', have received far less attention.

Nationalism in Africa always combined two agendas. The first of these, about which a great deal has been written, was the forced expulsion of colonial overrule. The second has a much slighter literature. That concerns its commitment to ushering in a new kind of state, freed not only of alien rule but also of what nationalists conceived of as the unprogressive elements of the past; in some respects this last ambition was a central plank in the entirely reasonable claim of many nationalists to be revolutionary.

African nationalists, like nationalists everywhere, used the clustered histories of their putative nations romantically and instrumentally. They did so partly to establish their own legitimacy; it was important to establish a genealogy of one's own political movement which established it as the ultimate heir of a long tradition of resistance to oppression. But nowhere in Africa, however, were nationalists in business to rehabilitate the dynasties, institutions, offices and practices of the pre-colonial past even if their use of history had drawn attention to, ennobled and even gilded that past. Their mission was to destroy what they regarded as antique, feudalistic and unprogressive. Nationalists were not about to surrender political power to the descendants of the kings and priests of the past once alien rule had been successfully expelled. This commitment went far beyond theory; it was no mere war of words but a series of real contests with the holders of ancient offices, both spiritual and temporal, and their followers. Those struggles with the modern political representations of *anciens régimes* have, however, enjoyed relatively little scholarly attention.

This book tries to suggest that the CPP's struggle against chieftaincy in southern Ghana was, by its own reckoning, at least as important as its dramatic, much better known and ultimately more successful combat with the British. Certainly it absorbed a very great deal of their political energies in the first 10 years of the party's existence first as a radical anti-colonial opposition and after 1951 as government. It is a story which has been in large measure set aside because it lies in the shadow of the inherent glamour of the anti-colonial struggle, a glamour which was real enough. But it is a story which we can perhaps more easily reflect upon more than 40 years after independence. Some might conclude that it provides a better context for understanding Ghana's modern political topography, for many of the older fault-lines continue to inform choice and allegiance in modern Ghana.

The unwillingness of most scholars to tackle this subject owes something to its complexity. As suggested earlier, generalization does no service to understanding; there is no single form of chieftaincy in southern Ghana and thus no singular history which does justice to the myriad histories of individual chieftaincies. The

7

reflexive response to that complexity might be the tackling of a micro-study of this or that kingdom or region; but that can hardly be satisfying, for who is to say whether a particular case study is the exception rather than the rule? Partly because of my earlier work on the modern history of Akyem Abuakwa[9] but more because it was in and around that kingdom that the most desperate struggle for power was fought, its history in the 1950s figures prominently in this account. But, as I hope is made clear, its history was particular and does not provide us with a springboard for generalized assumptions. The other more detailed examples are therefore also more widely drawn from the largely Akan-speaking chieftaincies of the southern half of Ghana. There is little here about the north,[10] about Ghana's eastern marches or about Accra itself. Those who might question the typicality of the area upon which I concentrate have a good point which I must concede; but it will become clear that this region was the battleground.

No less intimidating is the prospect of looking at the history of local government in Ghana. One of my students once commented that 'local government' was amongst the dullest phrases in the English language; she added that it was almost as dull as 'higher education'. In Africa as elsewhere, local government appears to lack the drama of the politics of the national arena and its actors are much less frequently well-known names; moreover, dealing with it requires mastering reams of sleep-inducing legislation and command of its pettifogging particularities. While I hope that I can avoid the dead hand of detail, it does become clear that the numerous fights, games and debates which raged around chieftaincy and hence local government in the period between the CPP's debut in government in 1951 through to the creation of the First Republic in 1960 actually constituted a very sizeable chunk of the national political arena.

This book is a study of that radical nationalist government's attempt to destroy southern chieftaincy. It is also a study of how some of Ghana's chiefs and their supporters attempted to survive that onslaught. It is, I fear, neither a pretty nor a happy account. But I would not have spent years studying it had I not believed that it was an exciting story and, more significantly, an important one, not least because it is the essential historical background for an understanding of chieftaincy and politics in modern Ghana.

[9] *Murder and politics in colonial Ghana.*
[10] The history of northern chieftaincy in the 1950s is extremely important but exceeds my research competence.

8

2

Colonial Rule & the Chiefs

Although it is a searching, relevant question, it is pointless to demand to be told precisely what a Ghanaian chief was or is. Some of Ghana's cultures, most notably that of the Akan,[1] had a long tradition of powerful monarchs supported by extensive aristocracies. The colonial and anthropological convention of referring to such people as 'chiefs', while adopted here to avoid confusion and reflecting current usage in Ghana, made little attempt to distinguish between 'chiefs' and also, perhaps intentionally, reduced their significance. The word 'chief' certainly packs less of a punch than 'king' or 'prince'. After Queen Victoria's death and the subsequent imperial supremacy of a sequence of British kings, the older colonial use of the word 'king' in West Africa seems to die out; the most obvious reason for this was perhaps the avoidance of the literary chaos which would have resulted from the coexistence of a British king with imperial subjects who were also kings; whatever the reason, the newer terminology diminished their status.

Even in a single, albeit extensive, culture like that of the Akan with whom this book is mostly concerned, the historical record provides us with examples of powerful rulers of physically large domains and large populations as well as much slighter figures who dominated tiny fiefdoms. We might, for example, contrast the powerful Asantehene, overlord of millions of Asante and much of the richest land in Ghana, with the Omanhene of Sefwi whose domain is very much slighter in terms of both area and wealth. Both of them are, however, Akan kingdoms ruled by Akan kings. All of these monarchs, great and small, acted within a bewildering variety of regionally distinctive hierarchies. Outstanding or unimpressive individual rulers could episodically enhance or diminish the clout of this or that chieftaincy. In other areas chiefs could be variously relatively powerless local headmen or ritual figures with extremely limited access to material, coercive and

---

[1] The Akan share a language, Twi, and an extensive culture which extends into modern Côte d'Ivoire. From ancient times they have been politically divided into numerous kingdoms, some small and some very large. Cultural identity did not prevent innumerable wars between these states.

other resources. For our immediate purposes what really matters is what colonial rule and indigenous politics made of these varied offices.

After the formal annexation of Ghana – or more properly before 1957, the Gold Coast – the British were faced with a dilemma confronted by all colonial powers. Briefly stated, this centred on how to create an effective administrative structure with inadequate local revenues. Recourse to strong central direction, to direct rule, implied the paid employment of large numbers of administrators and their staffs. It was quickly appreciated that local revenues from varied forms of taxation would not stretch to this. Furthermore, political considerations ruled out the financing of such an extensive and expensive apparatus from metropolitan funds; all governments are sensitive about increasing taxes and any metropolitan government proposing to do so in order to afford to govern far-flung populations in distant places understandably feared losing votes. And the abiding principle throughout Britain's governance of the Gold Coast was that its people would enjoy or endure only that administrative system which their own limited local revenue could support.

To this determining factor should be added the British perception of the considerable puissance of those they were to call 'traditional rulers' or 'natural rulers'. In some cases, most notably that of Asante,[2] this assumption was soundly based. The king of Asante, the Asantehene, was indeed a powerful ruler whose capacity to resist colonial rule was not finally ended until the defeat of the Asante forces in 1896 and the eventual extended exile of the Asantehene. Here it is worth noting the relatively late arrival of colonial rule in what came to be the Ashanti Region in comparison with other Akan areas over which colonial control had crept from the middle of the 19th century. But however we periodize colonialism in Ghana, British decision-makers had concluded that they could only rule the Gold Coast effectively with the assistance of the country's traditional rulers. In the absence of anything more than a skeletal police and military force, chiefly power was the best and, almost certainly, the only guarantee of what the British deemed to be law and order; this in turn and everywhere was believed to be the most essential ingredient of a propitious trading climate. Additionally, chiefs were seen as the centres of economic power controlling, as they claimed to do, access to land and the people who worked on that land. Land and what could be grown on it, or dug out of it, and the labour to do all of that work were the Gold Coast's most obvious economic resources.

The resulting devolution and dissemination of local authority was essentially pragmatic. It was not perceived as optimally efficient but it was felt to be the best system for which limited resources allowed. Although it was later to be elevated to being a hallowed principle and even a rather leaky philosophy as 'indirect rule', it was essentially the outcome of the quotidian administrative politics of 'make do and mend'. It was an unusual policy in that it could be presented as neutral, as neither especially riskily progressive or un-adventurously conservative; being

---

[2] The extensive cluster of kingdoms drawn together under the authority of a paramount chief, the Asantehene, who was also king of the constituent state of Kumase.

uncontroversial, it commended itself to Whitehall and Westminster. No right-wing critic in the metropole could claim that British taxpayers' money was being squandered on tropical adventures; this felt like minimalist governance. In turn, more liberally-minded Britons could be persuaded, however speciously, that this policy ensured that 'native institutions' and sensitivities were being respected and only minimally interfered with.

Not everyone regarded this policy as neutral. Over time the colonial authorities' predisposition to regard chiefs as central to the workings of colonial rule was to greatly offend the largely urban and coastal African professional elite. It was understandably galling for them to see their colonial rulers looking to mostly pre-literate chiefs rather than to educated men and women like themselves as stakeholders and auxiliaries in the evolving colonial enterprise.

An exact definition of chiefly power in the early 20th century is difficult. In towns and especially in the sophisticated, cosmopolitan towns of the Atlantic coast like Cape Coast and Accra, vigorous politics and eventually defiant anti-colonialism made rule through chiefs impractical; as a result a somewhat ramshackle structure of municipal councils, overseen by usually confused colonial officials, was created. The shambles that most municipal government proved to be, especially in the great capital city, Accra, contributed to an official view that rule through chiefs was preferable to more 'modern' forms of government. But for the vast majority of Africans throughout the colonial period, their most immediate contact with government was to be at the hands of chiefs. Until the 1940s, Ghanaians were governed by a dual system. Central government and local government, which was called Native Administration, were in effect separate powers 'which may co-operate but need not'.[3] Throughout Ghana and especially southern Ghana, local administration and justice was dominated by chiefs and their councils. This provided chiefs with comparative advantage but it scarcely concealed the fact that theirs were residual powers salvaged from the loss of autonomy under colonial rule.[4]

This rested in part on the evolution of a dual system of justice in which chiefs retained considerable legal powers. The British had extended their legal control over major crimes such as murder or arson but the vast majority of crimes of violence and crimes against property were heard in chiefs' courts or Native Courts as they came to be known. Many chiefs and their Native Authorities employed their own, usually small Native Authority police forces and established local jails. Additionally, the regulation of everyday life rested in large measure on the shoulders of chiefs. Matters relating to birth, marriage, death and inheritance fell within the purview of what was regarded as 'customary law'. Despite uncertainties about the boundaries of the domain of customary law, the concept of African law rather precisely defined those areas of African life where the British increasingly feared to tread. They had, it is true, empowered themselves to intervene where the

---

[3] Lord Hailey, *Native Administration in the British African Territories*, Part III, p. 205.

[4] As Kwame Arhin puts it: 'Colonial Government took away the power of the traditional rulers and gave them authority in local government.' *Traditional rule in Ghana: past and present*, p. 108.

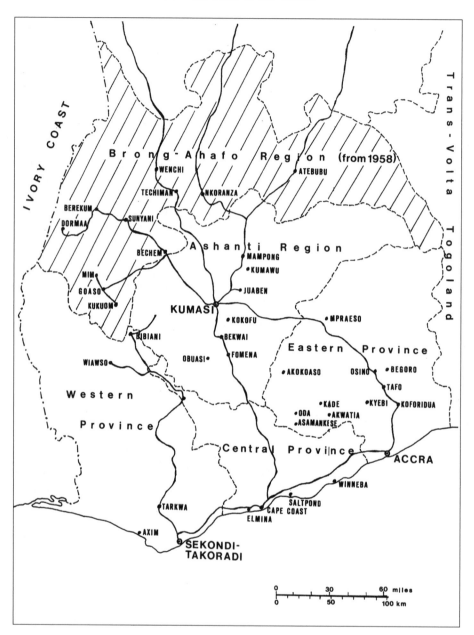

Map 2.1 Southern Ghana

judgments of chiefly courts involved processes or sentences which they deemed to be 'repugnant' or in breach of that most shadowy and, arguably, most culturally specific of concepts, 'natural justice'. Decisions to intervene, or to fail to do so, were frequently political rather than legal decisions; powerful or trusted chiefs were less likely to attract intervention than those who were weaker or unco-operative. In practice such interventions became rarer and rarer; this was because intervention carried with it the risk that it might undermine the local authority of significant local allies. Customary law was defined, interpreted and in some cases invented by Native Courts and it consequently varied considerably from area to area.

In terms of economic life outside the major coastal towns, chiefs retained considerable power. The British were intentionally reticent and even cowardly when it came to regulating Ghana's major economic resource, land. There were many discussions about the importance of land reform even if the precise objectives of such reform were never entirely clear; no such reform was ever to take place. So far as the vast majority of Ghanaians were concerned, land allocation, mostly in the form of usufructs, confiscation, taxation and rights were matters controlled by chiefs and their councils; and most disputes about these issues were resolved by Native Courts presided over by the same chiefs and councillors.

Beyond these powers, chiefs were loaded with a growing stack of civic responsi-bilities. They were required to ensure that the local physical infrastructure – and especially roads – was both extended and maintained. Under the various recensions of the Towns Ordinance they had to ensure the tidiness and sanitary respectability of their towns and villages. The nature of this was informed by the prevailing scientific attitudes towards matters like mosquito control. With hindsight many things chiefs were obliged to do now seem utterly absurd. They were expected to provide and then pay for the labour for these tasks. In addition they acted as licensing authorities for market traders, letter writers, purveyors of medicine and even for the establishment of animist shrines.

These obligations were onerous. Many of them involved the coercion, in greater and lesser degrees, of their subjects and generated a good deal of local resentment. Because colonial rule had deprived chiefs of the ultimate sanction of serious physical force, they universally enjoyed much less coercive power than they had once aspired to. Opposition to chiefs by those who were usually called 'mal-contents' in the colonial records accordingly became less risky; such defiance, which had once invited condign punishment, now courted nothing much more serious than fines or short periods in jail. Accordingly between 1904 and 1926 there were no less than 109 destoolments of chiefs in the Akan-speaking areas alone. The term 'stool' refers firstly to a real stool or throne, upon which a chief sits. It also serves as a synonym for a chief's office and the state or section of state over which he and more occasionally she ruled. Thus investment is called, somewhat inelegantly given that the surrounding ritual can be literally majestic, 'enstoolment' and deposition is known as 'destoolment'. In addition to local opposition, chiefs gradually came to be actively opposed by the precursors of the

13

radical nationalists, the coastal activists who deeply resented the close and largely unaccountable relationship between chiefs and the colonial state.

The reasons for this conflict are not arcane. In the late 19th century the coastal towns which had experienced centuries of both commercial and cultural interaction with Europe and the Americas were the homes of a rapidly growing, cosmopolitan modern elite. Their leaders were educated in the Western tradition, were mostly Christian and earned their livings by teaching, practising law or conducting commerce. Their backgrounds and achievements suggested to them that it was they who would and should be rapidly incorporated by the colonial state as its local agency. By the end of the 19th century, however, the growing professionalization of the British Colonial Service, the hardening of more systematic racism and the British predilection for working with chiefs had gradually excluded the coastal elite from such roles. Despite their credentials they were not destined to become tropical English men and women dominating a modernizing colonial state. Unsurprisingly they began to oppose colonialism and anyone who supported it.

Although the politics of the relationship between chiefs and this modern elite were complex and further complicated by the use made by the British of the useful possibility of *divide et impera*, the upshot was relatively simple. By the interwar period the competition for power between Africans in Ghana had polarized into a long-running battle between what might increasingly be seen as a nationalist elite and the chiefs.[5] As the former became more obviously anti-colonial and, by the 1920s, more patently nationalist, the British tended to rely increasingly upon their relationship with the chiefs for their legitimacy. In their usually static analysis of African life, 'natural rulers' were very precisely seen as just that. Africans who opposed chiefs were somehow acting unnaturally; the modern elite were cruelly, inaccurately if instrumentally, characterized as deracinated, anomalous and self-seeking by both chiefs and the colonial authority.

As the role of the colonial state increased after 1918, chiefs were seen as even more important to the maintenance of the colonial *status quo*. Accordingly their demands were listened to even if not always acceded to, whilst those of the coastal elite were stigmatized as the petulant bleats of a small but utterly unrepresentative minority. While this description, like all thumbnail sketches, ignores the sometimes tortured debates in African and colonial circles, it is right to regard the interwar period as one in which chiefs got their way in larger and larger measure. In an equal and opposite direction, the interests and aspirations of the town-dwellers were largely ignored.

None of this went without serious criticism. The antipathy of the coastal politicians has already been alluded to. But there were also colonial critics. Many colonial officials and especially those in daily contact with rural people came to regard, albeit discreetly, the disaffection of many Africans with their chiefs as at

---

[5] The polarization was far from complete. Beyond the immediate realm of politics, many of the intelligentsia were deeply involved in chieftaincy politics by dint of descent, their purchase of land in rural areas and through their involvement in rural litigation as lawyers.

least sometimes justified. Some, but certainly not all, chiefs ruled arbitrarily. They could use their considerable powers as patrons in a decidedly partisan fashion. Some were open to bribery. Others opportunistically sold communally owned land which they administered by custom as, in effect, trustees. None of this was surprising as the meagre stipends afforded them by the colonial state hardly matched the inherent obligations upon them to perform with all the dignity of princes. They were expected by their subjects and their colonial rulers to be 'big men' and that status demanded comparative wealth.[6]

Less excusably their courts were largely unregulated and their conduct often fell far short of basic universal requirements and understandings of fairness. Charges were sometimes trumped up so that eventual fines could be extracted; these were then shared amongst the chiefly members of the tribunals. More and more activities were subjected to the licensing functions of the courts so that the survival of many people and their families depended upon ensuring the legality of their economic roles by 'dashing' chiefs.[7] Chieftaincy had been transformed to the point where some incumbents regarded it as an opportunity to print money. In private many British officials shared the modern elite's essentialist view of the chiefs as corrupt and determinedly unprogressive even if some chiefs were undoubtedly innovative and progressive. But reforming the system had become an increasingly difficult undertaking. So reliant upon the chiefs had the colonial state become that alienating its African allies was felt to be too serious and even revolutionary a risk to undertake. Additionally chiefs were to become even more important in the course of the depression when years of low government revenue reduced the numbers of the colonial administration by about a third.

Although some *post hoc* political analysis might insist that chiefs were ultimately agencies of colonial government or of a more generalized imperialist agenda, few of them regarded themselves in this fashion. John Dunn was surely right to insist that chieftaincy 'neither behaved simply as an instrument in the hands of the colonial rulers nor that it ever drew its political power solely from its capacity to elicit the support of the colonial regime'.[8] To begin with, the vast majority of Ghana's pre-colonial states had become subjected to colonialism by treaty rather than by conquest. The major exception to this generalization was, of course, the Asante kingdom which was invaded by the British and their allies in both 1874 and 1896. Many chiefs in the interwar period would have argued with disarming dignity that they undertook the administrative roles they were asked to play because they chose to do so rather than because they were forced to do so. Writing of one of these states in 1928, the great Ghanaian lawyer-politician J.B. Danquah said 'Akim Abuakwa is one of several *independent* States in the Gold Coast.'[9]

---

[6] As Robert Addo-Fening brings out in his important book *Akyem Abuakwa, 1700-1943; from Ofori Panin to Sir Ofori Atta*, many chiefs had lost a considerable store of wealth as the application of the Emancipation Ordinance of 1874 saw many slaves leaving their chiefly masters.

[7] The giving of a gift of money or goods as a 'sweetener'.

[8] *Dependence and opportunity*, p. 93.

[9] *Akim Abuakwa Handbook*. The emphasis is mine.

Equally importantly, many of the more senior chiefs, and particularly those in the south of the country, had genuinely been involved in long-term struggles with the British to prevent further colonial encroachment into the freedom of action they claimed to enjoy by tradition as a right. In the interwar years especially, the chiefs and the British conducted a long arm-wrestling contest in which one side sought virtual sovereignty and the other greater control and accountability. In the process both sides conceded some ground as both possessed considerable armouries. The British ultimately ruled the Gold Coast and falling foul of the colonial authorities in any profound fashion risked retribution. In turn British reliance on chiefs had been constructed upon an ideology which over time had virtually sacralized chieftaincy. Chiefly influence in the colonial period had been built upon the elaboration of the notion of their natural rights; these ideas had become embroidered to the point where natural rights had become entwined with something close to divine right.[10] For credulous, nervous administrators, battling with chiefs could look perilously close to challenging the most profound of African sensibilities and that in turn risked costly riot and rebellion.[11] Taken together those largely misunderstood feelings became embodied in the colonial concepts of custom and tradition.

Those concepts had done the British and the chiefs signal service in facing down the challenges of coastal politicians. Their calls for a more democratic and accountable system of governance were countered by somewhat specious arguments about the inherent democracy of tradition[12] and of course the much contested insistence that 'natural rulers' spoke in a reliable and representative fashion for ordinary Africans; coastal politicians, colonial ideology insisted, could not be leaders as 'tradition' and 'custom' denied that possibility. But now 'custom' and 'tradition' came to haunt the British. In an era of heightened sensitivity brought about by the increasingly successful campaigns of the nationalists, overt assaults on what might be regarded as 'traditional' risked being perceived as affronts to all Gold Coast Africans; and a highly literate African press was ever ready to exploit such lapses. A weak colonial regime, and such it was throughout the inter-war period, fundamentally lacked the will and the resources to reform its all-important local government system. The flaws in the system which had developed since the 1870s were obvious enough well before the outbreak of the

---

[10] John Dunn memorably commented that the interwar period was one when 'the administration's moral sensitivity to traditional legitimacy was in a particularly inflamed condition'. *Dependence and opportunity*, p. 170.

[11] The unresolved problem was, as the Fabian critic Rita Hinden put it neatly, whether 'chiefs and native administrations derive their powers from their traditional position in native society, or by delegation from the government. Is the government the sole source of authority without whose recognition and approval they cannot legally function?' *Local government in the colonies*. p. 95.

[12] Specious because of the differential access of people to influence in the pre-colonial period. Women, slaves and non-royals enjoyed much less *prise* than royals. The same objections could be raised against notions of Athenian democracy which similarly excluded women and the unfree from the political process. A more modern insistence on the inherent democracy of traditional Akan government is to be found in K.A. Busia, *The position of the chief in the modern political system of Ashanti*.

Second World War. Although regulation of each individual chiefdom's taxation and tribute systems was required by the introduction of a number of externally audited 'Native Treasuries', few were actually established and even fewer actually kept books which were capable of audit. The chiefly councils, and their formal colonial administrative manifestations, the so-called 'Native Authorities', continued on occasion to pass by-laws which were oppressive, even when censured by central government. People were commonly tried by courts in which chiefs could be both complainants and judges. But it was another failure of rule through chiefs which pressed the British to begin to curb chiefly authority.

Even though the evidence had been available for decades, the demands brought about by the supply crisis of the Second World War finally revealed that the Gold Coast's economy was, at best, sluggish. Its role as a major supplier of vegetable fats and oils, of cocoa, gold and diamonds and its capacity to earn hard, foreign exchange by their export were perceived as important in Whitehall. Pressed by the metropolitan government to enhance production, the colonial government in Accra looked with a new degree of urgency to its local government agencies, the chiefs and their councils, for help in increasing the volume and value of its exports. Very quickly it was concluded that this mechanism simply did not work; chiefly rule was more of a hindrance than a help. It was hard to conceive of agencies less adapted to the work of what was now called development, the new buzz word, than the organs of chiefly rule.

The upshot was overdue reform made possible by the urgency of wartime. In 1944, the Native Authorities Ordinance was passed. The preamble to the ordinance stressed that 'it is expedient that ... provision be now made whereby ... chiefs may be enabled to take an effective part in the administration of the Colony'. But the ordinance also made a clear distinction between the local government functions of Native Authorities and the role to be played by what were now widely referred to as State Councils. State Councils, that is the councils of chiefs and their councillors, had previously dominated Native Authorities and in many cases were indistinguishable from them. Under the new ordinance, colonial government could attempt to control the constitution of Native Authorities and could closely supervise Native Authority finances. Although this took time and some rough contingent politics to work through, State Councils were now supposed to restrict their work to matters concerned with ritual and tradition. The intention was to gradually relegate chiefs to centrally defined roles which resembled, on a small scale, those of constitutional monarchy. The plan was for these reformed and in some cases federated Native Authorities[13] to become, *senso strictu*, local councils; their composition was supposed to be significantly larded with, and hence gingered up by, progressive, educated members drawn from the modern elite.

This change of heart or acquisition of courage was in part ordered by the growing awareness of the weakness of the older style of local government when it came to economic development. But it also drew on the highly critical confidential

---

[13] This was pressed when the old Native Authorities were felt to be too small to be effective.

report of Lord Hailey, 'Native Administration and political development in British tropical Africa', which was researched and drafted between 1940 and 1942.[14] Hailey was scathing about the lack of clear policy which had typified successive colonial governments' approaches to local administration in Ghana; this criticism repeated the clear rebukes rehearsed in his extended study *An African Survey*.[15] Hailey welcomed the demise of chiefs: 'the process of political development is likely to lie in the increasing acquisition of executive power by the representative elements of the Councils [by which he meant reformed native authorities] without any change necessarily taking place in the formal constitutional position of chiefs'.[16]

Although Hailey clearly had some expectations of organic change, the power now lay with the governor of the Gold Coast to designate as well as to appoint members of Native Authorities. For the first time the enstoolment and destoolment of chiefs and the composition of chiefly councils had to be specified, in writing, to the governor. Although such matters still rested on the proper working through of what was locally said to be custom, some of the older independence of chieftaincy was being curtailed.

As part of this drive to reduce the power of chieftaincy, reform of the customary law jurisdiction began with the Native Courts Ordinance of 1944.[17] That was initiated by a Committee of Inquiry appointed by the Gold Coast's Legislative Council in 1942.[18] Its report was utterly devastating. It itemized an unhappy story of frivolous litigation, endless wrangles between chiefs over jurisdiction, and arbitrary justice. The tribunals were almost universally composed of people who held such positions by hereditary right and to the exclusion of those with educational or professional qualifications. These tribunals, sometimes numbering 20 people, shared the sitting fees, the fines and other exactions. Hailey's reading of that report suggested that chiefs should no longer sit as court presidents.[19]

By the end of the Second World War, the tide of events was undoubtedly running against the chiefs. In many respects they had been authors of their own fate. It demeans them to suggest that they were simply victims of British policy, for they had cleverly played upon the huge gap between British effectiveness and intentions for decades. In the process many of them had acquired considerable local power and a few had amassed personal fortunes. Radical politicians insisted that they had done so whilst using the colonial presence as a protective shield. In the process, the argument ran, they had acquired far greater power than they would have enjoyed in pre-colonial days. Whether this was true or not hardly mattered; this was widely believed amongst those who were to be active nationalists and their supporters in postwar Ghana.

[14] The causative sequence is nicely brought out in PRO CO 96/810/6. The report was published as *Native Administration in British African Territories*.

[15] See bibliography.

[16] Native Administration, 5.VIII.

[17] Although the extent of that reform in concrete terms was, as we will see, severely limited.

[18] Native Tribunals Committee of Enquiry, Chairman, Sir Harry Blackall, Accra, 1943.

[19] Native Administration. p.204.

It was also increasingly believed by colonial government by the 1940s. Towards the end of the Second World War, the local colonial government, working with the Colonial Office, was preparing a new constitution for the Gold Coast. It was relatively radical in that it conceded, for the first time, a majority on the Legislative Council, the country's legislature, being composed of non-officials. Part of the electoral process included direct election by those enfranchised in the coastal municipalities. But the two great councils of chiefs in the Colony (the south) and Ashanti, the Joint Provincial Council[20] and the Ashanti Confederacy or Asanteman Council, also acted as electoral colleges after 1946. The hope of both the colonial government and the radical intelligentsia was that these chiefly councils would have the wit to understand that they were being asked to reform themselves and to return educated and otherwise qualified non-chiefs to the Legislative Council. This worked well enough in Ashanti where the Confederacy Council returned three non-chiefs and only one chief. In the south, however, the Joint Provincial Council returned seven chiefs and only two non-chiefs. While this was not the reason for the failure of the 1946 constitution, it was evidence of the unwillingness of many of the more powerful chiefs to respond positively to the need for reform.

As is well known, serious urban rioting broke out at the end of February and beginning of March 1948. The commission of enquiry which investigated the causes of these disturbances produced an important report[21] which provides us with some useful insights. The list of the witnesses the commissioners heard shows a disproportionate number of those who might have been expected to be irritated by or jealous of, and hence hostile to, chiefs. The Watson Commission's report concluded that chiefly rule was dying on its feet and the commissioners welcomed its demise. The Colonial Office was to respond later by arguing that the Watson commissioners had gone too far in criticizing the chiefs so harshly.[22] But that official response was partly caused by the growing apprehension about the increasingly radical tone of nationalism; chiefs were, after all, the devil they knew.

The Watson commissioners regarded Native Administration as 'residing largely in a hierarchy of vested interests jealously guarded by Chiefs and Elders'.[23] There was, they argued, 'an intense suspicion that the Chiefs are being used by the Government as an instrument for the delay if not the suppression of the political aspirations of the people ... The view is advanced that so long as the Chief accepts and supports the Government policy he will receive Government support however much he has become the object of dislike to his people.'[24] They encountered

---

[20] Joint because it was constituted by the amalgamation and recognition of the Provincial Councils of the Eastern and Western Provinces of the south, the Colony, by Order in Council in 1925. By 1944 it was no longer merely advisory but was statutory and executive.
[21] Watson Commission Report. CO 231. 1948.
[22] The senior Colonial Office official Andrew Cohen was manifestly angry on reading the report. 'The whole of the analysis suffers from the prejudice felt by the Commission against Chiefs ... The Commission greatly under-estimate the difficulties of forging a modern system of local government on the basis of the existing traditional system'. PRO CO 96/796/5, Minute, 29 June 1948.
[23] Watson Commission Report. para. 104.
[24] Ibid., para. 107.

'intense objection to chiefs being elected to and sitting in the Legislative Council ... the place of a Chief in society was ornamental rather than useful ... We are unable to envisage the growth of commercialization ... with the retention of native institutions save in a form which is a pale historical reflection of the past.'[25]

The Colonial Office felt that the commissioners had done 'substantially less than justice to the strength of the tradition and custom which a large part of the country still regards as essential to an ordered society'. The Colonial Office argued, with considerable justification, that the commissioners, all three of whom had previously been strangers to West Africa, had spent very little time in the Gold Coast, three weeks to be precise; they had not travelled in rural areas and had thus not had much chance to canvass opinion amongst rural communities 'which form the great bulk of the population of the Gold Coast'.[26] They might have added that the commissioners' views were also Eurocentric, derived as they were not only from the hostile views of the modern African elite but also from their own radical-liberal reading of world history. But of course the die was cast. The arguments of and the evidence used by the Watson commissioners were to condition both nationalist response and colonial policy for the years to come and the Colonial Office knew that there was no going back. In the British government's Statement on the Report there is a clear commitment to reform. 'It is the settled policy of the Gold Coast Government that Native Authorities ... should be made fully representative of the people of the area and the Chiefs are becoming increasingly alive to the necessity for this. Every effort is being made to speed up the process'.[27]

The Watson Commission's recommendations were catalytic and in large measure acceded to. Amongst their most important conclusions was that the 1946 constitution was dead and that a new and more representative constitution should be drafted by an all-African committee. That committee was duly appointed under the chairmanship of the Ghanaian judge, Sir Henley Coussey. The 'moderate' alignment of that committee and the fact that some senior chiefs were amongst its members assured that its treatment of traditional rulers was notably gentler and, some might argue, more 'African' than that of the Watson commissioners. Indeed so far as chiefs were concerned the committee rejected 'the status which the Watson Report would assign to them'.[28] In a paragraph that was to be much quoted in the years to come, the committee concluded that 'the whole institution of Chieftaincy is so closely bound up with the life of our communities that its disappearance would spell disaster. Chiefs and what they symbolise in our society are so vital that the subject of their future must be approached with the greatest caution ... Criticisms there have been, but none coming from responsible people whom we have known or met is directed towards the complete effacement of chiefs.'[29]

[25] *Ibid.*, paras 108–11.
[26] Statement by His Majesty's Government on the Watson Report, PRO CO 232, pp.2 and 6–7.
[27] *Ibid.*, p. 7.
[28] Coussey Committee Report, para 36.
[29] *Ibid.*

The Coussey committee's remit was to draft a new constitution and that body of proposals included the designing of a new structure of local government. It concluded that Native Authorities should be replaced by Local Councils of varying sizes consonant with local demography. The deficiencies of the old Native Authorities 'include the restricted basis of their membership, their old-fashioned procedure and their inadequate finance and staff[30] ... [they are] unequal to the demands being made on them'.[31] Chiefs, or more accurately 'the appointees of traditional councils', would continue to sit on these councils but would constitute no more and no less than one-third of council membership. But that concession apart, Chiefs' Councils, the State Councils, were to remain 'separate and distinct' from Local Councils and would be limited to 'declaring' what the committee called 'native customary laws' and settling 'constitutional disputes connected with stools'.[32] In many respects chiefs were being relegated to the marginal roles to which the Watson commissioners had referred. Obviously a major overhaul of the Gold Coast's local government system required serious planning and the Legislative Council rapidly set up select committees to both flesh out the Coussey committee's proposals and draft the legislation that would be required.

None of this occurred in a political vacuum. The modern elite which had pioneered nationalism in the Gold Coast had deeply resented the dominance of chiefs in the colonial councils of state and had done so for decades. But their suspicions were to be as nothing compared with the more complex distaste for chieftaincy expressed by what was becoming Ghana's most successful nationalist party, the Convention Peoples' Party (CPP) of Kwame Nkrumah which was founded in June 1949. While the CPP shared the anger of the older generation of nationalists with the colonial favour shown to chiefs in the past, their unease had two additional elements. Firstly in terms of social composition the CPP's activist support appears to have included a large number of people with no pretensions to membership of royal families and with no compromising relationships with chieftaincy; the humbly born Nkrumah himself provides just such an example. Very few of those who were to be returned as CPP Members of the Legislative Assembly (MLA) in 1951, for instance, had serious chiefly connections.[33] More of the CPP stalwarts had good reasons to be very resentful about chiefly misgovernance and contempt for commoners, as they saw it; a significant example was Nkrumah's lieutenant in the Ashanti Region, Krobo Edusei. A leader of the commoner Asante Youth Association, his vehement opposition to the Asantehene

---

[30] *Ibid.*, para. 31.

[31] *Ibid.*, para. 32.

[32] *Ibid.*, para. 83.

[33] There were exceptions. The father of A.E.A. Inkumsah, who sat for Ahanta, was a traditional priest before becoming a Methodist. A.E. Attafuah, the MLA for Western Akim, was the son of an heir to the Akim Kotoku paramountcy and the MLA for Akwapim-New Juaben, Ohene Djan's father, was Mankralo of Aburi. Abraham Mate Johnson, MLA for the Volta River constituency, was intimately connected with the Manya Krobo royal house but was a long-time opponent of the sitting *konor* or chief. The father of Yeboah Aukordieh, the MLA for Mampong North and an outspoken opponent of the Mamponghene, was a traditional priest.

and chiefly rule had been harshly rewarded by humiliating punishment from the Native Court on many occasions. He was one of a wider cohort; many of the best known CPP activists had made their political careers well before the foundation of the CPP, leading or being deeply involved in local struggles against particular chiefs.

But there was an additional element to their dislike of chieftaincy. The CPP was also a party which had been impressed by at least some of the thrusts of Marxism-Leninism. From the end of 1950, and for the first time, the anti-chief rhetoric of nationalism in the Gold Coast began to talk of feudalism. The newspaper of the party, the *Accra Evening News*, which first appeared before the formation of the CPP in September 1948 as a radical news sheet, constantly upbraided chiefs for their 'oppression of the masses' and especially for their 'collaboration with the imperialists'. While such attacks were generalized, they have a reasonably precise chronology.

At the time of the CPP's formation in mid-1949, occasioned by a split with the older United Gold Coast Convention (UGCC), there was clearly some expectation that some chiefs might make common cause with the CPP. It was merely a pity that they were so hesitant about supporting the party. Some chiefs did support the party and this almost certainly tempered what might otherwise have been more outright condemnation. But by October 1949, the *Evening News*' gossip column, 'The Accra Diary', written by the usually waspish 'Rambler', was able to refer to chiefs as 'our imperialists' who 'have oppressed and suppressed us for a century and have drained all the good elements in our God-given land to their own home towns'. The final stanza of a long poem by Kofi Aboagye, an ex-serviceman and primary schoolteacher from Agogo, published by the *Accra Evening News* on 22 July 1949 reads:

Chiefs and sages why in slumbers/ lethargic dost thou lie?/ Awake and join thy numbers/ to make this country free/ from the cruel crushing of our oppressors/ to get self-government this year.

When in November 1949 the CPP unsuccessfully demanded the setting-up of a constituent assembly, the Ghana People's Representative Assembly, the proposed membership of CPP members, trade unions, farmers' associations, ex-servicemen and youth associations very pointedly excluded chiefs. In the past nationalists had usually referred to the putative nation as 'the chiefs and the people of the Gold Coast'; in most cases the CPP now omitted that nicety and more and more frequently invoked the 'workers and peasants' or 'the masses'.

Chiefs were under increased pressure by the end of 1949 and there was much which ensured that they knew it. On the eve of the CPP's ultimately flawed attempt at a general strike, the Positive Action campaign of January 1950, the *Evening News*, which was formally published by the Party's chairman Kwame Nkrumah, who both wrote for the paper and approved its contents, was using much more obviously threatening language. 'Those of our chiefs who are with us ... we do honour ... those ... who join forces with the imperialists ... there shall come a time when they will run away fast and leave their sandals behind them; in other words

Chiefs in league with imperialists who obstruct our path ... will one day run away and leave their Stools'.[34] This was not a matter of simple one-sided bullying for, as is argued below, some sections of the Gold Coast's chieftaincy were increasingly acting in what they believed to be their and their country's best interests and in what appeared to the CPP to be a very provocative fashion.

The sheer vivacity of the CPP took both the colonial establishment, the old coastal elite and the chiefs by considerable surprise. For all three groups this was profoundly unwelcome but seemingly irresistible. The party of the old elite, the UGCC, in serious disarray in the run-up to the country's first general election in 1951, pragmatically and somewhat desperately buried the hatchet with their old enemies, the chiefs, as represented by their regional councils, the Joint Provincial Council and the Ashanti Confederacy Council. Indeed at a somewhat anguished meeting of the UGCC and the, by then, somewhat archaic and nearly memberless Aborigines Rights Protection Society held at Cape Coast in May 1950, these old sworn antagonists of the chiefs agreed that, in the absence of anything more exciting, chieftaincy must be the 'the most effective rallying point of sensible opinion in the country'.[35] Mutual dislike, let alone fear,[36] of the new radical forces represented by the CPP provided these old antagonists with a powerful reason for cooperation.

The CPP claimed to represent the aspirations of not merely the 'workers and peasants' but also 'youth'; while this rings seductively in any culture, it was an explicit language of exclusion in Ghana. The meaning of the word 'youth' in the Ghanaian political context merits a short diversion from the narrative. By the end of the 1940s the words 'youngmen' and youth had two conjoined meanings. 'Youngmen' was, and still is, a rather poor translation of the Twi words *nkwankwaa* and *mmerante*. Both signify something more wide-ranging than age. They are the usual terms for commoners, for non-royals. In the dominant Twi-speaking states of southern Ghana upon whom this book concentrates, being royal was at once something special and something routine. There were many who could and did claim to be royal. Technically anyone who could claim royal descent through his or her mother's lineage was indeed royal. As kings and chiefs took multiple wives, their descendants naturally proliferated over time; this genealogical timescale was considerable, for the formal histories of most of the Akan kingdoms begin in the early 17th century. There is no valid calculation of what proportion of the population of any individual Akan state or *oman* could boast, with some degree of confidence, that they were royal but they were certainly numerous. Claiming to be royal and having that claim widely recognized bestowed some privileges. These included being eligible to capitalize on the advantages of being a kinsman or woman of a reigning chief. Such privileges might range from some patrimonial

---

[34] Editorial in the *Accra Evening News*, 5 January 1950.

[35] Dennis Austin, *Politics in Ghana*, p. 134.

[36] The Asantehene reported to the chief commissioner that all his councillors 'are terrorised by the CPP'. W.H. Beeton, *Diary*. 24 September 1950, Rhodes House Mss. Beeton was assistant chief commissioner, Ashanti.

share-outs to paid positions in the palace, and before the 1950s, stool funding for education and the considerably enhanced chance of a job in the Native Authority; in many cases the officers of the Native Authority, the Native Authority police sergeant or the warden of the Native Authority prison were, for example, royal kinsmen. At the ritual level, access to certain rites and holy sites was reserved for royals. To be a 'youngman' was undoubtedly to be excluded from what were in most cases somewhat limited pork-barrels; but in rural areas these were all too frequently the only available pork-barrels. Unsurprisingly this distinction between royal and youngman was a point of friction in many *aman*. Commoners' associations, the *asafo* companies, were in the forefront of many destoolment attempts and, as modern politics took off in Ghana after 1945, commoners were almost certain to be identified with the CPP rather than with its more conservative opponents.

But 'youth' had acquired an additional meaning by the end of the 1940s. It was an almost emblematic word and even an icon in the Communist-dominated and -influenced world of those days. Beautiful, perfect young people held banners aloft, built dams and ploughed fields in much of the 'socialist realist' political art of the day. Youth were to be the vanguard of revolution and a great deal of the activity of the Comintern in the early days of the Cold War was directed at achieving links between Russian and Eastern European youth organizations and the burgeoning youth associations of the colonized as well as the Western world.

For many activists in the CPP, 'youth' had a depth of meaning which came close to the incantatory significance of 'worker' or 'peasant'. The party insisted that 'Youth everywhere are in action against the forces of evil, of suppression and repression, and we youth in the Gold Coast have not been found wanting. Together with the struggling youth of other lands we shall not rest until we have built the Brave New World'.[37] For all of these reasons the invocation of either or both 'youngman' or 'youth' was read as something close to a threat by the patriarchal Ghanaian 'old order' of chiefs and the middle class, the modern elite. In turn language was manipulated around this terminology and its meanings. In the press which represented the interests of the UGCC elite and its allies, the characterization of the CPP's 'youth' as 'hooligans' or 'verandah boys' was common. The term 'verandah boys' was initially widely used to describe the usually criminal groups of disaffiliated youngsters involved in petty theft or pimping in the big towns during the Second World War. The term derived from the fact that they hung around and even slept on the roadside verandahs of trading houses in the main streets of the larger towns. By 1950 'hooligans ' and 'verandah boys' were no more than the newest ways of talking about 'malcontents'.

The CPP's most senior officers recognized that 'youth' and their aspirations were unpredictable and in some cases uncontrollable. Some of the excesses of youth and especially the Asante Youth Association in disrupting Native Authorities and attempting to destool chiefs were notorious. The CPP at the national level, despite its suspicion of chiefs, was for some time eager to promote the notion of being

---

[37] The Ghana Youth Manifesto of the proto-CPP, the Committee on Youth Organizations (Accra, 1949).

widely representative and as keen to face down any suggestion that it was party to anything which might disunite the totality of 'the people'. The diary of W.H. Beeton[38] records the attempts of Komla Gbedemah and other CPP leaders to limit the localized onslaughts upon chiefs in the Ashanti Region. There were certainly some sections of the CPP leadership which remained open to the idea that they could take at least some chiefs with them. Certainly well into 1950, and thus before the election campaign hotted up, there was, in some areas, a struggle for the support of chiefs between the old, becalmed UGCC and the newer, more vital CPP.

But many chiefs felt that the constant attacks upon them and their status from below were orchestrated by the CPP. In some cases there was justification in regarding commoners' attacks upon chiefs as being ordered by local branches of the CPP. Certainly the proliferation of CPP branches in the closing months of 1950 resulted in a considerable degree of decentralization, a polite way of suggesting that the CPP's central committee was by then unable to control all of its branches as it grew very rapidly. This was a departure from the situation before the time when significant figures in the party hierarchy had been arrested and subsequently imprisoned for their roles in the Positive Action campaign of January 1950. Before this time the party's General Secretary, Kojo Botsio, exercised as much headquarters control over the regions as he could muster; but at this early stage the party was a much smaller organization than it was by the end of 1950. In these newer circumstances, the local representation of the national political struggle frequently reasserted older cleavages. Almost inevitably these reflected the tensions between the old, chief-dominated Native Authorities and sections of commoners. It was this as much as anything else which drove the UGCC and a sizeable number of prominent chiefs together in an uncomfortable and, as things worked out, a doomed alliance.

Foolishly perhaps, sections of the Gold Coast's chieftaincy began openly to oppose the CPP and some even began to take the UGCC's side. In June 1950, for example, it was alleged that some Northern Territory chiefs led by the Na Yiri were attempting to crush the CPP branch, recently opened in Tamale. Such attempts forced the issue of chieftaincy into the open. In an important speech to an enormous rally in Cape Coast on 6 August 1950, the acting chairman of the CPP,[39] Komla Gbedemah, turned up the heat. The party was not, he said, against chiefs: 'rather we are fighting to liberate them … Those of them who will be reasonable and willing to be emancipated and will come to our side we will bring home with honour … those of them who … choose to remain stooges … of imperialists must be left to their fate'. That fate, he said, was to be rather ominously like that of 'ostriches who … hide their heads … at the approach of the ominous desert sandstorm … we can have no reason to suppose that something different … would be the fate of those chiefs'.

The tensions were growing and the aggression was very far from being solely

---

[38] *Op. cit.*

[39] Nkrumah was serving what were to be uncompleted jail sentences of three years in total.

the work of the CPP. Almost certainly at the bidding of the UGCC, a meeting was held of the three Provincial Councils of Chiefs of the Colony, the Joint Territorial Council, on 15 August 1950 whose implicit intention was to flesh out the wish to provide a 'sensible rallying point' against the CPP. At this unusual joint meeting the chiefs were attempting to seize the initiative. They issued a seven-point memorandum which insisted that the Coussey constitution gave them the 'duty to lead and guide the people to the full status of a Gold Coast Nation'. They could hardly deny the existence of vigorous party politics but suggested that the creation of a national congress[40] would 'provide a forum for the exchange of ideas between the Territorial Councils and the various political parties'. This almost pathetic attempt to regain some control over the national tiller was immediately met by a clever CPP invitation to territorial council representatives to attend a CPP special delegates' conference on 2–3 September. Predictably this was rejected. At that Special Delegates' Conference in Kumase, a strong resolution, stimulated by the worrying prospect of an anti-CPP national congress of chiefs, determined that the chiefs' claim to national leadership was no longer acceptable; and the gap between the CPP and chiefs widened further. An editorial in the *Accra Evening News* concluded that 'We have now decided to carry on the struggle with or without the Chiefs ... we shall no longer continue to put our confidence in chiefs.'[41]

There was by now, in the CPP's opinion, strong evidence that the chiefs were playing an active role in party politics, something to which they had expressed their hostility in the recent past.[42] This position, consistently proclaimed throughout the 1950s, was a monocular condemnation; chiefly support for the CPP was, it seemed, not 'involvement in party politics' while support for their opponents very definitely was. Once chiefs had taken the step of opposing the CPP, as the CPP said had happened, the chiefs could look forward to no protection from them. 'We are not ... in favour of our *Nananom* [chiefs] being hooted at, booed or stoned, but it is natural that when a king condescends to take the role and perform duties of an ordinary citizen, then of course he must take the consequences.'[43] But even then, at national level at least, chiefs were still publicly regarded by CPP headquarters as the unwitting tools of darker forces and hence their own worst enemies. 'If they are not prepared to fight for their own rights, we shall fight for ours and theirs as well', trumpeted an *Evening News* editorial.[44]

It was widely known that a further Joint Territorial Council meeting on 21 October 1950 had discussed the possibility of banning of the CPP nationally;[45] they had only retreated from this extreme position when they recognized unhappily that an ineffective and illegal ban, for such it would have been, could only be very

---

[40] Almost certainly a ploy suggested by Dr J.B. Danquah.

[41] 6 September 1950.

[42] See *Accra Evening News*, 13 June 1950.

[43] *Accra Evening News*, 25 August 25 1950. This editorial suggests that a constitutional monarch such as George VI of Britain enjoyed respect because he stood apart from politics.

[44] 6 September 1950.

[45] The *Accra Evening News* reported that the CPP was discussed in 'a volley of abuses and curses' and that the idea was that of the increasingly demonized figure, Dr J.B. Danquah, 26 October 1950.

counterproductive. Even then the CPP Central Office resisted attacking all the chiefs directly; those chiefs hostile to the party were to be seen as no more than unwitting dupes. 'We find it hard to see why these imperialist agents are unable to come out boldly to the open ban on the Party but choose to use the old and decadent system of setting the chiefs against the people and the people against the chiefs.'[46]

At the major CPP meeting in Kumase on 2–3 September 1950 referred to above, it was reported that speakers had said that chiefs who did not agitate for the immediate release of those CPP activists jailed for inciting illegal strikes, including Nkrumah, in the Positive Action campaign, would be destooled by the CPP. Gbedemah was said to have advocated violence in a tirade against chiefs; Kwesi Lamptey was alleged to have said: 'eliminate chiefs from the system.'[47] In a matter of days this already alarming tone became even more threatening. Chiefs, the CPP argued, were now the authors of their own unpopularity just as they always had been. Their hostility to the CPP only made their rapid demise more likely. Their behaviour lured 'the younger people' into the 'temptation of marching into the homes of the chiefs and bring [sic] them to account, as what happened in the French Revolution when the women of France marched from Paris to Marseilles to bring down the King back from Paris to give account for his behaviour'.[48] Even more threateningly, the same editorial provided the party's supporters with something close to a legal 'get-out clause' when it came to normatively binding traditional loyalties. ' Once it can be proved that the chiefs are false to their oaths, the people are exempted by our ancient constitution from their allegiance.' There is no doubt that this was an open incitement to press destoolment charges against anti-CPP chiefs.

Although 'youth' had tangled with chieftaincy with some force, it was now becoming clear that the CPP leadership itself was becoming increasingly hostile, despite the fact that several chiefs had not only publicly supported the CPP but had actually joined the party. Several Kwawu chiefs, for example, did so in the course of rallies founding new branches of the party in Mpraeso, Aduamoa and Abetifi.[49] The party's newspaper actively encouraged such support. By the end of 1950 it is notable that articles began to appear in the *Evening News* which supported particular sides in contests over stools, an example of which is a partisan piece on the Juaso Stool contest,[50] or sided with 'sub- chiefs' who opposed anti-CPP paramounts.[51]

---

[46] *Accra Evening News*, 14 June 1950.

[47] W.H. Beeton, *Diary*, 2 and 3 September 1950.

[48] *Accra Evening News*, editorial 7 September 1950. No stranger to typographical errors, the newspaper presumably meant Versailles.

[49] If the *Accra Evening News* of 18 October 1950 is to be believed. The Kwawu Tafohene is alleged to have said: 'As your chief I have enrolled now and what about my subjects?'

[50] 14 December 1950.

[51] An example of which is the early support for the Dormaahene, a CPP stalwart, Nana Agyeman Badu, against the Asanteman Council, which the CPP correctly believed to be opposed to the party. See *Accra Evening News*, 13 December 1950.

A partial explanation for the increasing volume of hostility must lie with the party's inability to shut down the sometimes violent reactions against chiefs, especially in Ashanti in 1950. But an equally strong reason for the hardening of these attitudes must lie with the desperate, risky choice of some of the most important traditional leaders to throw in their lot with the doomed UGCC and to do so in the immediate run-up to the country's first general election. That could take pretty crude forms; for example, the Essumejahene, Nana Kwama Gyebi Ababio, refused the CPP permission to hold meetings in his town.[52]

Outside the big towns, election was indirect and the CPP feared that chiefs would have malign influence over the direction of the Electoral Colleges' choice in the countryside. It was worrying that highly influential chiefs like Nene Azzu Mate Kole and Nana Tsibu Darku, who was described by the *Evening News* as 'despotic ... a little Hitler in that area to lord it over poor people whom he is anxious to keep in perpetual fear and darkness',[53] were opposed to the CPP. In the event neither the chiefs nor the UGCC had the political acumen, popular attraction or organizational capacity to face down the sheer *éclat* and momentum of the CPP. In the 1951 elections, held on 5–8 February, the CPP was to sweep the board. It won all five of the municipal seats and had taken 29 of the 33 electorally contested seats. Chiefs retained a strong position in the Assembly, as under the new constitution the Joint Provincial Council had 11 seats in its gift, the Asanteman Council had six and the Southern Togoland Council one. Of these members, not all of whom were chiefs, at least four were to prove sympathetic to the CPP.

The Northern Electoral College returned 19 members, some of whom were chiefs or sub-chiefs. But the struggle between chiefs and the politically active had not been so marked in the north. Indeed the majority of the region's intelligentsia were in one way or another either chiefly or closely connected with chieftaincy.[54] With a clear CPP majority in the Legislative Assembly, the majority of the Northern members were to support the CPP in most divisions in the early years of the diarchic administration which led up to the achievement of internal self-government in 1954.

By February 1951 the chiefs of southern Ghana had been subjected to a decade of tumultuous change. In the course of a brief period they had moved from being powerful, indispensable central figures in the administration of their country to what must have felt like an increasingly marginal status. They had been rejected by their British allies and more importantly they had been rejected by an electorate voting in the country's first general election. From this election onwards they were also to deal with a government whose most important element, the CPP, was thoroughly out of patience with them.

---

[52] The *Accra Evening News*, 27 December 1950, reporting this, joyfully reminded its readers that he 'will be decorated with the insignia of the King's Medal for African Chiefs on Wednesday 20th December, 1950'.

[53] 13 November 1950.

[54] Access to education in the deprived Northern territories frequently owed a great deal to local privilege.

3

The Politics of Modernizing
Local Government

The 1951 general election in Ghana established a diarchic regime in which government was exercised jointly by the colonial power and elected Africans. The CPP's resounding victory had dictated that Nkrumah was released from prison to assume the office of leader of government business, the prime minister in all but name.[1] So far as chieftaincy was concerned, the direction of policy would now jointly lie with a receding colonial power intent on reforming local government and a political party which, as we have seen, was increasingly hostile to chieftaincy; this was to prove to be yet another serious blow to the chiefs. While the governor, Sir Charles Arden-Clarke, was constructing a new Executive Council, the country's Cabinet, the chiefs' territorial councils pressed him hard to include what they called 'regional interests', a new, less value-laden circumlocution for chieftaincy. They argued, quite accurately, that the Coussey constitution had not anticipated, and hence had not provided for, single-party control of government; while they were content to see four of the Executive Council seats going to the CPP, they wanted the four other African seats to be shared amongst the regions.[2]

Arden-Clarke resisted this request; but, in consultation with the newly released Nkrumah, it was agreed that the CPP should be allotted six portfolios in an Executive Council of 11 members, a clear majority, while allotting two seats to representatives of the Ashanti and Northern Territorial Councils. The territorial councils, bitter and unconsoled, continued to press for four ministerial posts. As the governor stood firm, the Territorial Council members told him that they would not co-operate either in or with the government and would refuse any Executive Council portfolios. Instead they would form a 'shadow government'

---

[1] He was formally to be made prime minister in 1952. For the detail see R. Rathbone (ed.), *Ghana; British documents...*

[2] For more on this see R. Rathbone: 'The transfer of power in Ghana, 1945–57'. unpublished doctoral thesis, University of London, 1968; and *Ghana; British documents...*

ready to be called upon when the CPP failed. They were not a party, they told the governor, and could not therefore regard themselves as an opposition. Arden-Clarke pointed out to them that such a plan was tantamount to political suicide and in this he was almost certainly correct. By 23 February, they had grudgingly concurred and the new ministers, including an Ashanti and Northern Territories representative, were sworn in on 26 February.[3]

An early policy obligation of the new government was to carry forward the reforms of local government outlined before the elections by the Coussey committee. On the basis of three reports by select committees,[4] the new Local Government Ordinance was drafted and then discussed in the Executive Council. In August 1951, following a debate in the Legislative Assembly, it passed into law.[5] There was nothing in the legislation to which the governor and his senior officials could object. Paradoxically perhaps, the new structure submitted traditional rulers to many of the kinds of explicit controls advocated by Lord Hailey in the late 1930s but which successive colonial governments had been too nervous to enact. Such radical change was only made possible by the legitimation afforded by the African domination of both the Executive and Legislative Councils.

For the British this reform was viewed as a welcome exercise in enhancing administrative efficiency and accountability. For the CPP, however, it was a first vital step in reducing the power of traditional bodies in the countryside. While the Coussey Committee had advocated a reduction in the local power of chiefs, it had envisaged giving chiefs a voice in national government through their membership of an Upper House or in regional councils. The Colonial Office had successfully opposed the creation of an Upper House and the 1951 Legislature was, like its successors, to be unicameral. Their view that an Upper House was an unnecessary layer of government was enthusiastically shared by the CPP. Regional councils were discussed in the Executive Council in 1951, but there African ministers argued, not without cause, that creating such bodies would erect an unwelcome barrier between central government and the newly created local and district councils.[6] Significantly the new law and its consequence, a new local government structure, removed many of the powers long held by chiefs.

While the new African minister of local government assured the nation that the new structure 'in no way means that any change is necessary in the traditional relationship between chiefs and their people ... customary service and allegiance

---

[3] Ashanti was represented by the distinguished Asante barrister, Edward Asafu-Adjaye, who was to remain in Nkrumah's Cabinets until 1957 and was to act as minister of local government in this first administration. The Northern member was J.A. Braimah, a chief. He was later to join the CPP and remained a Cabinet member until a scandal removed him from office in 1954.

[4] Appointed in December 1949, they submitted their reports on the Colony, Ashanti and the Northern Territories in October 1950.

[5] The best guide to the complexity of this measure is the booklet put out by the government in July 1951 with the snappy title of *Local Government Reform in Outline; being a summary of the 3 reports on Local Government reform and of the related proposals concerning regional administration*, Accra, 1951.

[6] Executive Council minutes. 24 August 1951. National Archives of Ghana (NAG) ADM 13/136.

will remain unaltered',[7] this was most assuredly not the sole intention. In the same information booklet the minister acknowledged that the reform 'contemplates a departure from the dominant influence of the traditional elements'. The new councils were to be 'efficient, modern and democratic bodies and to have an origin and existence wholly distinct from the traditional councils'. Traditional councils would remain in being but would only perform 'customary functions'. The ethical basis for the changes was manifestly shared by all of the Executive Council irrespective of party affiliation, regional base or race. Summing up the reforms, the minister wrote that they were based on two principles, decentralization and 'democracy, which implies the transfer of power from the official and the chief to the common man. This is the very essence of the new system.'[8]

This was all very appealing and it was expressed in notably moderate language. Few could cavil at the politically neutral invocation of democracy and efficiency. It was also to be the persuasive idiom adopted in the Executive Council, for here, despite their majority, the CPP were bound to attempt to carry the opinion of the British and the non-CPP ministers with them. In a memorandum considered by the council in June 1951, the Minister of local government outlined his ministry's plans for establishing new local authorities. The ordinance's 'cardinal aim' was 'to place the administration of local affairs on to a basis more democratic than that at present obtaining'. The creation of a 'sound structure of local government' was, he argued, 'essential to the future progress of the country'. The reforms moreover aimed at 'making the popular will effective'.[9] The election results could be, and were in a constitutional sense, rightly held to be a clear mandate for the CPP. To oppose their policies so soon after an election could justly be regarded as undemocratic and provocatively defiant. The new government's policies were to be understood as 'the popular will'.[10]

There was, of course, more to these reforms than met the eye. The details were significant. Under the ordinance, chiefs in the Colony (the South) and in the Ashanti Region effectively lost control of what were traditionally called stool lands, even if the general ownership of those lands remained vested in the stools and hence the communities which owed allegiance to those stools. The revenue from these lands, derived from local taxes on farmers, land and concession sales as well as from royalties on timber forests, auriferous and diamondiferous tracts, was the ancient basis of chiefly patrimony; from now on that revenue was to be collected by the newly created democratic local councils as one element of local revenue. Chiefs were no longer at liberty to alienate stool lands without the assent of local councils. The revenue from stool lands and from native courts would now go directly to the

---

[7] *Local government reform in outline*, p. 1. Foreword by the Hon. E.O. Asafu-Adjaye, MLA, minister of local government.

[8] All the above quotations are drawn from *Local government reform in outline*, p. 4.

[9] All quotes from a memorandum by Edward Asafu-Adjaye to the Executive Council. 28 July 1951. NAG ADM 13/2/1.

[10] It is worth pointing out that the CPP took office in 1951 on the basis of a poll in which less than 50 per cent of those enfranchised to vote actually registered and less than 50 per cent of that register actually voted. There is no agreement in the scholarly literature about why less than 25 per cent of the electorate chose to vote.

treasuries of local councils. And it fell to local councils to make annual grants to the traditional bodies, the state councils, for their administration and for the maintenance of chiefs and their retinues.

For the chiefs, the only sugar on the bitter pill of reform was the statutory reservation of one-third of the membership of the new local councils for 'persons, Chiefs or commoners appointed by traditional councils' and the reservation to paramount chiefs of the non-voting presidency of such councils 'on formal and ceremonial occasions only'.[11] All in all the whole reform package was a very significant reverse for traditional rulers.

Not surprisingly, chiefs and some of the senior British field administrators, the regional commissioners,[12] were deeply suspicious that the CPP was trying to construct local authorities for its own ends while trying to insulate these new authorities from the guiding influence and authority of the chiefs and of course the regional commissioners. At the same time there was growing evidence that the CPP was extremely suspicious of the support which it felt some expatriate officers were still affording the chiefs. In the entirely respectable guise of Africanizing the field administration, it was decided to create a cadre of African 'Executive Officers' who were 'to relieve District Commissioners of a great measure of their responsibility and who will in particular act as agents of the Minister of Local Government'.[13] One inference of this was that African officers would be directly answerable to a CPP minister while cutting chiefs off from direct and possibly supportive contact with expatriate administrators.

There was by now little doubt that the CPP was extremely hostile to chieftaincy. While ministers were publicly circumspect at this stage, many CPP Members of the Legislative Assembly were not. J. Hagan, speaking in the Assembly during the debate on the Local Government Ordinance, was cheered loudly by his own benches when he said: 'For the past 107 years our chiefs have been exercising their rights ... but that privilege has been abused ... our confidence is now gone ... their future is doomed ... we want them to abstain themselves from politics and wash their hands of financial matters.'[14] As we have seen, many of the reasons for that strident hostility were entirely reasonable. Some chiefs had exercised arbitrary power, had abused their positions and had been thoroughly resistant to anything approaching public accountability. As the undoubtedly dominant partner in a new government, the CPP confronted a tradition, especially noticeable amongst the major chiefs of southern Ghana, which continued to insist that the pre-colonial kingdoms were, in effect, sovereign powers. In many cases southern chiefs had asserted this kind of argument throughout the colonial period and, as we have seen, had enjoyed many powers which suggested if not sovereignty, then at least a large degree of autonomy. The mere

[11] Memorandum by the minister of local government for Executive Council, 14 July, 1951. NAG ADM 5/3/137.

[12] As the chief commissioners of the regions were to be called after the passage of the 1951 Local Government Ordinance.

[13] Legislative Assembly Debates, 22 December 1951.

[14] Legislative Assembly Debates, 4 April 1951.

fact that the CPP had swept to power on a considerable majority of votes should, the CPP felt, have altered that perspective profoundly.

Below the level of central government, however, CPP members and supporters in the rural areas showed, it was claimed, 'gross disrespect to Chieftaincy and a show of disrespect to established authority'.[15] That general proposition was certainly supported by the Gold Coast Police's Special Branch who believed that the earlier, localized campaigns against individual chiefs had, after the election, become a systematic campaign: 'in the Western Province, Eastern Province and even Togoland ... the Chiefs have been told that if they do not support the demands of the "masses" they will suffer ... As an instrument for maintaining law and order, should that term entail some form of sanction against his C.P.P. subjects, the average Chief in the Colony and Ashanti today is impotent.'[16]

The CPP strenuously rejected such accusations. It insisted that local attacks on chiefs were not CPP policy and, where they occurred, they were the direct result of the bad behaviour of individual chiefs. 'The Party', Komla Gbedemah said, 'has never shown any disrespect to the Chiefs but rather advocated and taught its members that due respect should be given to them; but of course, if a chief does not show the same tendency towards his people then of course the Party cannot be blamed for any conflict that ensues. *It might be said that this is the age of the Common Man.*' In this context there is little doubt that 'the people' and 'the Common Man' referred to CPP supporters.[17] It is extremely unlikely that such bromides fooled anybody. The party's newspaper continued to attack chiefs who were opposed to the CPP; and it also published articles which condemned chieftaincy *in toto* and even encouraged readers to take matters into their own hands. An article by an author using the soubriquet 'Orlando'[18] talked of the 'inglorious role our chiefs have played in imperialist post-war politics' and invoked 'the great democratic weapon DESTOOLMENT'.[19] The newspaper still named its publisher as Kwame Nkrumah and it was the official organ of the governing party; such an appeal was a clear incitement to local revolt. And this kind of name-calling was only the tip of a larger iceberg. The essential background to all of this is the ways in which the CPP had established itself in the countryside.

Following its founding in June 1949, the CPP had very adroitly attached itself to dissident groupings in the countryside. It could also be argued that dissidents had attached themselves to the CPP; it was of course a two-way process. Recruitment in the big towns was never a major problem, for here lay the CPP's natural constituency. In the country's rural areas, however, the home of the vast majority of the Gold Coast's citizens, it faced a more exacting task. Electorally it could not prevail without strong rural support; municipal seats alone could not furnish any

---

[15] Legislative Council Debates, 4 April 1951. The speaker was one of the Territorial Members, the Okyenhene of Akyem Abuakwa, Ofori Atta II.

[16] Special Branch Monthly Situation Report,. SB No. 27, April 1951, SF 873. Vol. VIII. The nature of this material is discussed in R. Rathbone, 'Police intelligence in Ghana in the late 1940s and 1950s'.

[17] *Ibid.* The stress is mine.

[18] From the tone of the piece Orlando Furioso might have been more apt.

[19] *Accra Evening News*, 29 August 1951

party with a majority in the Assembly. But rural areas were spatially immense, populations were scattered, were mostly illiterate and, like most farming communities, more preoccupied with everyday struggles with the market, the weather, pests and diseases than with abstract, distant arguments about democracy. Additionally, despite the romantic essentialism of some colonial assumptions of a rural harmony orchestrated by the uncontested legitimacy of 'natural rulers', virtually every chieftaincy, virtually every stool, was in reality a tense political cockpit.

Obviously the fault-lines of dissent differed from place to place. But squabbles and sometimes very dangerous confrontations were the essence of chieftaincy politics. There were many reasons for this. As we have seen, some were connected with utterly reasonable anger at the partiality and even the peculation of some traditional rulers. Some were the almost natural outcome of local administrative systems that had not responded to significant economic and social change; this led Dunn and Robertson to conclude that 'the persistence of chieftaincy as a focus of communal and factional strife is clearly in part a product of the protracted colonial experiment with indirect rule'.[20] Others undoubtedly had elements of class antagonism, for some local aristocracies had waxed fat by, for example, exploiting the sale of land which was not theirs to sell and by extracting excessive taxes from their subjects. But far more frequently the root cause of dissent was quite simply the fissiparousness that characterized Akan chieftaincy.

The great 19th- and early 20th-century jurists John Mensah Sarbah[21] and J.E. Casely Hayford[22] wrote extensively about Akan constitutional affairs and did so in the refined and derived idiom of Western parliamentary and legal niceties.That idiom was carefully chosen and was of course instrumental. Part of their brief was an insistence that Akan constitutional law was not barbaric and compared favourably with that of Britain. In those pre-relativistic days, that argument could only be pressed by analogy. The supposedly overarching legalism and regularity of process was picked up and then amplified by the 1920s and 1930s by Dr J.B. Danquah[23] and the great government anthropologist, R.S. Rattray;[24] it is important to remember that both of them were also British-trained barristers. Their accounts are immensely valuable and always fascinating but they are habitually normative. While not occasionally beyond question in detail, they tell us about what should happen and not what really happens. An exception might be J.B. Danquah's *Cases in Akan Law* which drew heavily on legal cases heard by the native courts of his half-brother, Nana Sir Ofori Atta, in Akyem Abuakwa. The excellent records of those tribunals in the Akyem Abuakwa State Archives in Kyebi show, however, that the guiding legal principles Danquah illustrates were as frequently ignored as adhered to in those courts. These major authorities are all worryingly silent about

---

[20] *Dependence and opportunity*, p. 93.
[21] See especially his *Fanti customary laws*.
[22] *Gold Coast native institutions*.
[23] See especially his *Akan laws and customs* and *Cases in Akan Law*.
[24] Most significantly his *Ashanti law and constitution*.

the politics as opposed to the rules of succession or deposition. In practice, very few rulers reached their stools with unanimous popular support. The Akan inheritance system ensures that there are almost always several legitimate claimants to a stool; frequently there are further candidates whose supporters would argue that what was assumed to be legitimate succession was in fact a perversion of custom or an unwarranted rewriting of local history.

Technically, the brothers of a dead king and his nephews, usually by his uterine sister, are eligible to succeed him. Few successions are uncontested; thus very few rulers take office without having triumphed over other claimants and their followers. The process seems almost inevitably to invite the formation of factions; in some cases these coalesce around a section of a lineage and in others they constitute personal followings of clients or people from the same town or village of the claimant. Successful factions get their man into office by making undertakings to those who support them; those promises need to be honoured, to be translated into patronage once success is attained. Accordingly all Akan rulers tread an extremely uncomfortable path. On the one hand, they must cultivate their supporters; past kindnesses demand present favours. On the other, such patronage inevitably further alienates those who have failed to get their way in the long and usually contested process of selecting a new ruler.

There are other fault-lines in most Akan states. Some are based on historical antipathies between towns in a kingdom. Although the official, chiefly ideology of most Akan kingdoms centres on a celebration of long-term homogeneity, this frequently and intentionally conceals powerful and often ancient antagonisms.[25] Very often there is popular suspicion that capital towns have accreted advantage by dint of being the site of the stool and the palace. During the period in which the palace and the Native Authority were virtually indistinguishable, there is no doubt that citizens of capital towns, the seats of paramount chiefs, benefited considerably from the job creation and the local expenditure that inhered in being administrative centres. Frequently such capitals were also to attract further employment by being designated the colonial state's district headquarters.

It was certainly not the case that the CPP initiated such divisions. Most of these had long, complex histories.[26] For some rulers, cultivating the CPP was seen as adding potentially valuable support to fragile tenure; after the CPP's success in the 1951 elections, such pragmatism could be seen as a continuation of the older, if risky, ploy of cultivating the colonial regime. But in the period 1949–54 it was more often the case that opponents of the incumbent chief declared themselves to be CPP supporters. Despite this, local political disturbances had in most cases little or nothing to do with national politics.

---

[25] For a detailed example see R. Rathbone, 'Defining Akyemfo; the construction of citizenship in Akyem Abuakwa, Ghana, 1700-1939'.

[26] David Apter's outline of the divisions in Wenchi and in Manya Krobo (between the ruler, the *konor* and the CPP activist Mate Johnson) in *The Gold Coast in transition*, pp. 257–72 and R.C. Crook's detailed elaboration of recent Offinso history in 'Local elites and national politics in Ghana', provide excellent examples .

Chiefs were usually destooled after the formal bringing of charges against them had been rehearsed and then supported in the relevant State Council. Schedules of such charges were drawn up and in some rare cases these are still open to consultation in the National Archives of Ghana. Three such cases merit a brief diversion as they give some idea of the extraordinary mixture of complaints. Some derived from this or that reading of 'tradition', whilst others were manifestly constructed out of immediate and very modern expectations.

In January 1953, the Adontenhene of Akim-Bosome[27] was faced with no less than 50 charges. A recital of all 50 would be very tedious. But they begin with 'That he told his elders that he would give up his stool for a woman' and continue with 'that he refused to take action when his sister in the menstrual period entered the *Ahenfie* [royal palace] ... that he sold ... all the cocoa farms being properties of the Stool ... that he did insult his Elders by charging them as wizards ... that he failed to repair the State Drums ... that he did steal a goat in company of some gangsters which goat he made feast of ... that he did have sexual connection with a girl ... in a car ... which vehicle was later brought to him to Brenase to purify ... that he does not take interest in Local School affairs and as a result the school has lost influence in the town', and so on.[28] This is a clear case of a chief being found generally offensive by his elders rather than local supporters of the CPP; here there appear to be no national political overtones.

For every such case in the 1950s, however, there are several others in which the whiff of national politics is rather more apparent. In March 1954, a mere 11 charges were laid against the Odikro of Amana Praso in Akim Kotoku.[29] These included a claim that he was clearly insane because he had thrown away his cloth and 'nakedly ran from street to street'. As Akan chiefs are expected to be physically perfect, a disability like insanity constitutes a good ground for destoolment. But the charges also claim that 'you do not love your town ... that you for many times play with small small girls pointing to each one of them ... with a stick ... "*kate wo twe kata wo twe*"' [roughly 'cover your vagina'] and then 'prior to the Local Council election you quarrelled with your Krontihene [a senior sub-chief] for refusing to canvas for the election of your grandson when he told you it was undemocratic if he did so'.[30] The grandson in question was an outspoken opponent of the CPP in the area. In this case, and in others, national political issues were becoming entwined with what had previously been a universe dominated by traditional concerns.

Even more transparently political are the charges levelled against the divisional chief of Otwereso on 14 May 1954. These included some traditional objections, such as 'you have taken ... the ancient Human Skull attached to the Atupan Drums ... for your own purposes'. But the second charge against him was that 'ever since the Establishment of the Local Council of the North Birim ... you have

---

[27] Nana Amoaben Oko II.

[28] See NAG ADM 36/1/118/75.

[29] Baffuor Yaw Antwi.

[30] See NAG ADM 36/1/118/ 94 and NAG ADM 36/1/118/95.

deliberately and maliciously ignored and failed to co-operate with the Local Council'.[31] That local council was dominated by CPP councillors and there is no doubt that these charges were provoked by the local branch of the CPP.

Local rulers and local aspirants to chieftaincy were in some cases quick to realize that the CPP, the winners after all, might prove to be a valuable ally. An 18-month-old stool dispute in Asiakwa between two senior chiefs, the Gyaasehene and the Nifahene of Akyem Abuakwa, was resolved at the end of May 1954 in the Gyaasehene's favour when he was able to press destoolment charges against the Nifahene for having instructed a local council member to vote against the CPP. But the CPP were also quick to realize that in disaffected groups and even towns they had potential rural allies. There can be little doubt that the divisive quality of stool politics was a potentially effective recruiting sergeant for a new political party.

The more chieftaincy could be publicly associated with colonial rule, the easier it was to extrapolate the CPP's anti-imperialism into an ideology and then a movement which opposed incumbent chiefs and those who were advantaged by chieftaincy. This was very firmly part of popular culture. The successful local peripatetic dramatic form, known to this day as 'concert party', whereby troupes of performers put on plays and musical performances in various venues, had picked up the theme by the late 1940s. The Axim Trio, one of the two most prominent companies, was performing two plays, back-to-back, around the time of the 1951 election. One was called *Kwame Nkrumah is our saviour* and the other *The D.C. and his Good Friend*.[32] The latter lampooned chiefs as dim-witted and unprincipled agents of the colonial establishment, as 'good friends' of the district commissioners. The play's title carried another meaning: 'Your good friend' was also the traditional, formulaic way of ending letters between district commissioners and chiefs. In the same period the Axim Trio was also performing another play called *The primitive chief*. Kwame Nkrumah's first public social engagement after his triumph in the 1951 election and his release from prison was to attend one of these performances.

By the end of 1950, the CPP presence in the countryside was almost always notable in areas of dissent. Its flags, and party flags which fluttered everywhere were very visible statements about local domination in this period, flew in those towns in the west of the Ashanti Region which were in contention with the Asantehene. They flew in Akyem Abuakwa in the towns of Asamankese and Akwatia which had tried to secede from Akyem Abuakwa in the interwar period, and in the area known as New Juaben which had resisted the control of Akyem Abuakwa's traditional ruling council for decades. Such lofty examples were matched by quite humble cases where factions opposed to village headmen, *adikro*, signified their dissidence by declaring for the CPP.

In many respects CPP support in the countryside in the first years after its foundation was a pretty certain indication of local tensions; and these tensions

---

[31] Destoolment charges against Nana Ofosu Kwabi II, NAG ADM 36/1/119/65.

[32] See *African Morning Post*, 1 March 1951, for a review of these plays.

were frequently accompanied by violence. The language of CPP insinuation into the countryside was frequently militaristic. The establishment of CPP branches and the holding of rallies were frequently expressed in an idiom of confrontation and conquest: 'Nkrumah invades Asikuma', *The Evening News* told its readers[33] and 'preparations are being made for a second invasion of Kibi'[34] are typical of the partisan journalism of the time.

The texture of these localized struggles differed widely. As suggested earlier, the fate of the state of Akyem Abuakwa and its king is a central skein in the unfolding history of the relationship between the CPP and Ghana's traditional rulers. It is to Akyem that we now turn. In an earlier work I tried to show how the king and royal family of a state which had been the most important and, in many respects, the most successful of the manifestations of indirect rule became dogged and implacable opponents of the colonial regime.[35] It was no coincidence that the state had produced two of the founding fathers of the United Gold Coast Convention, Dr J.B. Danquah and W.E.A. Ofori Atta. Danquah, a leading intellectual and lawyer and a long-term antagonist of British rule in the Gold Coast, was half-brother[36] of the state's paramount chief, the Okyenhene Nana Sir Ofori Atta, who had died in 1943. Ofori Atta was a son of the late Okyenhene. A further founding member of the UGCC was A.E. Akuffo-Addo, who was the late king's son-in-law.

Strong and resentful anti-British sentiment in the palace certainly pushed the new king, Ofori Atta II, towards anti-colonial nationalism by the end of the 1940s. That was certainly helped by his need to keep the support of a population which was very much divided over the issue of loyalty to the royal family. The majority of the people of Akyem Abuakwa were farmers and they were understandably up in arms over the particular and harsh ways in which the colonial government had addressed the menace of swollen shoot disease. The fact that the UGCC opposed the compulsory precautionary cutting down of cocoa trees was probably as pressing a reason for the Okyenhene's support for the UGCC as was any sense of loyalty to his kinsmen who were leaders of the party.

In July 1948, the UGCC's stalwart Willie (W.E.A.) Ofori Atta wrote to his kinsman the Okyenhene telling him that the Kyebi branch of the UGCC was to hold a rally there on 25 July 1948 and asked for his support.[37] Ofori Atta II readily agreed to this and wrote in return that he and his council 'heartily accepted your invitation and would give you all possible active co-operation in making your Rally, which is the first of its kind in Kibi, a golden success'.[38] The Okyenhene was breaking new ground by becoming so openly associated with a political party. His predecessor had been far more circumspect. Now there could be no confusion

---

[33] *Accra Evening News*, 29 November 1951.

[34] *Ibid.*, 7 November 1951.

[35] *Murder and politics in colonial Ghana*.

[36] Same father, different mother, as they say in Ghana.

[37] Akyem Abuakwa State Archives (AASA), Kyebi, 10/345. The letter is from his cousin W.E.A. Ofori Atta and is dated 11 July 1948.

[38] *Ibid.* Letter to W.E.A. Ofori Atta dated 23 July 1948. The orthography is confusing. Kibi is the same town as that now spelled 'Kyebi'.

about his support for the UGCC. He was to allow the UGCC to use the handsome walled courtyard of his palace, Ofori Panin Fie, for a further rally in November 1948.

By the end of the 1940s, the Okyenhene was therefore an unusually outspoken anti-colonial chief. He was, for example, to publish a strongly pro-UGCC article in an early number of *The Accra Evening News* on 8 February 1949. At this juncture it is clear that he was considered radical by nationalist politicians and not merely those of the UGCC. Indeed in June 1950 when the Joint Provincial Council was required to vote for two members of the Legislative Council, the CPP supported his candidature. He had 'been watched and tried by us, the common people and we have found that [he is] the peoples' man'.[39] A later *Evening News* editorial said that, whilst the party was in principle against chiefs being in the Legislative Council, 'we have to choose between two evils. We are supporting ... Nana Ofori Atta II because we know [he is a] chief of the people and [his] presence there will be to our best interest.'[40] This harmony had everything to do with the fact that the CPP had not yet begun its general election campaign and had, in fact, made few inroads into Akyem Abuakwa.

But the battle-lines between the CPP and UGCC were being drawn. The CPP had first entered Akyem Abuakwa during the last months of 1950. The first headquarters branch for the whole area of Akyem Abuakwa was set up in Kukurantumi on 13 October 1951 at a meeting chaired by the Osiemhene. The party now established support in areas which had opposed the Okyenhene during the previous decades. Its first successes were in Osiem where it had latched on to the faction which had eventually succeeded after a long and bitter contest over the election of a new Osiemhene. The Omanhene of Osiem, Nana Antwi I, was in the coming years to act as organizer and host to CPP rallies in his town, to the very great irritation of the Okyenhene. At one of these meetings where speakers included Komla Gbedemah and Krobo Edusei, Komla Gbedemah attacked the UGCC Members of the Legislative Assembly for Akyem Abuakwa, J.B. Danquah and Willie Ofori Atta, for putting 'party politics above local interests ... the huge revenue from rich soil should be used for the people'.[41] The CPP was able to increase its strength in Osiem over time. On 4 May 1951 the Mankrado of Osiem, Kwaku Bosumpen, the last office-holding opponent of the party in the town, was destooled. *The Evening News* reported that he had 'no interest in the welfare of the town ... he and one Kwame Dakwa (fetish priest) were the men who arranged a gang of ruffians to beat Osiem CPP members'.[42] The CPP also achieved strong support in Tafo, the centre of a long-term campaign against the palace. The CPP tried to establish a branch in the royal capital, Kyebi, itself but its flags were torn down at the Okyenhene's command. The Okyenhene had instructed his sub-chiefs

[39] *Accra Evening News*, 10 June 1950.

[40] 13 June 1950. Ofori Atta II was elected and was to return to the new Legislative Assembly in 1951 as a Joint Provincial Council member.

[41] *Accra Evening News*, 9 January 1953.

[42] 12 May 1951.

to tear down CPP flags throughout the Akyem Abuakwa state. Such incidents sometimes turned into cases before the Okyenhene's native tribunal. In June 1951 Kwabena Mensah, a local CPP activist, was charged with flying a CPP flag in Banso and fined nearly £20 for his offences. CPP meetings were, *The Evening News* reported, disrupted by lorry-loads of youngsters who were ordered to do so by the palace.[43]

The Okyenhene's animosity is not hard to explain. The UGCC had in effect become the royal family's party and the CPP was out to destroy the UGCC. Three of its most significant leaders, Danquah, Akuffo-Addo and Ofori Atta, were, after all, members of that family although this is only a partial explanation of the Okyenhene's support for the UGCC. There was, however, much that was personal in this struggle. There is little doubt that the Okyenhene behaved in a most irregular fashion in the course of the February elections. He was alleged to have harangued voters in the polling station to vote for the UGCC candidates, his kinsmen Danquah and Ofori Atta, and it was also alleged that CPP supporters were assaulted on polling day at his command.[44]

The Okyenhene was himself a Member of the new Legislative Assembly as one of the Joint Provincial Council of Chiefs representatives and on the floor of the House he lost no opportunity to attack the CPP for its active opposition to chieftaincy. But the over-exuberant and almost certainly incautious identification of the stool, the royal family and the king with the UGCC had an equal and opposite effect on the structure of politics in the state of Akyem Abuakwa. Thus the local CPP had become the party of opposition to the Okyenhene and to his rule from Kyebi. The Okyenhene railed angrily against the CPP's campaign in his state. It was, he said, all 'malicious propaganda'.[45] He continued to prevent the CPP, now the party of government, from establishing a branch in his capital. He continued to order CPP flags to be pulled down. And on the eve of local government reform he used his control of the Native Authority police to arrest CPP members on the grounds that they were 'trouble makers'. The Native Authority was asked to collect the names of CPP members so that the enemy could be easily identified, a somewhat Macarthyite commission it actually carried out. When local chiefs supported the CPP, they were called to account in the king's court, insulted, fined and in some cases destooled. The Odikro of Amampatia Akim was allegedly subjected to 'insulting words ... called him a traitor ... for being a CPP member ... cursed and declared him destooled with a fine of £36 ... The destooled Odikro is detained at Kibi until such time that the people of Ampampatia would come to say to the Okyenhene that they have all resigned from the CPP.'[46] By April 1951, the CPP newspaper was alleging not only that the king and

---

[43] Although I have heard of many such incidents, those at Ahwenease on June 4th 1951 and at Kyebi itself on 16 June are the only ones for which I have documentary evidence.

[44] See *Accra Evening News*, for 16 February 1951.

[45] AASA 10/345. Letter from Okyenhene to the UGCC Chairman, 7 March 1951.

[46] *AccraEvening News*, 31 October 1951. While this is a partisan and probably exaggerated account, the tribunal records suggest that it is mostly accurate; in addition there are too many such stories to discount it in its totality.

his supporters were engaged in an active campaign to sabotage the CPP government but, less plausibly, that they were actually making plans to assassinate the leader of government business, Nkrumah.[47] Nkrumah was to repeat the allegation about the threat to his life when speaking at a meeting in Osiem on 25 May 1951. These nasty spats were repeated throughout the kingdom and the provocations came from both sides. In May 1951, seven CPP supporters were arrested for insulting chiefs by openly praising Nkrumah.[48] Chiefs in Akyem Abuakwa who were supporters of the CPP or less than enthusiastic supporters of the UGCC were threatened with destoolment charges.

The CPP counter-offensive began at the bridgehead of Osiem. On 25 May, Nkrumah with a powerful entourage of his senior lieutenants, including Kojo Botsio, Komla Gbedemah and Nathan Welbeck, came to Osiem in a triumphalist procession. Gbedemah said that: 'The Okyenhene is still in darkness ... we go with chiefs who go with us'. Nkrumah denounced 'tyrant chiefs' who would get their come-uppance when local government reform was in place.[49] By September 1951, the local CPP leaders announced their intention to carry out a Positive Action campaign[50] against the state of Akyem Abuakwa, by which they meant the State Council, the Okyeman Council, of Akyem Abuakwa. In many villages the CPP stirred up feelings against village headmen, *adikrofo*, who remained loyal to the Okyenhene. Chiefs and headmen who were foolish enough to speak against the CPP or were unco-operative with the local party branch were threatened with destoolment. In a particularly unpleasant incident, the popular and well-educated chief of Asamama was threatened with destoolment and the row degenerated into a full-blown riot in which shots were fired. The ostensible reason for local CPP antipathy to this chief was that he had dared to charge a CPP member with a criminal offence. The chief refused to be intimidated into dropping charges against this man. These stand-offs made matters worse. Threatened minor chiefs turned to the Okyenhene and his council for support and resulting interventions, sometimes using the Native Authority Police, served to widen the gulf between the party and the palace.[51]

Some of the bitterness was undoubtedly fed by mischievous rumour. For example, the local CPP made great play of allegations of the dishonest financial dealings of the Akyem Abuakwa Native Authority which was still under the chairmanship of Nana Ofori Atta II. Older informants remembered that there was a strong local conviction that it had not distributed the considerable revenue collected in past years in an evenhanded way. In fact, there was an exhaustive historical audit of its accounts carried out by the government's senior auditor, E.L. Clegg, in September 1951. His report shows that the standard of book-keeping was very high. The same report also demonstrates that the widespread populist belief

---

[47] See *Accra Evening News*, 11 and 14 April 1951.

[48] The case was heard by the District Commissioner on 15 June, who threw out the charges.

[49] See *Accra Evening News*, 28 May 1951.

[50] What was meant by that was not spelled out.

[51] See District Record Book, Birrim District, 30 September 1951, NAG ADM 32/4/100.

that the native authority treasury, and hence the Okyenhene, was in receipt of large amounts of revenue and was a store of huge hidden wealth was a considerable distortion of a much more humble reality.

Part of the reason for such great sensitivity on an issue like this undoubtedly owed much to the implications of the impending changes to local government structure, which were being widely discussed; it owed even more to the impact of CPP propaganda. Both led some people, and most especially the young who had 'an awakening sense of civic responsibility', to refuse to pay local taxes to a Native Authority which was unfairly believed to have a somewhat tawdry financial track record and which was about to be replaced.[52] Chiefs in general were in serious trouble throughout Akyem Abuakwa in the early 1950s. That these problems were not confined to the Akyem Abuakwa kingdom is confirmed by a stern warning to the minister of local government from the chief regional officer, Ashanti.

> N.As [Native Authorities] are relaxing their efforts towards collecting revenue ... This is quite understandable since the present NA members are less prepared ... to court the usual unpopularity which goes with ... taxation, particularly since in some areas active opposition has been stirred up by political factions. The country-wide enquiries into the form and content of ... Local Councils have had the effect of arousing every parochial jealousy and tribal antipathy and it is certain that much dissatisfacton will be expressed ... by non-co-operation with the Councils when they are set up. ... the Minister's attention should be called to the need for the dominant political party propaganda machine to 'soften up' the opposition to direct taxation and all existing institutions.[53]

Things were, however, especially uncomfortable in Akyem Abuakwa. The district commissioner[54] by the end of 1951 reported:

> almost every week one Odikro or another was attacked by his people ... and often he or she was forced to flee from the village in fear of serious personal harm. Seldom were charges preferred against the chiefs and in all cases action seems to have been inspired and controlled by members of the same political group. As far as Chiefs were concerned, they had little opportunity for obtaining a fair hearing since ... people would not come before the State Council to prefer their complaints nor would they accept its authority. Action by one or two chiefs ... to have their assailants charged ... did not improve their relationship with their people and led to bitter accusations against the Native Authority.[55]

Disputes between 'youngmen' and chiefs raged throughout Akyem Abuakwa in the year following the general election. Riots in the towns of Abompe, Asamama, Osiem, Osino and Pomase were sufficiently serious to merit the intervention of the Gold Coast's national police. In most cases no one seems able to recall the precise circumstances which gave rise to these disturbances. But for those old enough to remember them, the root cause was, predictably, either the CPP or the Okyenhene and his state council. This was undoubtedly an unpleasant period. The Okyenhene,

[52] *Ibid.*

[53] Chief Regional Officer A.J. Loveridge to the minister of local government, 11 December 1951, NAG ADM 13/2/2.

[54] P.S.G. Smith.

[55] District Record Book, Birrim District, 31 December 1951, NAG ADM 32/4/100.

who had minor surgery in Accra in January 1952, remained absent from Kyebi, perhaps wisely, for much of the first half of 1952. And, more mysteriously, he left for Guinea in French West Africa, where it was rumoured that he consulted the priests of the great 'fetish' at Kankan, in August 1951. It would be interesting to know what advice he was given.

The essential background to these events, and similar events throughout many parts of the colony and Ashanti, was the attempt to put a new system of local government into operation. The new ordinance seemed simple enough and thoroughly sensible on paper. In reality it was a cumbersome reform package and chiefs and their state councils were in some cases, most notably in Akyem Abuakwa, able to exploit this for political gain. The new local councils were essentially hybrids. The old native authorities were to be run down and their powers assumed by newly constituted and largely elected local councils. But the new legislation had not bitten on the bullet and had not totally excluded the chiefly element from the new structure, which surely was what the CPP would have wished. As already noted, one-third of the membership of the new local councils had to be composed of those returned by the local traditional council. This concession paid some deference to chieftaincy and to the spirit of the Coussey committee; but in so doing it courted chaos.

This transition, or supersession as it was called in administrative circles, required local councils, which took over the revenue-raising powers enjoyed by the old Native Authorities, to come initially to some agreement with their local traditional councils over the actual extent of that revenue. Not surprisingly, such agreements were hard to come by; newly elected local councillors, often CPP supporters, insisted frequently that the old order was not declaring all of its assets and was concealing sources of income. Local councils and traditional state councils were also supposed to agree on the proportion of that revenue which would be devoted to traditional council expenditure. Anyone reading the numerous accounts of bitter disagreement in district after district would be led to an analogy with debates over financial settlements in the course of rancorous divorce. The government believed, quite literally, in a clean break. The minister of local government's 'Notes on the supersession of Native Authorities' stated unequivocally that 'there is no inter-regnum between the disappearance of the Native Authority and the establishment of a Local Council in any area'.[56] The practical problems of disentanglement were, however, to make a mockery of such an euphoric expectation. The evidence suggests that government had a longer-term ambition. There is little doubt that central government also had its eyes on the royalty revenues of those traditional states which enjoyed gold or diamond concessions. In Cabinet on 5 March 1953, the minister of commerce and industry commented that 'it is not in accordance with modern economic policy that revenue accruing to a Government from the exploitation of a mineral ... should be diverted to ... individual landowners'.[57]

[56] 14 February 1952, NAG ADM 36/1/99/70.
[57] NAG ADM 13/2/10.

Throughout 1952 the ministry of local government was overwhelmed by a series of distinctly messy problems initiated by the new legislation and in many cases exacerbated by local political interests. The first of such problems emerged from the attempt to 'fit' the new local councils alongside the old Native Authorities. There is no reason to doubt the general intention of creating efficient and accountable organs of local government. But parochial loyalties were re-awakened and enlivened by the imminent prospect of change.

For example an age-old struggle over jurisdiction between the rulers of Manya Krobo and Akyem Abuakwa flared up once again. The heart of this matter lay in the fact that something like 30,000 Krobo people had bought land in Akyem Abuakwa, around Begoro, in the first few years of the 20th century. This land and its inhabitants were matters of long if spasmodic dispute between the two rulers. Now it was revived. Manya Krobo suggested that, by dint of long occupation, this area should fall within the administrative area of the new Manya Krobo Local Council. The Okyenhene and his council, *per contra*, argued that the only solution lay in the creation of a new and separate local council. In this squabble, Cabinet dismissed the arguments of the Akyem Abuakwa stool and in so doing worsened its relationship with the traditional rulers of the area.[58] It was not surprising that the CPP had created a significant political presence in Begoro.

Other cases indicate that in a substantial number of areas in Ashanti and the Colony there was such antipathy between the elected members of new local councils, very many of whom sailed under CPP colours, and the traditional elements that everyday local administration was impossible. In Wenchi, for example, charge and countercharge were made by the Wenchi stool and by the new CPP-dominated divisional council. The government intervened and suspended the traditional bodies pending an enquiry into allegations of abuse of power by Wenchi's ruler, the Wenchihene. This was perceived as partisan and elicited a strong response signed by most of those members of the Legislative Council who had been returned by the regional councils of chiefs. 'We strongly protest against the decision ... it ... not only undermines chieftaincy but it also strikes at the very foundation of democratic rule in this country. We consider that the Executive Council has used its power in a dictatorial and arbitrary manner ... no encouragement [should be] given to the disregard for law or to totalitarian practices in this country.'[59] In Denyase, the enmity between the CPP's eight elected local council members and the Denyasehene resulted in an impasse in which the council could no longer function and during which the Denyasehene was destooled by a faction led by the local CPP branch. As 'local government administration in the area has completely broken down', the minister asked Cabinet to suspend the local council and to impose a management committee on the area.[60] The same process was

---

[58] Memorandum by the minister of local government, 'Establishing a Manya Krobo Local Council', 25 February 1952, NAG ADM 13/2/4.

[59] Letter enclosed in Cabinet Papers, 25 February 1952, NAG ADM 13/2/4.

[60] Cabinet memorandum by the minister of local government, 'The suspension of Denyase Local Council', 9 September 1952, NAG ADM 13/2/7.

followed in Agona[61] and in many other areas. In each case the new committee of management was 'agreed' by the chief regional officer in consultation with the minister and resulted in something very close to direct rule. In some cases these periods of suspension amounted to an interim arrangement during which the opportunity was taken to shake out troublesome traditional members. Such suspensions were to become commonplace in many local government areas in the southern Gold Coast.

There can be little doubt that local government reform had become a political battleground. The letter quoted above resonates strongly with another letter sent to the British Secretary of State for the Colonies[62] just over two months later by the Ghana Congress Party, which was the new style of the old UGCC.[63] This complained about the 'intimidation, violence and frequent destoolments to which Chiefs throughout the country have been subject. Recently the Prime Minister threatened in public all chiefs who dare to give support in any form to the Ghana Congress Party with dire consequences.[64] Chieftaincy today is threatened with extinction.'[65] There is no doubt that claims by chiefs and their supporters to local political as opposed to ritual power were regarded as hostile by the government and against 'the current trends towards popular representation ... a tendency towards democratic government'.[66] At a purely pragmatic level, such complications were profoundly unwelcome to a government which, like all governments, wanted change to advance on smooth ground.

These were not isolated examples. Innumerable complaints about the lack of 'fit' between the new local government structure and what was claimed to have been tradition were made. But even more disturbing were the number of cases in which the financial implications of reform became bogged down by the refusal of local councils and traditional bodies to agree to a final financial settlement. At the heart of this mess lay the government's unwillingness to specify the exact proportions in which stool land revenues were to be distributed between councils and stools. Both parties were required to agree these amounts, but it was clear that in many cases there was such mutual hostility that agreement was impossible. In the case of Akyem Abuakwa innumerable meetings were called throughout 1952 by the chief regional officer of representatives of the successor councils to what had been the Native Authority and the stool. An early suggestion by the minister for local government that a financial split giving one-third to the stool and two-thirds to the successor local councils was made in June 1952; this was, probably predictably, vehemently rejected by the stool.[67] In March 1953, the chief regional

---

[61] See Agona (Colony) Local Council Suspension and Transfer of Functions Order, 1954, and Cabinet memoranda, 7 January 1954, NAG ADM 13/2/15.

[62] Oliver Lyttleton, who personally visited the Gold Coast in May 1952.

[63] Its chairman was Dr Kofi Busia, the sociologist. It was no coincidence that he was a Wenchi royal.

[64] I have been unable to find any reference to this alleged statement by Nkrumah.

[65] NAG ADM 13/2/5.

[66] Cabinet memorandum by the minister of local government, 'Akwamu Native Authority', 10 October 1951. NAG ADM 13/2/2.

[67] The gross land revenue of Akyem Abuakwa in 1952–3 was estimated at a maximum of £90,500.

officer wrote that: 'owing to the political situation in Akim Abuakwa it is possible that the Stool and Councils may not be able to reach agreement in which case the Minister ... may have to make a decision'.[68] As late as May 1953 the stool was still contending that it should receive two-thirds of the revenue, a view which was rejected. Not until June 1953 was the earlier proposal for a two-third/one-third split actually imposed upon the area.[69] But the final distribution of assets was clearly still incomplete as late as March 1954 and the stand-off between the traditional and elected elements was still unresolved.[70] For over two years the funding of local government and hence local development in a sizeable part of the eastern region of the colony had been held up by intractable squabbling.

The CPP was a party in a hurry and became a government in a hurry. The evidence suggests a growing sense of impatience with what it regarded as traditional intransigence. Cabinet had no doubt that these problems were being deliberately created by chiefs and their supporters and that such campaigns were politically inspired. Forced by the need to satisfy their British co-rulers, perhaps, there had been some expression of public respect paid to traditional rulers in the early days of the post-1951 administration. That position was undoubtedly eroding. By July 1952, the minister of local government was digging in his heels.

> There is a danger that traditional authorities may attempt to continue powers which have been transferred to Local Councils particularly where there was no doubt that the majority on the Council is confined to persons with political affiliations unacceptable to the traditional authorities[71]... unless clear and unequivocal directives can be given from a Central Government Office and conveyed to the traditional authorities ... an important part of local administration falls to the ground and may bring down local government with it.[72]

In thinking through the problems of creating councils which were larger than the Native Authority they were superseding, the minister in the same memorandum wrote 'whenever there is a conflict between geographical factors and traditional allegiances, the former should prevail if that would lead to more efficient administration'.[73]

Government policy began to dump the assumption, part of the hitherto seemingly sacrosanct inheritance of the Coussey committee deliberations, that traditional authority should be recognized in all reformed local government structures. While it is impossible to prove this, the fact that the CPP grew stronger in office between 1951 and 1954 seems to be one of the reasons why their formal deference to chieftaincy became less apparent over time. By the end of 1952 the

---

[68] NAG ADM 36/1/99/174.

[69] See Subsidiary Supplement No. 27 to the *Government Gazette* No.42 of 30 June, 1953.

[70] See Government Agent, Birrim District, to Regional Officer Eastern Region, 9 March 1954, NAG ADM 31/1/99/15. The impasse was publicly acknowledged – and lamented – by the Minister of Local Government at the inauguration of the new headquarters of the Akyem Abuakwa District Council at New Tafo on 27 March 1954.

[71] A circumlocution for the CPP.

[72] Cabinet memorandum by the minister of local government on 'Progress in the introduction of Local Government Reform', 11 July 1952, NAG ADM 13/2/6.

[73] *Ibid.*

first draft of the White Paper on reformed municipal councils actually omitted all mention of traditional authorities. Cabinet eventually rectified that to some extent but a history of seriously burnt fingers prompted a draft which stated that municipal councils should 'make suitable financial contributions to the maintenance of Traditional Authorities ... *to the extent to which the Minister shall deem necessary.*'[74] Such decisions were to be made at the centre and were no longer to be subjected to the caprices, as the minister saw it, of partisan and unprogressive traditional interests.

In April 1953, the minister took an important memorandum to Cabinet. He agreed that whilst 261 of the proposed 280 new local councils had been established, there were still major problems, although none of them had been running for more than a year when he wrote. He itemized the difficulties with considerable honesty. Interestingly, he began by looking at the numerous councils whose work was at a standstill because of conflicts between elected and traditional members. It is a very fairminded summary: 'In some cases these have arisen out of the failure of the traditional members to accustom themselves to the new order ... in others, out of attempts by elected members to assert their authority'. But the minister went on to deplore 'a reluctance to accept the principles of democracy in local affairs ... the principle of majority rule is not yet understood'. While not alluding to the politics of widespread non-compliance, he suggested that the new local councils' attempts at revenue-gathering had been 'not encouraging'. Overall, this important setpiece of CPP policy, the democratization of local government, was 'in danger of breakdown'.

This reflective and extremely circumspect document, characteristic of the elegant drafting of Edward Asafu-Adjaye and his ministry in this period, brings out the central significance of the challenge to this major plank of CPP policy which was on foot in the countryside. The reforms prompted by the Coussey committee and then the select committees of the House had prompted the drafting of legislation which had unwanted repercussions. Chiefs had inadvertently been allowed considerable room for disruption so long as legislation continued to require them to agree to be compliant. Local government was the arm of administration which most affected the everyday lives of the vast majority of the population. The CPP had promised root-and-branch reform, efficiency and democracy at the local level. After more than two years in office, the net result was undoubtedly extremely messy and hence considerably embarrassing.

The attempts to limit chiefly powers in the day-to-day administration of the countryside were, as we have seen, being resisted. But, as indicated earlier, chiefs also exercised power through their domination of the Native Courts system. The CPP government's management of that vital issue merits special attention and we turn to that matter in the following chapter.

---

[74] Cabinet memorandum on the Municipal Councils Ordinance, 28 November 1952, NAG ADM 13/2/8. The emphasis is mine.

4

The Erosion of Chiefly Jurisdiction

The fate of the system of Native Courts was deeply imbricated in the more general destiny of chieftaincy in Ghana. There is a long history to this which can be dealt with reasonably economically. We have already touched on the evolution of a binary legal system. Its major implication was that much of the law which touched upon the lives of ordinary Ghanaians was deemed to be customary law by the colonial state and by chiefs. Although the plural cultures of what became the Gold Coast had developed numerous and different patterns of legal values, customary law in the Gold Coast was 'Akanized' throughout the colonial period; that process, which merits further research, was and is part of the workings of a more generalized story of the growth of Akan hegemony in many areas of Ghanaian life.[1] In practical terms customary law cases and cases involving minor offences brought many thousands of Ghanaians annually before the so-called Native Courts.

So far as the Colony, the southern third of the Gold Coast, was concerned, Native Courts constituted, as M.J. Field argued, an 'intensely personal system of jurisdiction'.[2] These courts were, however, largely unregulated and scantily reviewed by the colonial state; this lack of intervention persisted into the post-war era[3] and their conduct could fall far short of the basic universal requirements of any definition of fairness. As we have already noted, there is much evidence,

---

[1] More immediately it owed much to the fact that John Mensah Sarbah's *Fanti customary laws*, published in 1897, was for many years the only written authority on *any* customary law in the country.

[2] M.J. Field, memorandum to Secretary of Native Affairs, 15 April 1939. From Ashanti Social Survey Mss. Copy in the possession of T.C. McCaskie, to whom I am grateful for sight of this important text.

[3] This is clear from the Report of the Commission on Native Courts, 1951, para 82. Administrative review of Native Court decisions by either district commissioners or the judicial advisor in the Colony and southern Togoland was carried out in only 0.24 per cent of cases in 1946–7, 0.15 per cent in 1948–9, 0.20 per cent in 1949–50 and 0.21 per cent in 1950–51. The corresponding available figures for courts in the Ashanti Region give 0.88 per cent in 1949–50 and 0.54 per cent in 1950–51. Courts in the Colony and Ashanti heard just over 93,000 cases in 1949–50.

generated most especially by aggrieved Africans, which suggests that charges were sometimes trumped up so that fines could be exacted; these were then shared out amongst the chiefly members of tribunals who were for the most part otherwise unremunerated. They were not only unpaid, but also lacked security of tenure; many analysts of justice systems regard such tenure as one of the major guarantors of independent judgement. We have also seen that more and more quotidian economic activities were subjected to the licensing functions of these courts; market vending, hawking, letter writing, the sale of 'native medicines' and the operation of shrines, matters touching on the economic survival of many, increasingly depended upon the legality of their economic roles. That could only be secured through the courts and this sometimes carried with it the need to 'sweeten' chiefs on those tribunals with bribes.[4]

By the interwar period many were arguing in the pages of Ghana's many newspapers that chieftaincy had been transformed to the point where some chiefs regarded high office as an opportunity to print money; in turn, the chiefs' courts were held to be amongst the most productive of their mints. But weak colonial regimes and the politics of devolution to the chiefs ensured that reform remained a distant goal.[5]

The court system demanded reform but the administration was both too weak and too nervous to set reform in train. Throughout the interwar period, the colonial regime lacked the will and the resources to reform the local court system. The weaknesses in the system were obvious enough well before the Second World War. As we have seen, chiefs' councils, Native Authorities and Native Courts continued to produce by-laws which were sometimes oppressive, and did so even when censured by central government. Ordinary Ghanaians could be brought to court on charges levelled by chiefs who were then to sit on the tribunals which heard those charges.

For the same reasons which explain the beginnings of the reform of local government, the Native Court system was eventually seen as something which needed to be radically altered. As we have seen, that was initiated by a committee of enquiry appointed by the Gold Coast's Legislative Council in 1942.[6] Unlike many of its dreary kind, this commission's report reads like good investigative journalism. Well argued, it suggested that it was stretching the imagination to describe the Native Courts as a justice system. There was little justice here. Too many of these tribunals were self-indulgent in every sense of the phrase. Not all of the blame for this rested on the chiefly adjudicators. It was a structurally weak system. For example, statute insisted that professional lawyers were excluded from hearings.

---

[4] *Kalabule* is a more common expression nowadays.

[5] M.J. Field records: 'I was recently asked by the Secretary of Native Affairs what I "Thought of the doctrine that the time had come to insist that native chiefs had no inherent rights but derived their authority entirely from Government"'. This, she replied, was 'like the doctrine of man's right to shear the wolf, "lawful, but not expedient".' Memorandum, 15 April 1939. Ashanti Social Survey Mss. Copy in the possession of T.C. McCaskie.

[6] Native Tribunals Committee of Enquiry, Chairman Sir Harry Blackall, Accra, 1943.

Their exclusion owed much but not all[7] to the sometimes well-founded belief that lawyers ran up fat bills by complicating and prolonging simple processes; ultimately those fat fees came out of the pockets of thin people. These tribunals, sometimes numbering 20 people, shared the sitting fees, the fines and other exactions. Hailey's reading of the 1942 commission report resulted in the tactfully phrased suggestion that so far as chiefs sitting as court presidents were concerned, 'every consideration was in favour of relieving them of this position ... it is unnecessary to enlarge on this indictment of the ... procedure for its truth was generally admitted'.[8]

The political crisis of 1948–9 intervened in what a depressing history of governmental dilatoriness suggests might have been a very slow process of legal reform. As we have seen, in the aftermath of both the Watson Commission and the Coussey Committee, the Legislative Council rapidly set up a series of Commissions both to flesh out the Coussey committee proposals and to draft the required legislation.[9]

Amongst those commissions, one concerned with Native Courts was appointed in December 1950. Under the chairmanship of the great Ghanaian jurist K.A. Korsah[10] and consisting entirely of African lawyers, this commission submitted its report in September 1951. It recommended significant reform, including giving Native Courts the more politically sensitive name of 'Local Courts'. Interestingly. 'native' was a word whose use had, with rare exceptions like that of this jurisdiction, mostly fallen into disuse in the Gold Coast by the late 1930s. It is unusual to encounter its use in official correspondence in the Gold Coast where 'Africans' or more precise ethnics were more regularly deployed even in informal official correspondence. This might tell us something about the nature of the particular colonial regime the Gold Coast endured or enjoyed. More importantly, the Korsah Commission stipulated the replacement of the extensive and frequently condemned chiefly 'benches' by stipendiary or lay magistrates and recommended a mixture of the two. This seemed to herald the beginning of the end of chiefly domination of local justice. Amongst other recommendations it repeated the recommendation of the Coussey committee that, in effect, chiefs should not be appointed as members of courts with the exception of the Northern Territories jurisdictions.

That there was something anomalous and frequently improper about the way the Gold Coast's binary legal system operated had been, as we have seen, apparent for decades. But progress in the direction of reform was extremely slow. The Watson Commission had advocated a radical, probably impractical as well as politically untenable merging of customary law into the general laws of the country. The Coussey committee, with a large number of lawyers in its ranks,

---

[7] It was, after all, part of the more general 'logic' of indirect rule and one of its repercussions was to deny lawyers involvement in the governance of a huge proportion of the population of the Gold Coast.

[8] *Native Administration*, p.204.

[9] For more details see the final sections of Volume I and the opening sections of volume II of R. Rathbone (ed.) *Ghana; British documents on the end of Empire.*

[10] Later Sir Arku Korsah, who was to become Ghana's Chief Justice.

regarded Native Courts as outmoded and recommended that a special committee should look into the future of the legal system; as noted above, the Korsah Commission was duly appointed to carry that forward.

Interview evidence[11] suggests that the ambitious and hence crowded legislative timetable of the diarchic administration relegated the Local Courts issue to the back-burner; that seems logical enough. Although the Korsah Commission submitted its report in 1951, it was destined to gather dust until 1952 when the Acting Chief Justice commented briefly on the report to Cabinet. And it waited even longer, until 1953, before the Chief Justice was to prepare a more detailed memorandum on it for Cabinet. In 1953, another committee, this one composed of officials,[12] was created to bring recommendations for reform legislation to Cabinet.[13] Those recommendations were designed, the minister of local government told Cabinet, to bring Native Courts 'into line with the general march of progress in the land'.[14]

What was being considered was of considerable importance. As we have seen, the vast majority of Gold Coasters seeking justice or judicial relief of any kind did so, initially at least, in Native Courts. In 1950–51 alone, the 300 or so such courts heard more than 83,000 cases. The case-load of these courts fell in 1950–51. The higher figures for 1948–50 are best explained by chiefs regularly summoning local 'malcontents', in some cases proto-CPP members, for disorder offences in those very volatile years. Native Courts were therefore thoroughly interwoven in the day-to-day life of many communities and, as importantly, in the everyday lives of the country's citizens as individuals. These courts were the workhorses of the Gold Coast's justice system and they were relatively inexpensive. They were cheap because the members and registrars of such courts were very poorly rewarded; this is a major factor in any understanding of the frequency of allegations of these court officials' venality. Overhauling so extensive and so inexpensive a jurisdiction constituted a very large step and the slow progress towards reform required reflection and care but, as importantly, a weather-eye on costs.

The reform measures eventually envisaged by Cabinet were undoubtedly intended to end the domination of Native Courts by chiefs. In many respects the drafts followed the general lines recommended by Korsah and his commission in their 1951 report, even if it had taken over three years to consider those proposals properly. The new courts were be called local courts. Their areas of jurisdiction would harmonize not with the old traditional jurisdictions, which tended to correspond with what local chieftaincy politics had constructed as the boundaries of 'native states', albeit most uncomfortably,[15] but with the newly constituted local and urban council areas. The courts would be served by either single stipendiary magistrates or benches of no more than five honorary, volunteer magistrates,

[11] With Kojo Botsio on 18 May 1991 and Komla Gbedemah on 27 June 1991; both in Accra.

[12] Composed of six administrative officers, two of whom were legally qualified, and a law officer.

[13] They did so on 30 April 1954. Cabinet, NAG ADM 13/2/16.

[14] *Ibid.*

[15] For more on contests over jurisdiction see R. Rathbone, 'Defining Akyemfo; the construction of citizenship in Akyem Abuakwa, Ghana, 1700–1939'.

members of the 'great and the good' appointed by the governor on the chief justice's advice. Appeals would not go beyond the Supreme Court in land and succession cases and not beyond the district magistrates' courts in other cases. Lastly Cabinet resolved to move towards the colossal task of what they called the crystallization, that is to say the unification and codification, of customary law.

No one who had read the succession of damning reports about the nature and conduct of the Native Court system since the early 1940s could fail to recognize that radical reform was urgently needed. Although commendably cheap, the system all too frequently failed to provide even the crudest approximation of natural justice in the eyes of many. But reform was going to prove to be slow to mature and was not to occur until after the achievement of independence.[16] Even then the Local Courts Act of 1958 left 'much of the basic structuring of the old system of Native Courts ... intact'.[17] Why was this so?

Enforced reform was, in reality, taking place in a rather more covert fashion well before any substantial legislation was drafted. The minister of local government was beginning to use his powers to 'vary', by order, the composition of several Native Court panels. The membership of such panels consisted of long lists of names which almost invariably closely corresponded to the membership of the local, traditional state council. All of those empanelled were entitled to sit in judgement in Native Courts. But as a consequence of the reform of Local Authorities, such listings now required the approval of the minister and, in turn, he could appoint new members to such panels. I would argue that this available and entirely legal methodology allowed the sequence of CPP governments to alter the alignments of Local Courts without a formal battery of legislation, and as importantly, without any discussion in the Legislative Assembly[18] but, in effect, to reform their essence, their structure, very little. That essence continued to resonate with M.J. Field's earlier observation that this was an 'intensely personal system of jurisdiction'.[19] What had been proposed by reformers was intended to transform that personal system into a network of dispassionate territorial jurisdictions. But as things turned out, the form, the personal system, of local justice was to be little altered; but from now on, those administering that justice were to be nominees of the minister and thus in large measure the nominees of local CPP branches.

Well before the advent of internal self-government following the second general election of 1954, the minister of local government was tinkering with the membership of these courts. The legislative use of Native Court Variation Orders to wrest control of those courts from traditional office-holders gathered pace before and immediately after independence. The first case I encountered involved the Native Court panel in Sekondi Takoradi. With the approval of Cabinet and hence the law officers, the minister removed 17 members of the panel, of whom at least six were

---

[16] With the enactment of the Local Courts Act (No. 23) of 1958.

[17] W.B. Harvey, *Law and social change in Ghana*, p. 222.

[18] Such changes were merely notified in the *Government Gazette*.

[19] See footnote 2 for citation.

traditional office-holders. With Cabinet assent, he replaced them with 12 others, only one of whom was a royal.[20]

A more comprehensive sweep was, however, conducted towards the end of 1953. In the course of a single Cabinet meeting, the minister, using his capacity to make variation orders, altered the membership of nearly 20 Native Courts. As it bears on the ways in which CPP governments tried to reduce the powers of chieftaincy without all of the ensuing fuss and trouble of grand legislation, the detail which follows matters a great deal.

In the Anlo Native Area court, the minister deleted six names from the old panel list, all of which were those of chiefs. He then added the names of six members, none of whom were chiefs. In the Keta court, three panellists' names were deleted, including that of a chief, and the names of three non-chiefs were added. In the Dzodje, Penyi, Ave-Aferingbe and Hevi Native Courts, five members were removed from the list of whom four were chiefs; five non-chiefs were then empanelled. Five of the names on the list of the Manya Krobo panel were deleted, including a chief, and five non-chiefly names were imposed. The Dormaa Native Court saw five panel members, including two chiefs, struck off followed by the addition of five new names, only one of which was that of a chief. In Djebian, three commoners and two chiefs were removed and six non-chiefs substituted. The Suisi court lost three commoners and two chiefly panel members who were replaced by a slate of five commoners. The Painqua and Akuse/ Kpong court lost three commoner members and two chiefs and, in their places, gained four non-chiefs. The Akwenor court saw three chiefs and two commoners deleted from the panel, who were replaced with five non-chiefs. The Shama court lost six chiefly and one commoner member and gained seven new members, none of whom were chiefs. A similar story comes out of the change to the Akwamu Native Court whose panel lost four chiefs and two commoners and gained six new names, none of whom were chiefs.

This procedure was to be followed even more energetically after the 1954 general election and the advent of internal self-government. Well before that time it would have taken an unusually impercipient chief to fail to recognize that the elections of 1951 had been merely the prelude to a more sustained attack upon them and their old privileges. They were, in effect, being removed from court membership without the intervention of major draft legislation and the wider discussion which would have been prompted by such a bill. There is no evidence which can be relied upon which suggests alternative and more cogent reasons for the delay of legislation, rather than adjustments, on this matter. Reform was taking place, and so far as the chiefs were concerned it was radical reform. But it was taking place within the existing provisions of the old colonial Native Jurisdiction ordinances. It was this methodology which, perhaps, led the minister of local government to describe this (with some degree of self-congratulation) as an 'unobtrusive process of adapting existing institutions'.[21]

[20] Cabinet, 11 July 1952, NAG ADM 13/2/6.
[21] Cabinet memorandum, 30 April 1954, NAG ADM 13/2/16.

At this stage it is worthwhile recapitulating the paper trail which led up to this situation of reform without new legislation: the Watson Commission and then the Coussey committee had recommended reform and the Korsah Commission was set up to make recommendations about reforming legislation on local jurisdictions. It reported on time. In 1953 the chief justice, Sir Mark Wilson[22] and a committee of officials made further reports to Cabinet on precisely how the local court system should and could be reformed. These were discussed by Cabinet but it was decided there that 'it was not appropriate that a caretaker Government should take decisions on issues which might prove highly controversial'. In this context 'caretaker' clearly meant a government on the brink of a general election and hence in its last days of office.[23] In effect the diarchic government of 1951-4 evaded drafting legislation on local justice despite the possession of a formidable battery of very detailed and informed critical commentary from a variety of sources all of which demanded change and a decent set of proposals for legislation to bring such change about.

Despite the possible inference that a non-caretaker government, such as that constituted in the wake of the 1954 general election,[24] would and certainly could tackle the issue, there was a remarkable reticence on the issue. While the emergence later in that year of the National Liberation Movement might account for a more cautious approach to far-reaching reform affecting the role of chiefs, the diffidence is notable even before October 1954. For example, when the newly-elected Cabinet first turned its mind to what they agreed was necessary local court reform after the 1954 elections, it relied once again on the 'unobtrusive' use of the Native Courts variation order procedure it had successfully adopted previously.[25] Once again, however, Cabinet's decisions provide the clearest evidence imaginable of the removal of traditional office-holders from local court panels and the substitution of a majority of lay figures, many of whom are relatively easily identifiable as CPP supporters. In the course of that meeting, Cabinet agreed to the minister of local government's recommendations that the following changes should occur.

In the Manso Akroso court, 14 names were deleted from the panel, five of whom can be identified as chiefs; 21 names were added to the list of whom only three could be considered to be 'traditional'. Five names were removed from the Awutu court panel, one of whom was a chief; 11 names were added to that list and none of them was that of a chief or royal. The Upper Denkyira court panel lost 15 names, four of whom were chiefs, and 22 new individuals were newly placed upon that panel, none of whom were chiefs. On this occasion Cabinet went on to approve major changes of this sort to the court panels of Northern Denkyira,

---

[22] Who had submitted his report on 30 April 1953.

[23] As the minister of local government expressed it in his memorandum to Cabinet on 5 October 1954, NAG ADM 13/2/18.

[24] Which was after all believed by all parties to be the government which would negotiate a new constitution and then take the Gold Coast into independence.

[25] NAG ADM 13/2/17, Cabinet agenda, 3 August 1954.

Central Denkyira, Southern Denkyira, the Eastern and Western Gomoa courts, the Western, Eastern and central Agona courts and the Dangbe court.

In all of these cases, large numbers of traditional office-holders were removed from court panels only to be substituted, for the most part, by non-traditional figures. There are, of course, serious problems surrounding the identification of local royals in such listings. But the schedules were habitually very pernickety about titles.[26] In some cases where chiefs or elders were either retained on the panels or were newly empanelled, the evidence suggests that they were usually CPP allies. These changes were justified by the minister as being 'in pursuance of my policy of having the membership of Native Courts altered to conform with modern conditions'.[27] This methodology was consistently adhered to throughout the period between the 1954 and 1956 elections, the period between the 1956 election and independence and even after independence.

By mid-1955, it was clear that the earlier intention of totally reforming Local Courts, signalled in so many ways from 1948, had been largely abandoned.[28] CPP governments had not reformed the courts, despite the volume of well-attested complaint about the procedures; rather, they were simply altering the composition of those courts. At the level of material explanation, this owed much to two particular problems. First, reform implied new and considerable costs. It was the cheapness of the old Native Court system which had, amongst other things, endeared it to the British; that factor proved to be no less attractive to a self-governing and then an independent CPP regime. It readily became apparent that while the local council rating (local taxation) system would meet some of the additional costs, a significant additional vote would have been required from central funds to meet the needs of a seriously reformed system.

Secondly, there were serious manpower implications in total reform. Despite the mythology about vast numbers of lawyers in the Gold Coast, there was, rather, a dearth of senior lawyers who might have been willing to act as stipendiary magistrates. Such lawyers who were prepared to act as magistrates were implicitly prepared to forgo the rewards of growing private practices in return for a steady but relatively low salary; unsurprisingly, there were few such volunteers who were also good lawyers. The scale of the proposed change was formidable; 'If all Native Court panels are to be abolished at once, I will have to appoint about 300 stipendiary justices', the minister conceded in a Cabinet paper discussed on 10 May 1955.[29] In reality there was a desperate need for more lawyers, a matter noted in the Elliot Commission's recommendation of the establishment of a West African faculty of law some years earlier. In 1946, for example, of the 136 Gold Coast

---

[26] Without exception those I have seen identify individuals as Omanhene, Ohene, Opanin, and so on. As a rule of thumb I have regarded anyone with such a title as either 'royal' or, in one way or another, a traditional office-holder.

[27] NAG ADM 13/2/17. Cabinet agenda, 3rd August 1954.

[28] See Cabinet memorandum by the minister of local government on the reform of Native Courts. 14 June 1955, NAG ADM 13/2/23.

[29] NAG ADM 13/2/22. This perhaps explains why the 1954 CPP election manifesto includes a commitment to establish a law school at the University College.

students studying in the UK, only 12 were reading law. Two years later, out of a Gold Coast cohort of 253 reading for degrees in the UK, only 29 were destined for the law. It was not until 1956 that the University College decided to establish a law faculty at Legon in the quinquennium beginning in 1958 even if some law courses were already being taught in the economics faculty.[30] In addition, the Gold Coast had no tradition of an unpaid lay magistracy on the British model; this had been among the ideas floated by Sir Henley Coussey and other senior Ghanaian jurists who had recommended the use of justices of the peace from the late 1940s. Accordingly, there were few educated people who could be counted upon to undergo training and then to give up time for no financial reward, beyond expenses, in order to play such a civic role.

Thus even by 1958, after independence, the minister of justice, within whose portfolio the local courts system now fell, admitted to his colleagues that 'the reform of Native Courts [*sic*] has been proceeding unobtrusively by the *reconstitution of Court panels*,[31] by the alteration of areas of jurisdiction, by improving the standards of knowledge and efficiency of registrars and by bettering the physical amenities of Courts'.[32] This suggested, quite remarkably, that despite the considerable volume of criticism mounted against the system since the 1930s, the government was prepared to insist that it was procedural shortcomings and shabby premises alone which had brought local justice into contempt. This ran counter to the recommendations of each and every commission which had examined the system since the 1940s. Even more strikingly, it should be contrasted with the CPP's earlier commitment to extensive reform.

But even earlier in the independence era, in May 1957, the minister of local government had presented yet another memorandum on local courts to Cabinet. This quite explicitly admitted that the root-and-branch reform, advocated in the Report of yet another Korsah Commission, this time a report of October 1955, could not be contemplated largely because of the cost implications. 'I ask my colleagues', he wrote, 'to agree that any action to implement the recommendations of the Commission on Native Courts, desirable as these may be, should be postponed for the time being but that the position should be reviewed from time to time.'[33] The reality of the situation was caught, and very honestly so, a full year later by Ako Adjei, whose ministry of justice had now taken over responsibility for local courts from the ministry of local Government. 'The new Local Courts', he wrote, 'will exercise jurisdiction in the same area as their predecessor native courts and *will differ from them only in nomenclature and in the persons constituting them.*'[34]

---

[30] I owe this point to a personal communication from Katya Leney, whose study of the establishment of the Gold Coast University College and the University at Dakar is eagerly awaited.

[31] My emphasis.

[32] Cabinet memorandum on Native Courts by the minister of justice, 13 May 1958, NAG ADM 13/2/48.

[33] Cabinet minutes of the meeting on 21 May 1957, NAG ADM 13/2/38. Anyone who has sat on a committee will recognize that a commitment to review anything 'from time to time' is very close in meaning to 'no further action'.

[34] Cabinet memorandum by the minister of justice, 24 June 1958, NAG ADM 13/2/49. The emphasis is mine.

The Cabinet meeting which discussed Ako Adjei's frank admission also agreed to a set of new orders he proposed; these once again used the variation procedure discussed above. They dealt with a number of courts in the Akyems, in Kwawu, the Krobos, Akwamu, Ada and in Akwapim. He proposed, and Cabinet agreed, a raft of new panels for those courts. These new lists provide us with a grand total of 721 new nominees on such court panels; only 50 of these could conceivably be regarded as chiefly or royal but, importantly, these seem in almost every case to be pro–CPP chiefs. At a further Cabinet meeting a month later, the minister of justice presented a further draft dealing with another clutch of Central and Western Province courts. Of the 139 'persons forming Local Courts', only eight could be conceivably regarded as chiefs.

CPP governments' inability to carry out the radical reform of the system, something which was urged by commission of enquiry after commission of enquiry for years, is immediately revealing. The history of that diffidence demonstrates some of the unfolding characteristics of CPP government methodology. Amongst these perhaps the most important is the rehearsal, well before independence, of the use of what later came to be called executive instruments rather than fully debated legislation in the pursuit of policy gains after March 1957.

Throughout this narrative the CPP government can be seen effecting significant changes in the composition but not the nature of an important jurisdiction through the very skilful and undoubtedly constitutional use of existing colonial legislation; and one might stress especially the continuing use of the residual but authoritarian powers once vested in the Governor-in-Council. After the elections of mid-1954 this effectively meant Cabinet in virtually all domestic political matters. Gubernatorial decisions were always taken on the advice of the Cabinet and there is no evidence which suggests that this advice was ever rejected. Taken together and over time, the corpus of variation orders amounted to government by *diktat*, for the organizing principles – let alone the details – were never discussed in the House. The old and authoritative law-making role of the Governor-in-Council had been embraced by Cabinet in the new democracy.[35] In this respect a very great deal hung upon the advice Cabinet received from the government's law officers. Their very significant roles, especially after 1954, have received virtually no scholarly attention but on which more research should be devoted.[36]

The Native Courts issue suggests the CPP's impotence every bit as much as it deals with its skilful manipulation of power. There is a great deal of evidence which suggests just how much they longed not only to end the continuation of chiefly power in the local government system but also to resolve the mess that a binary legal system had delivered. Financial concerns certainly inhibited the kinds of full-blown, modernist reform for which they wished. They remained tied in to

[35] Why this was not subjected to British official criticism remains unclear. Perhaps what appears anomalous to us today was not so regarded by those whose colonial careers had developed in such authoritarian systems.

[36] The role of Nkrumah's attorney-general after independence, Geoffrey Bing, was especially significant. His own controversial account of those years is to be found in his autobiography, *Reap the whirlwind*.

systems of both local government and local justice which combined uncomfortable elements of the colonial view of traditional governance with elements of modern, elective and more obviously accountable systems; needless to say, the eventual compromises satisfied nobody. Along with the numerous contingent political constraints dealt with elsewhere in this book, all these factors go some way towards explaining the strange survival, well into the independence period, of what was in effect the old colonial Native Court system with all its undeniable defects. They also reflect a serious diminution in chiefly control over justice in the countryside. That involved far more than just deciding whether Kofi had stolen Kojo's screwdriver or whether the market stall belonged to Effua or Ama. Courts are sites and occasions where values are allocated. The removal of chiefs from courts undermined them by denying them a formal role in conciliation and the maintenance of the ethical basis of customary law. These local courts were now the creations of government and the links with the mandate of history, however unfairly that might have been exercised in some cases, were broken.

5

The Fusion
of Local & National Politics

We now return to the main narrative. In terms of the grander story of the transfer of power it was widely understood that both the constitution and the diarchic administration brought into being by the 1951 general elections were transitional. In the course of that administration, discussions were to take place between the British and Gold Coast governments which would lead to the drafting of a new constitution. This would both confer virtual internal self-government on the Gold Coast and be the prelude to the granting of independence. Although the detail was undecided, there was widespread agreement that the election scheduled for 1954 would usher in a period in which the majority party, and few doubted that it would be the CPP, would hold all the portfolios in an entirely African Cabinet.[1] In many respects the struggle against colonial rule was over. 'Self government for the Gold Coast', argued the *Daily Graphic*, the country's most reliable newspaper of the time, 'is no longer a political issue but an administrative and constitutional exercise. Our problems are more of an internal nature rather than an external one.'[2] This comment was both extremely acute and prescient.

The national discussions about the shape of a new constitution were accordingly seen as of great significance. The government drafted a White Paper on constitutional reform which was widely circulated for comment. Not surprisingly, the chiefs' territorial councils, which were formally approached, used this as an opportunity to make their mark. The Asanteman Council and the Joint Provincial Council collaborated in their response. This argued, *inter alia*, for a statutory role for the chiefs' territorial councils, for all local government decisions to be made in the name of the local chief as the 'head of his people' and the formal recognition of traditional authorities as essential elements in local administration. While territorial councils would continue to decide 'local constitutional matters', they argued that appeals should go to a local judicial committee rather than to the

[1] For more detail on these developments see R. Rathbone (ed.), *Ghana; British documents...*
[2] Leader article, 2 February 1954.

59

Governor-in-Council. They also represented the case made by the Coussey committee for an Upper House of the Assembly, which had been rejected in the final drafting of the 1951 constitution.

To strengthen his hand when dealing with the Colonial Office and a British Conservative government, Prime Minister Kwame Nkrumah was eager to be seen to be carrying the country behind his government's proposals. Shortly after receiving the memorandum from these two territorial councils, he personally visited them both in June 1953. His own account suggests, and the records of the councils do not dispute this, that he was able to talk them out of the idea of an Upper House by agreeing that territorial councils should be strengthened. At both of these meetings there was apparently agreement that chiefly affairs, usually referred to by the somewhat pompous circumlocution of 'local constitutional matters', should be kept out of national politics even if this was rather precisely what was making the lives of so many chiefs extremely difficult. This, Nkrumah agreed, could be best done by ensuring that appeals from territorial councils could be dealt with by 'an impartial committee ... appointed to deal with appeals from State Councils' and territorial councils.[3] These two undertakings were to be considered after the 1954 election by the government along with the suggestion that the whole issue of the Upper House should be examined by a commission of enquiry. Neither of these undertakings was ever to be honoured by any CPP government.

It is important to note that Nkrumah was now personally involved in matters which might have been regarded as falling naturally within the purview of the ministry of local government. This owed something to the mounting frustration felt by the government at the time. But it was also an attempt to use the CPP's heaviest artillery to silence an irritating pocket of resistance to what it regarded as progressive change in the countryside. Cabinet had already agreed that local government reform had been only patchily successful. By the middle of 1953 there is little doubt that chiefs were seen as the major stumbling-blocks on the path to radical reform and thus to the smooth attainment of independence. Despite the apparent success of his emollient words to the territorial councils, Nkrumah was much more sceptical in the privacy of the Cabinet room. He doubted the importance and the sincerity of the territorial councils' representations. He wrote:

> My impression is that the motive behind the proposals is the fear of the Chiefs that, unless certain practical steps are taken by the Government to recognise and visibly strengthen their present position with regard to Central Government on the one hand and Local Government on the other, they will be forced into a situation where they have neither powers nor functions. ... I am far from satisfied that there is any real support by the territorial councils for the detailed recommendations ... nor am I convinced that the recommendations are truly in the sphere of constitutional reform ... the Minister of Local Government should bring a paper to Cabinet on this matter...'[4]

[3] Prime Minister's Memorandum to Cabinet, 15 June 1953, NAG ADM 13/2/12. The appeals referred to concerned wrangles between chiefs over issues like precedence, stool boundaries, enstoolments and destoolments.

[4] Memorandum to Cabinet, 14 August 1953, NAG ADM 13/2/13.

These were not doubts he shared with the British government.

As the chiefs could not be brought round by the prime minister, the government's tactics shifted to an attempt to marginalize them further. The prime minister's suggestion that the future of the chiefs was now seen to rest somehow outside the remit of constitutional drafting and lay, rather, within the far more confined bailiwick of the Ministry of Local Government marked a serious if covert political development and a departure from the principles laid down by the Coussey Committee. There is no doubt that this relegation was intentional and there is little doubt that the Cabinet accepted this position. Some months earlier, in a markedly testy memorandum to Cabinet, Nkrumah spelled out his position even more clearly. Commenting on another demand from the Asanteman and Joint Provincial Councils asking for clear assurances that the status of chiefs would be enshrined in the new constitution, he wrote with obvious irritation:

> If chiefs were to perform their functions in a manner acceptable to their subjects as being 'constitutional' there would be no need to seek any protection in the Gold Coast Constitution ... The Government does not understand in what way 'the status of chiefs' can be safeguarded in the Constitution ... the most effective safeguard of this status lies in the extent to which a chief is considered by his subjects, in the changing conditions of the Gold Coast, to be acting in a constitutional manner...[5]

Things were far too fraught for such private thinking to be translated into unambiguous public statements by the prime minister. In a somewhat defensive statement to the Legislative Assembly on 11 March 1954, Nkrumah reminded the House of a statement he had made in September 1952 which had echoed the spirit of the Coussey committee report in agreeing that 'chieftaincy is ... deeply bound up with the life of our community'. But that statement had firmly thrown the blame for rural disorder on to the shoulders of the chiefs themselves. Chieftaincy could not remain static, he argued, but 'must adapt itself to the changing requirements of the present time'. His speech suggested that government and chiefs could strike a bargain: 'this Government is determined to assist and support Chiefs. In return we shall expect a more thorough adaptation of their functions to the changing conditions in the country which will bring independence to the Gold Coast.'

'Changing conditions' and 'changing requirements' were now serving as synonyms for CPP activism in the party's official rhetoric; similarly the frequent invocations of the discontented 'subjects' were frequently neat and evocative ways of expressing the often utterly justified frustration of local CPP branches with their local traditional rulers. Chiefs would have to have been blind to their predicament, which worsened in the run-up to the general election. For example, speaking at a CPP rally in Apedwa on 6 June, the managing director of the Cocoa Purchasing Company, A.Y.K. Djin, said: 'Chiefs have no power at this time. All the powers are now in the hands of the majority party which goes into the Assembly.'[6] Both

---

[5] Prime Minister's Memorandum to Cabinet, 11 January 1954, NAG ADM 13/2/15.

[6] *Daily Graphic*, 9 June 1954. Djin was later to be disgraced for corruption in 1956 by the Jibowu Commission of Enquiry into the affairs of the Cocoa Purchasing Company. For more detail on the hostility of Apedwa to the royal family see R. Rathbone, *Murder and politics...*

the venue and the platform were significant. Apedwa lies only a few miles from the capital of Akyem Abuakwa and was historically opposed to the paramount of Akyem Abuakwa. And as Djin shared the platform with Aaron Ofori Atta there would have been few doubts in the minds of listeners that the speech was extremely hostile to Nana Ofori Atta II, the Okyenhene. At a CPP rally in Kumase, the chief regional propaganda secretary of the CPP[7] told a large crowd that 'if the chiefs amalgamated with the other political parties to oppose the CPP during the General Elections then the CPP would be justified to consider those chiefs as their political enemies'.[8] The CPP candidate for Akyem Abuakwa Central, Aaron Ofori Atta, at a party rally on 29 May, stressed that his party was 'not against chieftaincy yet it will not support any chief who would not co-operate with its members'. Aaron Ofori Atta's biography matters considerably. He was a son of the late Okyenhene Nana Sir Ofori Atta I and cousin to the incumbent Okyenhene, Ofori Atta II, who was then president of the Joint Provincial Council. He was also a nephew of Dr J.B. Danquah and half-brother of Willie Ofori Atta, both stalwart opponents of the CPP. Aaron Ofori Atta was to serve as minister of local government in the post-election CPP government and played a considerable role in the attempts to reduce chieftaincy. He was widely regarded by the Akyem Abuakwa royal family and by other chiefly figures as a dangerous renegade. At a Ghana Congress Party rally in Kukurantumi on 3 June 1954 Danquah denounced him in a fashion which played well in a culture which makes much of family loyalty and obligation. 'He has run away from his father's house and is insulting those who gave him his education.'

While it may have been logically perverse, political reality determined that in practice any co-operation by chiefs with the CPP was not to be seen by the party as 'involvement in party politics'.[9] Seen through CPP lenses, chiefs who supported the CPP were somehow not involved in party politics, whilst those who opposed the CPP were. The CPP press was, for example, utterly uncritical when the regent of Denkyira, Nana Kojo Odei II, chaired a rally (at which Nkrumah was present) for the CPP candidate for the local constituency.[10] There was no CPP objection when on 11 June 1954 the Bechemhene introduced Nkrumah to a large gathering by begging him to 'carry on the good work' and by pledging the support of the Bechem state for the CPP and its local candidate Yeboah Afari.[11] Similarly no criticism was levelled at the chief of Nkansu when he 'promised that he and his people would support the official party candidate as we want roads and means of communications'.[12] Nor did Nkrumah apparently feel any sense of irony when he

---

[7] Kwabena Ampofu Twumasi Ankrah. He was eventually to be tragically stabbed to death by an NLM activist in a political brawl.

[8] Reported in the *Daily Graphic*, 30 January 1954.

[9] Indeed *The Accra Evening News* had for years welcomed such affiliations with enthusiasm. For example on 1 May 1951 they applauded the comment of the chief of Peki-Djake, Fia Ofori Yao, 'I shall follow Kwame Nkrumah wherever he goes and will stand behind him with all my people through thick and thin.'

[10] *Daily Graphic*, 22 May 1954.

[11] *Daily Graphic*, 12 June 1954.

[12] *Ibid.*

asked the Offinsohene to support the CPP candidate, C.C. Addae, in the forth-coming election.[13] The stigma of 'involvement in party politics' had become a encoded way of expressing chiefly opposition not only to the government but also to the local CPP organizations. Quite evidently it was a one-way street.

The president of the Joint Provincial Council, Nana Ofori Atta II,[14] addressing the Council on 19 January 1954, was trying to be cautious when he said: 'the time has come for the chiefs to put things right. Speak your mind and die for it is better than keep quiet and lose your traditional heritage. Politicians may come and go but chieftaincy will ever remain.' In the period immediately before the election, the Joint Provincial Council had spent a good deal of time bemoaning the declining position of chieftaincy. By losing their ex-officio membership of the Assembly under the 1954 constitution,[15] chiefs had been forced to surrender power to 'youth' and they, unhappily, 'no longer obeyed their traditional elders' said Nana Blay VII, Omanhene of East Nzima, to the Joint Provincial Council.[16] But chiefs, the JPC President had stressed with his tongue in his cheek, 'were not supposed to indulge in party politics. We do not intend to depart from that policy.'[17]

But the simple division of chiefs and CPP had become ever more complicated. The politics of regions began to undermine the CPP's invocation of 'the people' and its understandable and entirely sympathetic wish to maintain national unity. In a rare moment of harmony, the Asanteman Council and the Asante Youth Association, who at been at each other's throats from the mid-1940s, presented the government with a demand for special treatment for the region;[18] this argued that the Ashanti Region deserved a larger number of constituencies and hence a greater number of members than the adopted allocative formula of population to seats would allow. By August 1953 the Ashanti CPP branches had also agreed on a letter making exactly the same point. These proved to be the opening shots in a campaign which ended with the formation of the National Liberation Movement (NLM) in 1954.[19]

The vigorous arguments were based on a somewhat specious claim that the region of Ashanti had contributed and would continue to contribute an absolutely and relatively disproportionate amount of national wealth. The argument was specious because the figures which might have supported or contradicted the claims were confusing; moreover, the numbers which were paraded ignored the

---

[13] *Ibid.* The request was completely at odds with the party's manifesto which opposed chiefly involvement in politics. At the same meeting Nkrumah said: 'If the Ashantis do not help to win the majority to form the next Government ... the country will suffer ... but Ashantis will suffer a double agony.'

[14] And as we have seen and will see, the most outspoken anti-CPP chief in the Gold Coast.

[15] The reserved seats for territorial councils representatives which figured in the 1951 constitution were removed, as had been widely expected, in favour of an entirely and directly elected Legislative Assembly under the 1954 constitution.

[16] Minutes of the Joint Provincial Council for 5 May 1954.

[17] Minutes of the Joint Provincial Council. Speech by Nana Ofori Atta 11, 5 May 1954.

[18] This sensitivity had been flagged as long ago as 17 September 1951 by the *Accra Evening News* in an editorial which noted Asante discontent with the share of development funding accorded to the region.

[19] For a full account see Jean Allman, *The quills of the porcupine.*

multi-regional provenance of the capital which enhanced the infrastructure which facilitated economic growth in the Ashanti Region. It was, however, a case that had been pressed by successive chief commissioners for Ashanti in the interwar period.[20] It also suggested that the indisputably glorious history of the Asante merited a larger number of members. Lastly Ashanti's rather thin population as a region doomed it to under-representation in comparison with the Colony and the North. Both memoranda concluded that Ashanti deserved 30 seats in the post-1954 Legislature. This was a tricky issue for the party and an awkward one for the government. This rare example of regional unity between chiefs and people in Asante revealed a propensity to regionalism which had seemed unlikely in the previous two years. The party's hostility to any fragmentation of the country was apparent from its foundation. The third of the aims proclaimed at the inception of the CPP was: 'To secure and maintain the complete unity of the chiefs and people of the Colony, Ashanti, Northern Territories and Trans-Volta'. To pacify the region by concession would have required the party to agree that wealth bought greater representation and, *ceteris paribus*, that poverty diminished the number of seats in a region; this was hardly a proposition that a party speaking the language of socialism could endorse. On the basis of a sensible memorandum by the prime minister, Cabinet decided to stand firm against both of these resolutions.[21] By so doing it paved the way for a brutal struggle between the party executive and some of its Asante branches in the run-up to the 1954 election which was to be one of the strands in the foundation of the NLM in Ashanti by the end of the year. It also widened the gulf between government and the chiefs in the region.

It is extremely difficult to assess the significance of these perturbations for ordinary people. We have seen that the CPP enjoyed a comfortable majority in the first general election of 1951 even if that 'comfortable majority' was numerically made up of less than 50 per cent of the ballot of only half of those entitled to vote. Similarly, we will shortly see the CPP convincingly win another election in 1954. But were chiefs and their cause proving to be a rallying point for localized disaffection in the Gold Coast? The nature of chieftaincy in the Akan areas at least made such polarization unlikely. While individual chiefs were undoubtedly supported by their close kin and their dependents, there were always numbers of disaffected royals and their dependents whose collective noses had been put out of joint by the election of particular incumbents. As suggested earlier, such groups were likely to embrace the CPP as an organized vehicle of local opposition. Accordingly, supporting chiefs and supporting the CPP was never to be a simple matter of class identity or of royal or commoner status.

Elements within some chiefly families were strong supporters of the CPP; commoners who stood to do well out of the success of this or that chiefly figure would almost inevitably oppose the CPP if it was in contention with their patron. Nor was such support necessarily undivided. In the run-up to the 1954 elections it is clear, for example, that the state of Bechem was a CPP stronghold. But that

---

[20] An issue upon which Professor Ivor Wilks is currently working.
[21] Prime Minister's Memorandum to Cabinet, 28 August 1953, NAG ADM 13/2/13.

support was split between the CPP's official candidate Yeboah Afari and a 'rebel' candidate, J.K. Antwi-Kusi, also claiming to stand on the CPP ticket.[22] The faction led by the Bechem Youth Association, which called itself the 'CPP of Commons', supported the 'rebel' candidate. The faction which supported the official candidate was led by the Bechemhene and called itself the 'CPP of Lords'.[23]

Chiefs had, however, always exemplified place and identity for many Ghanaians. Despite or possibly because of the onrush of modernization in the Gold Coast, people retained strong loyalties to their places of origin. Such loyalties were enormously varied and could be expressed in different contexts as regional or town and village identities. Such attachments are not neatly explained by sledgehammer concepts such as primordial ties or slippery ideas like ethnicity. While it is impossible to show what people felt 40 or so years ago, it is the case today that many Ghanaians feel 'at home' when revisiting their childhood homes. Here they not only can discharge their family responsibilities but can also dress and behave in a more relaxed fashion than they feel they can in towns. Like many of us, they are relieved to be away from the noise and bustle of the city. We have no need of exotic explanations of why many Ghanaians maintained strong affection and loyalty for their roots.

At a more obviously political level it is clear that strong feelings of regional deprivation, however erroneously arrived at, were emerging in the run-up to the 1954 general election. We have already seen the rumblings in Ashanti. Now in the north a growing suspicion that the CPP was much more concerned with its southern heartland and not much bothered by the relative underdevelopment of the north paved the way for the formation of the Northern Peoples' Party in February 1954. It was more than merely symbolic that it was launched in the house of a chief, the Tolon Na, and that some of its leaders were chiefs. In the years to come the Northern Territorial Council of Chiefs meeting hall was to act as its headquarters.[24] It was not, however, simply a chiefs' party; it was, rather, a strong expression of what appears to have been a widely shared feeling in the North of being treated ungenerously by an administration whose concerns were perceived to be firmly rooted further south. Even if it was not a chiefs' party, the strong presence of chiefs within its leadership ensured that further reform of chieftaincy and local government, in so far as it touched the north, would be interpreted as yet more proof of the CPP's cavalier attitude to the region. For some Gold Coasters there is no doubt that chiefs were to come to symbolize or embody place at the moment at which the CPP in Accra became suspected of feathering its own geographical nest whilst ignoring the nests of others.

The CPP manifesto for the 1954 election, in contrast with that for 1951, explicitly singled out chiefs for criticism. Local councils would have to become entirely elected:

---

[22] The struggle between the party's executive and some party branches over nominations and the entire issue of 'rebel' candidates is dealt with very fully in D. Austin, *Politics in Ghana*, pp. 216–25.

[23] *Daily Graphic*, 27 May 1954.

[24] See D. Austin, *Politics in Ghana*, p. 186.

with a view to eliminating the continual friction which occurs ... this will save chiefs from being dragged into party politics against their dignity and integrity ... it is not the intention of the CPP to destroy chieftaincy but rather to adapt it[25] to its democratic practices by clearly defining the functions of the chiefs in our new society ... A spirit of liberty, of national consciousness, pervades the country and the *Common People* have come to feel that they are as good as the so-called aristocrats who have ignored and despised them...

The CPP 'strikes fear, despondency and alarm in the hearts of tribalists, racialists, communalists, imperialists and other reactionaries'. Nkrumah was feted in the manifesto as being, amongst other things, 'the Hope of the Common Man'.[26]

The election itself, admirably analysed in Dennis Austin's *Politics in Ghana*, resulted in another unequivocal CPP victory. Something close to 50 per cent of the enfranchised population, 1,225,603 people, had registered to vote. Of that number, 706,710 actually went on to cast a vote. And the CPP polled 391,817 of those votes, or just over 55 per cent. It is impossible to explore fully the problematic of either the low registration figures or the poor turnout; so long after the events it is unlikely that research will now yield useful answers to these mysteries. The Gold Coast was, however, wedded to a first-past-the-post, simple majority electoral system of the sort practised in Britain; and beyond any reasonable doubt the CPP had secured a clear majority and was constitutionally, and entirely properly, the country's government as a result. But with hindsight it is clear that nearly 2 million Gold Coasters had not registered or had not voted or had voted against the CPP in that election. It is also the case that the seven opposition parties and the independent candidates had secured 314,903 votes or 44.6 per cent of the poll.

This election was believed to be the last before independence in London as well as in Accra. The new government was expecting to embark upon the negotiation of an independence constitution with the British government and there is abundant evidence to suggest that full independence was expected to be granted at the end of 1956.[27] The election results seemed to signal that there was now little that the internal opposition could do to upset the CPP government or to halt its general intentions.

The Gold Coast's government now entered a stage in which the country was effectively internally self-governing. Its external relations were still under colonial control as were its police and armed forces; the law officers also continued to be expatriate colonial civil servants. But from mid-1954 Cabinet was basically an all-African committee. Its deliberations were no longer reported as a matter of course to London as Cabinet agendas, working papers and minutes were now both internal and secret documents. It is, however, clear from both his private and formal correspondence that the governor was selectively briefed, most probably by Nkrumah, on what happened in Cabinet during their private evening meetings on

[25] The use of this verb in its active voice is important.
[26] *Accra Evening News*, 4 May 1954.
[27] See for example, Prime Minister's Cabinet memorandum, 'Celebration of Independence', 26 November 1954, NAG ADM 13/2/18.

the battlements of the governor's residence, Christiansborg Castle. The constitutional domination of CPP ministers in Cabinet is reflected in an apparent and important change in the nature of Cabinet meetings. The cautious, managerial and almost apolitical nature of Cabinet deliberations in the period 1951–4, when several British official and non-CPP ministers sat in Cabinet, was replaced by a more robust and much more self-consciously political body. This was now unequivocally party government and that shows up very clearly in the archival record of that period.

From that record it is clear that the CPP was determined to reinforce its electoral victory by extending its control of the state, a state which all believed was shortly to be independent. That the party was aware of the forces gathering against it is obvious from a notable discussion in late August 1954 of a proposed bill 'restricting the titles and membership of religious, regional and tribal organisations represented in the legislative Assembly'.[28] In many respects the bill, proposed by the prime minister, was remarkably similar to the later Avoidance of Discrimination Act which did not become law until December 1957, well after Ghana achieved its independence.[29] The prime minister wrote that he had been 'disturbed by recent occurrences ... where various dissident groups showed signs of combining in a regional alliance calculated to attract Ashantis in opposition to the measures of the Government. The regionalism of the NPP had put ideas into the heads of others ... it had proved necessary to find means of safeguarding public unity'.[30] This proposal was opposed in a Cabinet subcommittee by the acting attorney-general, A.G. Forbes, but it was nonetheless recommended that the minister of the interior should proceed to prepare this legislation.

Such a bill became politically unfeasible by the beginning of 1955 and three years were to pass before it became law. The evidence suggests that the eventual 1957 act was not merely a reaction to the disruptive power of the party formed at the end of 1954, the NLM, but was originally intended to be a pre-emptive strike, for this proposal was originally tabled several months before the foundation of the NLM. The proposal does, however, suggest two things. Firstly, the CPP was apprehensive about the growth of opposition to government and the regionally divisive nature of that opposition. Secondly, it was ready to contemplate tabling increasingly robust legislation to wear down its enemies now that virtually all internal policy was under its direct control and now that it enjoyed a huge majority in the Legislative Assembly.

This is the context in which the policies aimed at bringing dissident chieftaincy more comprehensively to its knees were generated. But there was a wider context which suggests why such policies were seen as a matter of urgency rather than gradualism. Between 1951 and 1954 the government had enjoyed the fruits of a buoyant economy rooted in unprecedented increases in the world price for cocoa.

[28] Which suggests that D. Austin was not entirely correct in saying: 'The sudden formation of the NLM took everyone by surprise', *Politics in Ghana*, p. 281.

[29] This legislation was to outlaw the NLM and forced its reconfiguration as the United Party.

[30] Minutes of the Legislation Committee of the Cabinet, 26 August 1954, NAG ADM 13/2/18.

By June 1954, the minister of finance was predicting that this would not last. 'I am quite certain that the price will fall. When it does fall, I am equally certain that it will fall heavily. I do not however believe that it will fall much if at all in the crop years 1954–5 and 1955–6. As I see it therefore, we have before us two or three years of immense prosperity to be followed by a very doubtful future.' He argued that the safest course was the pegging of the price paid to farmers to 72 shillings per load of 60lb. This was agreed by the prime minister and Cabinet. But the proposal was initially withdrawn; this was after all the immediate pre-election period and it was decided that this important matter, obviously a potential vote-loser in cocoa-growing areas, should be left to the new government.[31] It was, however, discussed at the first post-election Cabinet meeting[32] and was there agreed. Once this policy was unveiled, it was to provide the proximate cause for the foundation of the NLM. The CPP government's wish to control the countryside was henceforth to prove extremely difficult to achieve.

That it wished to control chieftaincy is beyond doubt. The earlier palliative promise by Nkrumah to the territorial councils to create a local constitutional committee to act as a final arbiter in chieftaincy cases found its way into the governor's speech at the opening of the new Assembly on 29 July 1954. By the end of August the matter was again before Cabinet. The minister of local government tabled a draft in which a commission composed of a government-appointed chairman, a judge and one nominee from each of the Asanteman, Joint Provincial, Trans Volta Togoland and Northern Territorial Councils was proposed. In discussion, minister after minister frowned upon giving this body such extensive powers. They feared that they might thus lose what they hoped would prove to be their growing control over traditional constitutional affairs. But they had committed themselves to this policy. A draft was bounced around the territorial councils for their comments. The political situation from the middle of 1955 and the numerous but contradictory objections raised by these chiefly bodies enabled the government to avoid carrying this legislation forward.

Although the creation of the NLM was to provide the CPP with its greatest test, it was, as government, already presiding over a countryside in which things were either unravelling fast or making no discernible progress. Despite the intention to wrest power from chiefs, traditional rulers retained considerable powers both because some genuinely attracted respect and because the rate of reform of both local government and local courts was markedly slow. Had chieftaincy been in the process of simply withering away, it is doubtful whether the chaos in the countryside would have been so apparent. But the disarray was not simply the upshot of a CPP government onslaught on a set of anachronistic institutions. Some chiefs were acutely aware that the CPP was not merely a formidable adversary but also a potentially useful ally.

Some traditional states and even more factions within chiefly states overtly allied themselves with the CPP. This was not, as suggested earlier, a recent

[31] Cabinet memorandum by the minister of finance on cocoa duty, 8 June 1954, NAG ADM 13/2/17.
[32] On 27 July 1954.

68

occurrence. But now such allegiance had a new edge. The most obvious example of this was the attempted defection of a number of states in the Ashanti Region, led by Dormaa, from the control of the Asantehene and his Asanteman Council. The origins of the dispute go back into deep history but were exacerbated by decisions made in 1935 which incorporated the so-called Brong states within the reconstructed Ashanti Confederacy. The ostensible reason for the dispute was the contested ownership of nine villages.[33] The secession was certainly being mooted well before the CPP came to power. A federation of 5 Brong states had been formed in 1950 even if it enjoyed no formal recognition.[34] The new government's position was initially to insist that this was essentially a matter for the Asanteman Council to resolve. In time its support for what amounted to Brong secession was to be a major weapon in its struggle with the Asantehene and the chiefs of the core Asante states.

Although the CPP, like all political parties, was happy to receive support from any quarter, the party as government recognized that the support of some chiefs brought significant costs. As a party in opposition to the colonial regime, the CPP had of course welcomed rural disorder; indeed it could reasonably claim that such disorder was strong evidence of its rural support and the colonial government's waning authority. Once involved in government, it had an increasing interest in rural order not least because so much of the national wealth was created in the countryside. In the course of a meeting of newly elected representative ministers and the Asanteman Council on 3 July 1951, Nkrumah assured the members of that council that he and his colleagues were most perturbed about the wave of destoolments sweeping through the region and there is no particular reason to doubt the sincerity of that. For government, rural chaos was particularly unwelcome if local government reform was to succeed.

But rural disorder was not a spasmodic aberration; it was, as we have seen, the very stuff of local politics. There was a disjuncture between the CPP government's wish for calm in the countryside and the local activities of the party branches. Some of the CPP Legislative Assembly members were, for example, openly siding with the Brong secessionist states by as early as March 1951 just because they aimed at denting the power of the Asantehene. They adopted this position partly because of the history of antagonism between the Asante Youth Association, the forerunner in many respects of the important, centripetal CPP branch in Kumase, the local CPP and the Asantehene. The Asantehene's traditional local enemies, the Dormaahene and the Tekyimanhene in particular, were by definition their allies. This dispute was an example, on a very grand scale, of the innumerable cases throughout the southern Gold Coast where the local CPP branch became quite intentionally embroiled in the partisan politics of Akan stools. In 1951 alone, CPP activists, with the support of local CPP Members of the Legislative Assembly, were in the forefront of movements to depose the chiefs of significant states like Bekwai, Denyase, Ejisu, Kokofu, Mampong, Offinso and Wenchi. Although there

[33] It is a dispute that continues to this day. It flared up very dangerously in 1996.
[34] See also the entry for 26 December 1950 in W.H. Beeton, *Diary*.

is no evidence which suggests that such campaigns were orchestrated from Accra, the prominence in these matters of some of the CPP's most influential politicians, Bediako Poku and Krobo Edusei in particular, is beyond doubt. CPP veterans of this period insist that the tensions between the central committee and branch activists over these issues were intense.

The political importance of the rise of the NLM from the last months of 1954 is beyond question. Its history has been handsomely recorded and analysed elsewhere[35] and it would be tedious to repeat the well-known facts about its origins and career. But there is no doubt whatever that the close involvement of prominent chiefs especially in Ashanti with this new opposition party both exacerbated and complicated the relationship between the CPP and chieftaincy throughout the country. Although the history of the NLM is not the subject of this volume, it is important to stress its impact. It presented the CPP government with a series of far greater challenges than any it had so far encountered. The context is of immediate importance to an understanding of both opposition and government tactics in the period.

The widespread assumption that the 1954 general election was the last before independence would have presented any opposition party formed after that election with a profound quandary. Formally the NLM had no members of the Legislative Assembly even if the majority of the handful of opposition Members of the Legislative Assembly were to behave as though they were in subsequent years. But in a formal sense the NLM's political activism was boxed in. Even with the support of a few MLAs, the huge majority the CPP enjoyed in the Assembly meant that the opposition was legislatively impotent not least because the government's party discipline in the House was far more effective after 1954. The NLM's stated wish to alter the constitution in a very significant fashion[36] appeared to have very little chance of success. It was the CPP government and not the opposition that was embarking on discussions with the British government on the drafting of the independence constitution. That CPP government had the mandate to negotiate because of its recent, massive electoral victory. While there is no reason to doubt that both the CPP and British governments wished any new constitution to enjoy national support, that support appeared at least formally to have been tested at the polls in 1954; once drafted, the constitution would be tested in an Assembly in which the CPP majority assured the successful translation of any draft into eventual statute. In these circumstances it is hardly surprising that much of the NLM's political career was essentially extra-parliamentary.

Extra-parliamentary activity was especially difficult for the CPP government to counter. Rural politics, as we have seen, had always been robust and sometimes violent. That tradition was to continue; but at least at the level of perception it was now definitively altered. The conflicts in rural areas from the end of 1954 through to independence were now to be re-labelled. CPP factions, already strong in many

35 By J.M. Allman, *The quills of the porcupine.*

36 It argued for a federal constitution with strong regional powers. The CPP and the British were wedded to the continuation of a unitary state.

rural areas, were to be in contention from now onwards with factions which declared that they were not merely local contenders in local disputes but were also NLM supporters. The formation of the NLM made available a more extensive national identity to the numerous and widely differing local forces with which local CPP organizations had been struggling for the past five years. A wide range of essentially local wrangles, including stool disputes, were now reconfigured as elements in a national struggle for power.

In this situation the CPP had to tread with some delicacy. In most circumstances a democratically elected government confronted with extra-parliamentary action, some of it notably violent, would turn to the courts and the forces of law and order to maintain the peace. Just as the NLM was weakened by its lack of a parlia-mentary presence, the CPP also found itself on thin ice. In the first place, the politics of the terminal colonial period in Ghana were not those of an independent democratic state. Britain remained the colonial power; Ghana's present consti-tution and its future independence hung on the active consent and support of the British government, which in turn was reached partly on the advice of the governor. The CPP government's every move was under critical scrutiny by the power that ultimately held the keys to full independence.

From 1951, Britain had elected Conservative governments. They had perse-vered with the previous Labour governments' colonial policies so far as West Africa was concerned. But some back-bench opinion and some opinion in Cabinet, moved perhaps by ideology as well as the campaigns mounted by some of the business community, was hostile to the winding up of empire and particularly hostile to Nkrumah and the CPP who they regarded as hand in glove with Moscow. Nkrumah had to work hard to maintain the support of the governor, the Colonial Office and by extension that of the British government. Already accused of Stalinism by some of the more rabid right-wing press in Britain, he would have made his opponents in Britain extremely happy had he attempted, as he was undoubtedly sorely tempted to do, to smash the NLM by main force. At the same time, even had he wished to do so, it is unlikely whether this would have done other than provoke a local constitutional crisis. The control of the forces of both internal and external security rested with the British as it was to do until the day of independence itself. The use of force accordingly would have required the complicity of the British governor and a largely British senior officer corps in both the police and the military; and ultimately that would have needed the tacit agreement of the British government. Consequently the rising tide of violence in the countryside was especially difficult for the CPP to control.

But the CPP's war of attrition against chieftaincy preceded the foundation of the NLM and was almost certainly a major reason why the NLM was to attract a large number of Akan chiefs in the course of its brief career. That war was being fought on many fronts. During and immediately after the 1954 election, CPP ministers made it clear at public meetings that 'the Gold Coast was being developed in a socialist way'.[37] Chiefs should co-operate with their local MPs 'so that their

---

[37] The minister of communications, Aaron Ofori Atta, to a CPP rally in Kumase on 6 July, as reported in

grievances and problems might be solved by the Government'. If chiefs 'co-operated with their representatives in the Assembly their states would no doubt be developed';[38] by implication non-co-operation presumably risked incurring communal punishment in the form of the withholding of development expenditure in areas of opposition.

In less obvious and strident fashion, chieftaincy was being undermined by local government reform and by the somewhat covert alteration of the old Native Courts system. But such reforms had significant local embellishments. In the state of Akyem Abuakwa, whose fate will loom large in the later stages of this book, the identification of the royal family with anti-CPP causes from the late 1940s was very apparent. We have seen the construction of the CPP's antagonism to the paramount, the Okyenhene, who was also the president of the Joint Provincial Council. This was manifest in petty as well as in more serious moves.[39]

More significantly, the ministry of local government was actively seeking to undermine the Okyenhene's power by its particular reform of the Akyem Abuakwa Native Court system. In May 1954, Cabinet agreed with the minister that the new court should sit at New Tafo rather than the kingdom's capital, Kyebi. This decision appears to have been made at the behest of the newly constituted and almost entirely CPP membership of the relevant local councils. These councils' ostensible reason for demanding this was that they 'feared injustice and intimidation if the court was not removed from the king's palace and from his capital.'[40] As we have seen, there was more than a little justification for this accusation.

The order transferring the seat of the court from Kyebi was accordingly a highly charged political decision. It was, moreover, a decision that smacked of partiality in other respects. New Tafo is the neighbouring town to Tafo, the town of Aaron Ofori Atta's mother and hence his town. Standing as the CPP candidate, Aaron Ofori Atta had defeated his famous uncle, Dr J.B. Danquah, for the Abuakwa Central seat in the Assembly in the 1954 election. Aaron Ofori Atta was to be minister of communications and then minister of local government in the CPP administrations after 1954. Danquah argued bitterly that his nephew wished to 'destroy the authority of his father in Kibi', a reference to both the present Okyenhene[41] and to Aaron Ofori Atta's late father. It is clear that politics in Akyem Abuakwa fed off divisions in families as well as between towns in the traditional kingdom.

The area around Tafo also falls under the traditional control of the divisional chief, the Adontenhene, Nana Kwabena Kena II. Kena was a highly educated man who had successfully taken a correspondence course which led to a university degree and had a background in accountancy. He had not been amongst those

---

[37] (cont.)the *Daily Graphic*, 7 July 1954. The speech went on to insist that socialism 'would make everybody happy and free when full self-government was attained'. The same newspaper reported a very similar speech by J.E. Jantuah on 6 September 1954.

[38] The minister of local government, Edward Asafu-Adjaye, speaking on 11 July, reported in the *Daily Graphic*, 12 July 1954.

[39] Such as his removal from the Vernacular Literature Board in 1952.

[40] Quoted in the *Daily Graphic*, 23 July 1564.

[41] Who was actually Aaron Ofori Atta's cousin.

Akyem Abuakwa chiefs who had been antagonistic to the CPP from its earlier days. He had dissented from the decision by the Okyenhene's council, the Okyeman, to prevent the inauguration of the CPP in Kyebi.[42] By his own account he had allowed the CPP to establish itself in his town, Kukurantumi. Although the Adontenhene was not to join the CPP formally until June 1956, he was in active contention with almost all of the rest of the Okyeman Council over the issue of the removal of the court from Kyebi to New Tafo.

How much of Nana Kwabena Kena's politics was personal or pressed upon him from below is unascertainable. All too frequently chiefs, like most of the world's politicians, claimed that they did this or that because this was the will of their people. But given that the area around Tafo had a long history of opposition to Akyem Abuakwa's paramount chief and to his capital city, Kena's claim to have been acting in accordance with the popular will is unusually convincing. And it led him to refuse to endorse the Okyeman Council's resolution of 12 July 1954 demanding the restoration of the Court to Kyebi. For his pains he was threatened with destoolment by the Okyeman Council. From this moment onwards the Adontenhene, one of the most powerful of the kingdom's divisional chiefs, and the CPP member for Abuakwa Central, Aaron Ofori Atta, were to make common cause. Their objective was now the complete defeat of the Okyenhene and his supporters.

While this particular passage of arms was to end in a very dramatic showdown after independence, it was symptomatic of the complexity of the situation in which chiefs now found themselves. The government had grown increasingly impatient with them and some members of government were now publicly hostile to the entire institution of chieftaincy. Government policies undermined both their old administrative and legal authority. Those who opposed individual chiefs in local disputes found a welcoming home in local CPP branches as well as the promise of future favours. The CPP had in turn proved much more skilful in adapting to new circumstances and had been successful in gaining control of a large majority of the new local councils. In many cases the CPP's opponents had not bothered to take part in elections to local councils.

It was as though the old binary colonial state continued despite the trans-formative political changes since 1951. On the one hand, there was a modern political universe in which modern political processes, like elections and election-eering, dominated. But on the other, there was another world in which political power was apparently regarded as inherent and not elected by manhood suffrage. The ideologies of both universes as well as their methodologies were poles apart and there was little dialogue between the two. It is tempting to see virtue in the potentially democratic nature of the modern universe and to see none in that which maintained the significance of kingship and kinship. This, however, is an outsider's view. Both sets of views were held strongly and with an equal measure of conviction and resolve. The resulting dialogue of the deaf frustrated both the CPP and its enemies. Both claimed to have right on their sides; both claimed the

[42] His evidence on this to the Jackson Commission of Enquiry into Akyem Abuakwa affairs on 24 February 1958 is borne out by the records of the Okyeman Council.

moral high ground. The logical basis of the arguments of either side derived from differing understandings of rationality or were derived with equivalent logic from different premises; thus there was little shared language and hence little chance of exchange and persuasion. It would be entirely wrong to see this struggle in solely materialist terms. Both sides had intellectual arguments and strong principles as well as material interests But this kind of conviction politics is a stranger to compromise. Too much of the resulting debate was accordingly carried on by violent means.

The statutory relationship between many local and traditional councils was therefore almost inevitably poisonous. At the same time the possibility of a national alliance between chiefs against government was persistently undercut by the growing propensity of some chiefs to seek support from the CPP. In some circumstances this could prove to be a boon in local disputes, as it was for the Adontenhene in Akyem Abuakwa. In others, such as the Brong example and that of the state of Attebubu,[43] the CPP as government could prove to be a valued ally in much higher-level constitutional wrangles. A good CPP connection also appeared to assist states in their constant search for local development funding.[44]

Deciding which way to jump was a painful process for many chiefs. Some veterans of this period suggest that while the political urgency of the day made neutrality impossible, there were palpable costs attached to public adherence to either the CPP or the NLM. By their own accounts some chiefs were forced in public to side with one or other party against their wishes in circumstances which sound remarkably and uncomfortably like 'recantation' sessions during China's Cultural Revolution. The Asokorehene[45] alleged that his public support for the NLM at the Asanteman Council meeting on 19 October was the result of the threats from 'a crowd of youngmen... I found my life was in danger and I had no choice but to support the National Liberation Movement to save my life'.[46] His decision split the town, led to attempts to destool the Omanhene by the town's NLM faction and eventually to very serious rioting in February.

By the end of 1954, the Bechemhene also had changed his mind and decided not to support the newly formed NLM. He was summoned before the Asanteman Council, which by then had thrown in its lot with the NLM. He was summoned because 'some of the young men of Bechem, Tanoso, Dwomo, Techine and Kwasu had complained about him. The grounds for complaint were not ostensibly about his support for the CPP. The complaints were, rather, that for the 22 years of his reign he had failed to go regularly to the banks of the Tano River to pour libation for the 'good health' of the Golden Stool. He had also failed to have the horn called *Asante kotoko se me nim de* blown every 40 days, as was customarily required.

---

[43] Whose state council reaffirmed their support for the CPP. They were not interested in the demand of the Ashantis' because they have long ago seceded from the Ashanti due to the bad treatment ... by the Asanteman Council'. *Daily Graphic*, 24 September 1954.

[44] As in October and November 1954, when a number of the pro-CPP states of the south, like Bechem, received the funding they desperately needed for new water supplies.

[45] Nana Yaw Gyimah II.

[46] Reported in the *Daily Graphic*, 26 November 1954.

His wife was accused of not wearing the appropriate state regalia when libation was poured every eight days. Lastly he had taken the 'fetish' *taa bekoe* through Bechem in daylight contrary to custom.[47] It was no coincidence that these alleged offences committed over a period of 22 years should result in charges being laid at precisely the moment when the Omanhene declared his support for the CPP. By 19 November, the Bechemhene and his state council had decided to secede from the Asanteman Council and the authority of the Asantehene. They were now and always had been Brongs, they said. In mid-December the Asanteman Council destooled the Bechemhene.

Bechem was not the only state to resist the NLM's attractions after its inception. In November 1954 the Amansie state council announced its hostility to the NLM. 'The government', they said, 'is ours and of our own making.'[48] In giving his reasons for supporting the CPP and the government, the Akwamuhene of Anwomaso said 'there may be development projects to be implemented in the town by the Government and in view of that if they supported the Liberation Movement they would be denied those services'.[49] That particular argument is to be found frequently in such exchanges; it suggests that coercion and rewards were not, as the CPP later insisted, the political methodologies of the NLM alone.

The list of traditional areas in the Akan-speaking areas which resisted the NLM is a long one and each case has its own particular history. For example, the Kumawuhene, Barima Otua Acheampong, under pressure from the area's MLA, Krobo Edusei, first declared that he intended to secede from the control of the Asanteman Council and join the Brong federation. Both Dormaa and Kumawu were, he said, historically ruled by members of the Aduana matriclan and had both once been part of the state of Akwamu which had eventually been conquered by the Asante. Two days after this announcement, and days after a great deal of pressure had been applied upon him by the Asanteman Council in Kumase, he agreed that he was indeed a clan relative of the Dormaahene but remained a member of the Asanteman Council.[50]

Few of the specific explanations one might derive from narratives such as these have much to do with the central or national issues which ostensibly divided the CPP and the NLM. These specific local struggles were for the most part recensions of older factional or inter-state disputes. To some extent there is a resemblance between the civil struggles in imperial Rome between factions supporting this or that charioteer. In those encounters being a supporter of the Reds or the Greens had little to do with chariot racing and everything to do with city politics. For many chiefs and for many of their councils the great struggle for national power in the Gold Coast afforded them potentially useful national identities in conflicts over what had previously been essentially parochial issues. This is not intended to demean those issues. They loomed large in the minds of

---

[47] See *Daily Graphic*, 10 and 16 November 1954.
[48] *Daily Graphic*, 12 November 1954.
[49] *Daily Graphic*, 22 November 1954.
[50] See *Daily Graphic*, 8 February 1955.

participants. But it is misleading to believe that national politics provided, in their entirety, the proximate causes of local dispute even if involved factions sailed under those national flags of convenience.

6

The Politics of Polarization

The formation of the National Liberation Movementl has been analysed in considerable detail elsewhere. Most analyses of that movement have stressed, entirely reasonably, the leading role of the Asante in that opposition movement. Its brief career was to prove a further if extended moment in which chiefs and their supporters, not only in the Ashanti Region but also from further afield, would either join the bandwagon and support the CPP government or would risk all in opposition. Despite the government's support for the convention that chiefs should be, like constitutional monarchs, politically neutral, there was no possibility of that in the years to come.

The advent of the NLM certainly hardened the battle-lines between government and chiefs. Ministers were stirred to reaffirm their strong hostility to a society where 'class distinction [was] based on accident of birth'.[1] But the rift was a much more complex affair. As we have seen, chiefs and their supporters were making uncomfortable choices about where their best interests lay. Part of the information upon which decisions about which way to jump were made was derived from equivocal readings of the future; chiefly hostility to government might steer government towards the punitive withholding of much needed local development capital – or worse. On the other hand, although the NLM and its supporters' expectations were euphoric rather than practical, events over time began to suggest to some that the CPP's command of government might not be as permanent as it appeared to be in the immediate aftermath of the 1954 election. The defection of major CPP figures to the NLM in February 1955 – R.R. Amponsah, Joe Appiah, Victor Owusu, J.C. de Graft Johnson and E. Kurankyi Taylor – must have reinforced that sense of possibility. By the end of 1955 large numbers of CPP councillors, especially in Ashanti, had joined them in the NLM. But such readings were tempered by necessary readings of the past. The leading position of the Asante nobility in the NLM allowed the chiefs of some individual

---

[1] From a speech by J.E. Jantuah quoted in the *Daily Graphic*, 6 September 1954.

77

states to express their resentment of Asante hegemony by declaring their positive support for the CPP government. In many cases apprehensions about the future and the redressive potential of the current impasse were interwoven. For example, the Attebubu State Council publicly declared its opposition to the NLM in late September 1954. The Attebubuhene said that his people 'were not interested in the demands of the Ashantis because they have long ago seceded from Ashanti due to bad treatment ... by the Ashanti Confederacy Council'. The linkage of old antipathies with the expectation of government favours is apparent when, in the same statement, he appealed to the government 'to give them pure water, hospitals, roads and more secondary and primary schools'. When his paramount issued the blunt instruction to join the NLM: 'Inform your Elders, men and women to sign Federation, failure the people will be dealt with by the Asanteman. Flags will be given to you later',[2] the Akwamuhene of Anwomaso[3] declined to do so. At a public meeting he said that 'there are many development projects to be implemented in the town by the Government and in view of that if we support the Liberation Movement we will be denied those services'.[4] This palpable awareness of the possible local disadvantages of declaring for the opposition is very obvious in case after case.

The most obvious beneficiaries of this polarization were a cluster of states to the west of Ashanti usually referred to as the Brong States.[5] As we have seen, these were states which had once been conquered by Asante, a status reinforced when the British restored the Asante Confederacy. In that process the Brong States were brought under the traditional authority of the Asanteman Council and its chairman, the Asantehene. Although the idea of a separate Brong region had been floated before, it was not an idea that had been supported by first the British and then the CPP. But the Brong chiefs were quick to realize that the deepening political crisis afforded them an opportunity to press this case again. The overture for this was an early expression of considerable hostility to the NLM and a series of effusive expressions of support for Kwame Nkrumah. The Dormaahene, speaking on behalf of his fellow Brong chiefs in October 1954, argued: 'any move against Nkrumah and the CPP government is the greatest political blunder any ungrateful people could commit for never in the history of this country has any person or body been able to unite the whole country for a common purpose as has been done by Nkrumah and the CPP government'.[6]

When making *ex cathedra* statements about allegiance to either the government or to the Asantehene,[7] it cannot be inferred that chiefs ever reflected anything like complete local unity of local purpose. The endless internal tensions within individual states simply took on the new national labels. Those internal tensions

---

[2] *Daily Graphic*, 22 November 1954.
[3] Nana Kwame Amoake.
[4] Quoted in the *Daily Graphic*, 24 September 1954.
[5] The most important of these were Dormaa, Tekyiman, Drobo, Suma, Odumase, Wiase and Aboase.
[6] Quoted in the *Daily Graphic*, 28 October 1954.
[7] By the end of October 1954 Asante allegiance to the Asantehene was a coded way of stressing support for the NLM, as the Asanteman Council had declared its support for the NLM on 20 October.

were frequently accompanied by a considerable amount of bullying and threats. Coercive politics of this sort were practised by both sides. As we saw earlier, the Asokorehene was undoubtedly a victim of serious personal threats and he was far from the only chiefly victim caught between the upper and nether millstones of national politics. The resulting violence between the Omanhene's supporters and the local NLM branch in Asokore town was so severe that a permanent police presence was drafted there in February 1955 from the neighbouring towns of Effiduase and Mampong.

Intricate politics such as this and the Bechem case referred to in the last chapter were not confined to the Ashanti Region. In Akyem Abuakwa, a state whose royal family were firmly attached to anti-CPP political groupings, the hostility to the CPP was maintained. Publicly the Okyenhene, Nana Ofori Atta II, had been more circumspect than he had been in the first two years of CPP government. As president of the Joint Provincial Council of Chiefs, the Okyenhene had, for example, been careful to insist upon the political neutrality of the JPC. 'We are not against any political party but are conscious of our sacred duty as custodians of the interests of our people,' he said at the opening of the JPC meeting on 2 December 1954. But weeks later while celebrating the Odwira festival in the state capital Kyebi, he very publicly honoured his uncle, Dr J.B. Danquah, who immediately on his return from the USA in December 1954 had pledged his support to the NLM. Having lost his parliamentary seat to his nephew Aaron Ofori Atta in the 1954 general election, Danquah had left the Gold Coast on 10 September to take up a United Nations fellowship. At the festival Danquah was not only welcomed home but was also somewhat provocatively installed as a senior divisional chief of the Adonten division.

Whether such an appointment was customarily legitimate was a fine point of Akan law. What was more pressing was the fact that this was undoubtedly intended to insult and weaken the authority of the head of the Adonten division, the Adontenhene, Nana Kwabena Kena II. As we have seen, Kwabena Kena was distinctive in the Akyem Abuakwa kingdom as being the most senior chief who had supported the CPP in defiance of his paramount's clear political support for the NLM. Kena had not been consulted about the enstoolment of Danquah and was, not surprisingly, infuriated by it. He inferred that this decision was made not merely to dignify the Akyem Abuakwa state's most famous son but also to retaliate against Kena's support for the move of Kyebi's local court to the CPP stronghold of New Tafo.

The extent to which Danquah and another of his nephews, William Ofori Atta, who was also a staunch NLM supporter, were using the Akyem Abuakwa stool to further the ends of the NLM is difficult to judge. Any analysis of Danquah's rhetorical style over time would certainly suggest that some of the Okyenhene's most provocative anti-government statements were drafted by Danquah. On 21 February 1955 the governor, Sir Charles Arden-Clarke, visited Kyebi. At the Durbar he was harangued at length by the Okyenhene's chief *okyeame*.[8] The

---

[8] Usually translated as 'linguist' but in effect any Akan king's mouthpiece, advisor and confidant. This *okyeame* was Baffuor Kwesi Dua Sakyi.

government, he was told, should set up a constituent assembly comprising the chiefs and the people, with a view to the transfer of power to 'a sovereign authority designated by the chiefs and the people'. The *okyeame* complained about 'our grave concern with the revolutionary, even radical changes brought about by the Local Government Ordinance, affecting local administration and the native courts and also with the spread of the practice of corruption and bribery as well as the mismanagement of affairs which is going on today'. The address closed by reiterating some key NLM demands such as the raising of the cocoa price. How moved Arden-Clarke was by this address is hard to judge. But at a meeting of the Berekum State Council on 27 March he was reported as saying: 'It is true that the Government made the pledge to maintain chieftaincy; how far and by what they intend to implement the pledge I do not know.' This certainly suggests some personal concern with the drift of events.[9]

Events in Akyem Abuakwa focused government hostility in the direction of the kingdom and that became increasingly dangerous. In a debate in the Legislative Assembly, Aaron Ofori Atta[10] said that 'chiefs were losing their respect owing to their own attitude to chieftaincy' and singled out the elevation of Danquah, his uncle, to a divisional chieftaincy as an example of unacceptable authoritarianism and contempt for customary law. He suggested that Danquah was being paid £600 per year for this office[11] and that this was, amongst other things, a misuse of public money. This hostility was visible in a less formal fashion; the area of Akyem Abuakwa was manifestly not regarded by government as a priority area for the distribution of development funds; this was a matter of concern as, for reasons rehearsed above, local council taxation proved hard to collect and local revenue had to be supplemented from central funds. Attention was constantly drawn to this localized developmental neglect, for obvious reasons, by the pro-NLM activists. But it was also a matter of concern for the CPP members of the Legislative Assembly for the area and by the CPP-dominated local council. From their point of view, the defeat of the NLM in Akyem Abuakwa would have been facilitated by government generosity rather than punishment. Instead, as the CPP Member for Akyem Abuakwa North, C.E. Nimo, suggested in the House on 29 July 1955, roads, medical services and education were being neglected in the kingdom. The Member for Akyem Abuakwa West, S. Owusu-Afari, supported Nimo's argument and said that there was strong local feeling that nothing had come their way under the 1951 development plan. Although none of the speakers in this debate made the point explicitly, they were openly criticizing a policy which increasingly obviously rewarded friends but no less apparently punished enemies.[12]

---

[9] This account is derived from the extensive report in the *Daily Graphic*, 22 February 1955.

[10] The minister of communications at this stage.

[11] This was unlikely; £600 was the government stipend for paramount chiefs and Danquah's post fell far short of that level of seniority.

[12] There were exceptions. Cabinet agreed in March 1955 to restore the government grants to Ashanti local authorities, which had been reduced in 1954, to 1953 levels. Nkrumah noted: 'in these circumstances in the face of the pressure from Ashanti ... it would be impossible completely to ignore Ashanti.' Cabinet, 22 March 1955, NAG ADM 13/2/21.

While the government formally took note of the protest, it was to do little to meet these complaints from its own benches in the years ahead.

Although the increasing stridency of the NLM was the most immediate cause of more and more government aggression towards the chiefs, it was, as we have seen, part of a longer struggle. While it is impossible to prove, it seems very likely that the government was using its members in the House and outside to increase the volume of decidedly threatening rhetoric. In August 1955 at the sixth annual CPP delegates conference at Kpandu in the Volta Region, motions advocating the removal of any national financial support from the Asanteman and Okyeman Councils were tabled to considerable applause. Speaker after speaker condemned both of these chiefly councils for using 'undue influence' in politics. In November 1955, the Member for Akyem Abuakwa East, K. Amoah-Awuah, demanded the amendment of the Local Government Ordinance to abolish the appointment of traditional members to local councils other than those who had stood for election as ordinary members.[13]

Such public menaces more than closely mirrored what was being conjured in Cabinet. These public statements by rank-and-file CPP members were almost certainly 'planted' by senior party officials and were designed to suggest that Cabinet policy-making was simply reacting to the wider will of the party and hence the country. Although only parts of Cabinet thinking ever found their way on to the statute book, what was being hatched in the course of 1955 was very profoundly threatening to chieftaincy in general and some chieftaincies in particular.

The general drift indicated a real resolve to reduce drastically the remaining power of traditional authority in all its manifestations. First, the government sought to sidestep the widespread breakdown in local administration in many areas, which was the result of irreconcilable differences between the new and largely CPP local councils and traditional authorities. As we have seen, these differences were usually the result of local councils and chiefs being unable to agree on the annual payment councils were expected to make to traditional authorities. In effect, local councils now had a monopoly of local revenue-raising and that included the income from stool lands. Many chiefs, and especially those of the richer stools, regarded this as appropriation and defiantly stood out for much larger grants than local councils were prepared to make. The result was that little business was transacted and, importantly, little revenue was raised; a large number of local councils were close to bankruptcy. Many local councils were suspended by the government in this period and local administration was taken over by committees of administration appointed by the minister of local government.[14] Such suspensions were not discussed in the Assembly and were made by Cabinet order, a legislative relic of the order in council. They amounted to the imposition of direct rule in many areas of the country. It effectively ended the capacity of chiefs to defy local councils and hence the wider intentions of government.

---

[13] This reform was to wait until 1959.

[14] See for example the cases of Nkoranza, Tongu and Asokore local councils discussed in Cabinet minutes, 19 April 1955, NAG ADM 13/2/22.

Second, it is clear that from the middle of 1955, the government was actively moving towards the break-up of the Ashanti Region by supporting the notion of creating a separate region for the Brong states. Several of the Brong states had been agitating for such a separation for many years. The archival record of such petitions goes back to 1949 and runs to no less than 545 pages. Before the rise of the NLM, the CPP had, like the British before them, done little more than acknowledge receipt of these arguments. On 25 March 1955 Nkrumah told the Assembly that legislative action would have to follow the secession of several Brong states from the authority of the Asanteman Council.[15] At this juncture he went no further than suggesting that the government would 'examine the possibility of setting up a Brong Kyempem traditional council'.[16] There was something awkward about that prescription. Such a council could hardly be traditional, as there had never been such a council in the region's history. As a consequence it could only have been a statutory body[17] with no traditional powers.

By late August, Cabinet was going well beyond this initial, modest proposal. It is striking that the memorandum proposing the creation of a new region was presented by Nkrumah to Cabinet and not the minister of local government. It is no less striking that the memorandum is entitled 'Two administrative regions for Ashanti'. It is a strange document which makes no mention of the politics of the region, but argues for such a development as being 'in line with Government policy of devolution, enabling a greater degree of participation by the local inhabitants'. That such a division was being actively courted is suggested by the prime minister's recording of a number of detailed planning meetings on the issue in the region. He concluded that 'the Goaso area of the Kumasi District and Sunyani and Wenchi Districts and the Kintampo area of the Mampong District together with a northern portion of the Mampong District containing Attebubu would all be in the Western Region of Ashanti'.[18] That 'Western Region' would in due time become the Brong Ahafo Region.

Thirdly, the government had been seeking a method of reducing the powers of chiefs and their councils over what the Coussey constitution had called 'constitutional matters'. Many of these matters were slight issues. But they covered a range of concerns which related to some of the key causes of rural unrest. As we have seen, competition for traditional high offices had become coloured by national politics. Under the 1951 constitution which in this respect remained unamended, the resolution of many of these conflicts continued to lie with the paramount chiefs and their councils. Major matters like destoolment and the recognition of newly elected chiefs was a matter, the Coussey committee had decided, for the senior chiefs of the traditional areas of the Gold Coast.

The government's first attempt to wrest many of these powers from the ultimate control of chiefs preceded the rise of the NLM by well over a year. The

---

[15] Those states were Dormaa, Tekyiman, Abease, Odumase, Drobo, Suma, Wiase, Sunyani and Bechem.
[16] In the Brong language Kyempem means something like 'Confederacy'.
[17] Set up by order in council.
[18] Cabinet minutes, 23 August 1955, NAG ADM 13/2/24.

proposal for the creation of what was to be called a local constitutional committee was first publicly mooted in the government's proposals for constitutional reform of July 1953. It argued that the determination of these sensitive issues should be removed from the realm of politics. This curious formulation suggested a totally fictitious universe in which 'politics' was defined as that which was ostensibly 'modern' and only occurring at the national level. Despite the obvious fact that chieftaincy issues were now clearly embedded in even the most restrictive definition of politics, this alternative discourse was one which suited the CPP very well indeed.

The creation of such a committee came before Cabinet on a number of occasions. On both 3 and 31 May 1955 Cabinet decided that it would quietly drop this promised reform from its legislative programme. The time was 'not opportune to introduce the Bill' which was obviously a reference to the ferment occasioned by the NLM in Ashanti. But by July the matter was reopened, not least because of the legislative implications of supporting the secession of the Brong states. Cabinet papers relating to these discussions leave little doubt about the government's intentions. Even when the notion of a national commission with judicial powers was being mooted, Cabinet insisted that its agenda and its decisions would be steered firmly by government. While the commission, as a judicial body, would only hear government representations, there would be 'a convention that the Commission should accept Government representations'. The minister also argued that many commission decisions would be 'closely related to the maintenance of law and order, a basic responsibility which ... Government must hesitate to delegate to a statutory body'.

While the government steeled itself to abandon a commitment made not only in its 1953 constitutional reform White Paper but also in its election manifesto, it canvassed three acceptable variants. The first was that any 'Commission be so arranged that there is a majority of Government nominees on it, in which case it would be possible to give it the powers to make final decisions'. The second was that it could be composed of independent commissioners but only on condition that they could merely make recommendations to government. The third option was to appoint a minister for local constitutional affairs, who would appoint commissioners, who in turn would make recommendations to Cabinet.[19]

At the heart of these discussions was a recognition that the governor retained a power from the 1944 legislation 'to grant, withhold or withdraw recognition' of paramount and other senior chiefs. Although no colonial governor had exercised those powers since 1944, he could now only make such decisions as 'the Governor-in-Council'. As the council was now Cabinet, such decisions could quite legally be made by Cabinet who would then 'advise' the governor; as the Gold Coast enjoyed internal self-government after the 1954 elections, only an extraordinarily politically inept governor, which Arden-Clarke was not, would choose to ignore that advice.

This complex legal and political account is the essential background to the

19 Cabinet memorandum by the minister of local government, 12 July 1955, NAG ADM 13/2/23.

drafting of the inflammatory amendment of the States Councils Ordinance. In many respects the amendment did little more than unify the laws of the entire Gold Coast[20] while emphasizing many of the rights of the governor and his government which had lain uncontested on the statute book for over 10 years. The amendment basically allowed subchiefs to appeal over the heads of their paramounts 'at the discretion of the minister' to appeals commissioners[21] and was understood quite correctly by many paramounts as intended to undermine their authority. Although much of the content of the amendment was, as we have seen, no more than a restatement of law and the extension of laws covering the Colony, the Northern Territories and Trans Volta Togoland to the Ashanti Region, the timing of the legislation, as much as its contents, was widely regarded as a political manoeuvre to weaken the powers of paramount chiefs and their councils, especially in Ashanti. From the government's point of view there were in reality only two paramount chiefs and two state councils which needed to be broken: the Okyenhene and the Asantehene and the Okyeman and Asanteman Councils were manifestly in the CPP's gun-sights.

In late November, the regional chairman of the CPP, Harry Asafu-Adjaye, the scion of a distinguished Kumase family, resigned from the party in protest against the State Councils (Amendment) Ordinance. He spoke for many opponents of the CPP when he said: 'By this Act the leaders of the CPP have proved themselves wreckers of the Ashanti nation which took many years of toil, tears and blood to build.'[22] Defections such as this became commonplace in the wake of what was widely presented by the opposition as an unequivocal declaration of war against Ashanti. The NLM greatly benefited from that in the Ashanti Region. By the end of 1955, the CPP, who had initially dominated the Kumasi Municipal Council, were in a minority.[23] Sporadic violence and widespread coercion made it increasingly difficult for CPP supporters to show their hands, let alone their faces, on such bodies. Only two CPP councillors could bring themselves to attend the municipal council meetings on 3 December 1955 and 6 February 1956. Although the ostensible reason for postponing many local council elections, routinely scheduled throughout May 1956, was the troubled security situation, there is no doubt that the CPP's fears of losing more local councils to the NLM was a powerful additional, if unstated, motive for the government's decision.[24] Such postponements were described, with some justice, in the debate on the wonderfully

---

[20] And fundamentally to bring the laws governing Ashanti into line with those already applying to other regions of the Gold Coast.

[21] Before appeals commissioners were appointed such appeals were heard by government-appointed Committees of Enquiry. Such committees were in operation, before the amendment, enquiring into stool disputes. In mid-1955 there were no less than six such enquiries running at the same time.

[22] Quoted in the *Daily Graphic*, 28 November 1955. His resignation was followed by several prominent CPP local councillors in Ashanti including A.E. Boakye, J.W. Acheampong and E.K. Senchere.

[23] The NLM had 17 councillors and the CPP only 11 by this stage.

[24] Such elections were postponed in March 1956 in Akyem Abuakwa, Ashanti, Anum, Akwamu and the Northern Territories firstly until October 1957 and then 'until convenient' by the minister of local government in early May 1956. See Cabinet, 12 May 1956, NAG ADM 13/2/80.

entitled enabling legislation, the Local Government Councils (Extension of Tenure in Office) Ordinance, as 'a danger to democracy' by the Opposition MLA for Anloga, Modesto Apaloo.

In tandem with these discussions, Cabinet was moving towards the removal of traditional members from local councils. The entrenched right to one-third of the seats on such councils for the nominees of state councils had been established in the local government reform legislation of 1951. On 9 September, at the prodding of the minister of local government, Cabinet agreed that traditional members should be removed 'when the Government was satisfied that such action was expedient in the interest of fully representative democratic local government'. A month later, following discussions between the minister and Nkrumah, the minister concluded that it was 'likely that any debate in the Legislative Assembly on the proposal ... would be misunderstood and would [be] likely to alienate the sympathies of chiefs in the country as a whole; for the amendment might be construed as an attempt by Government to do away with Chieftaincy.'[25]

The abandoned draft amendment was a potentially draconian measure which undoubtedly sought to weaken the last vestiges of chiefly influence in local councils. Amongst other things it would have illegalized 'the use of oaths, fetishes, spells and the gong-gong to influence people in the way they should vote in local government elections' and would have remitted any disputes over stool lands to a government-appointed land court. But the proposed legislation risked undermining 'the amicable relationship between representative and traditional members now existing in many areas'; that was a scarcely encrypted way of saying that where chiefs supported the CPP and CPP-dominated local councils there was every reason to respect chieftaincy. Throughout the final months of the colonial period, the government had to balance the advantage of keeping pro-CPP chiefs sweet whilst sapping at the legal foundations of the power of those chiefs who opposed them.

The minister had, however, no need to rely upon new legislation. Cabinet had powers under the Local Government Ordinance[26] to vary, at his discretion, the proportion of traditional members on any local council. 'By proceeding in this way', the minister suggested, 'the desired result can be achieved without amending the Ordinance and so provoking an embarrassing debate in the Assembly ... the Minister ... should use his existing powers to reduce to the legally permissible minimum the traditional members appointed to councils.'[27] This quite legal method of regulation allowed the Minister to retain pro-CPP chiefs on local councils whilst culling those who were obviously supporters of the NLM. This methodology mirrored that already being used to remove unfriendly chiefs from local court panels.

---

[25] Cabinet paper by the minister of local government (A. Casely-Hayford), Cabinet minutes, 18 October 1955, NAG ADM 13/2/25.

[26] Section 7(2).

[27] Cabinet paper by the minister of local government, Cabinet minutes, 18 October 1955, NAG ADM 13/2/25.

The government was fighting antagonistic chieftaincy on several fronts by the beginning of 1956. In addition to the measures already mentioned, Cabinet was also increasingly clear about its support for the creation of a further region which would eventually be called Brong Ahafo. Such a move could be presented as a reaction to popular feeling in the putative region against unwanted Asante domination. Its effect was to split the old Ashanti Region in half, thereby reducing the Asantehene and his Asanteman Council's national political clout. The government's absolute commitment to the creation of a new region emerged in yet another Cabinet discussion on the establishment of a constitutional commission to deal with friction between traditional rulers and states.

A White Paper on establishing such a commission had been circulated to the chiefly councils of the Northern Territories, Trans Volta Togoland, Ashanti and the Colony. The responses had been predictably negative and, even more interestingly, considerably contradictory, which suggests that there was little liaison between those councils. The divided nature of chiefly opinion encouraged the government to pursue its own course. The powers of such a commission would be severely limited. Its role would be confined to 'the determination of appeals dealing with [chieftaincy] disputes ... and that the executive powers now vested in [the Governor in Council] ... should not be transferred to the Commission'. In addition, the minister of local government was supported when he proposed that 'the Brong Kyempem Federation'[28] should be included within the commission's remit as a region in its own right.[29]

At the national level the government was walking a tightrope. The NLM had enjoyed considerable success in their public relations offensive outside the Gold Coast. They had worked skilfully on the remaining British official suspicions about Nkrumah's trustworthiness and, in some more extreme cases, had sown doubts about the wisdom of the imminent transfer of power. Despite the governor's assurances that the results of the 1954 elections still represented the will of the people, it was widely believed in London that the NLM's successes might well represent a change of heart by a significant number of Gold Coasters. The Colonial Office was eager to support any initiatives which would reduce such doubts. An element of this was the despatch, following the formal request of the CPP government, of a constitutional advisor, to examine the merits of the NLM's insistence upon a federal system of government.

Although the advisor, Sir Frederick Bourne, was formally boycotted by the NLM, he was able to meet and hear a number of NLM officers in secret. His eventual report was something of a masterpiece of equivocation. It deferred to the demand for devolution by proposing the creation of regional assemblies but his recommendations fell very far short of supporting the NLM's case for full federation. His proposals were eventually discussed at a round-table conference at

---

[28] Which he defined as Abeasi, Atebubu, Banda, Berekum, Dormaa, Drobo, Duan, Mo, Nkoranza, Nkwanta, Suma, Techiman, Wenchi and Weasi.

[29] Memorandum by the minister of local government, 6 March 1956, NAG ADM 13/2/29.

Achimota, which the NLM again boycotted, and in their absence those meetings agreed with Bourne's proposals.[30]

The CPP was essentially hostile to any form of regional devolution. It was a centralizing party with a strong commitment to a unitary country. Of course its centralism went beyond its eagerness for national unity. In March the CPP central committee issued the following statement: 'owing to the fact that the NLM ... have ... mischievously misconstrued the term "democratic Centralism" (the guiding principle of the Convention People's Party), the Central Committee is anxious to explain ... that the term is synonymous with ... "Parliamentary Democracy"'.[31] But so far as the wrangle over federalism was concerned, it could hardly reject the advice of the expert it had invited. It endorsed the idea of regional assemblies and did so without too much discomfort, as their powers were to be extremely limited.[32] But Bourne and the Achimota conference were also sensitive to the NLM's case that chiefs had a role to play in national government. Bourne's primary emphasis was, however, on regions. The proposal that each region should, in effect, establish a House of Chiefs[33] appeared to echo the earlier demand of the Coussey committee that the country should have an Upper House. While that had been rejected by the British as well as the CPP, it seemed as though chiefs might play such a role not in a national legislature but in the new regional assemblies.

The government agreed to the establishment of Houses of Chiefs in each of the regions,[34] but was extremely careful to provide them with terms of reference which very severely limited their powers. They could consider matters referred to them by government; they would advise on African social customs and customary law. A House of Chiefs could consider Bills 'affecting its functions and referred to it'.[35] These were very slight powers indeed. The notion of Houses of Chiefs with designated functions that related to regions rather than national issues was actually very welcome to the government. It had the potential to further balkanize, by regionalizing, the national chiefly constituency.

But chiefs were already balkanizing themselves. In December 1955, the Joint Provincial Council of Chiefs, representing the Colony, met in Dodowa. At the start of business they considered a letter from the general secretary of the NLM inviting them to mimic the Asanteman Council's denunciation of the States Council (Amendment) Bill as 'inimical to the interests of the people'. Their long

---

[30] For a fuller account of these manoeuvres see Vol. II of R. Rathbone, *Ghana; British documents...*

[31] This gem was reported without comment in the *Daily Graphic*, 2 March 1956.

[32] The assemblies were, as we shall see below, destroyed almost immediately after Independence.

[33] Bourne argued for this 'in the first place to safeguard their position and in the second place to provide a means whereby their experience can be utilised for the general good of the Region'.

[34] Including one for 'the Brong Region if such a Region is established...'. Cabinet, 12 April 1956, NAG. ADM 13/2/30. Bourne had in fact been hostile to the creation of a Brong Ahafo Region: 'I cannot see any administrative justification for creating a separate region ... local opinion on the subject is far from unanimous.'

[35] Memorandum on 'draft response to the Report of the Constitutional Advisor and the Report of the Achimota Conference', 12 April 1956, NAG ADM 13/2/30.

discussion was cautious, even nervous. Many chiefs reiterated the importance of chiefs remaining outside national politics. The Omanhene of Dutch Sekondi reminded the council that the Joint Provincial Council 'had no political allies' and then that 'chiefs should support the government at all times'.

While many supported the Omanhene, there were others who worried about the implications of not supporting the Asante. The Omanhene of Akwamu warned that 'some of us have relatives and friends in Ashanti. We should not do anything which would hurt the feelings of the Ashanti.' To do so, he argued, encouraged a rift between Ashanti and the Colony. After much discussion, the JPC came up with a resolution which was duly sent to the government. This stated that it was 'at one with the Asanteman Council and the NLM in demanding its [the bill's] repeal' and added that the publication of the bill had created 'public unease' and suggested that the timing had been inappropriate. But it tempered that criticism with a statement that the Bourne mission provided an opportunity 'to examine and discuss dispassionately proposals for a constitution', an idea with which the NLM strongly disagreed.

But the rift referred to by the Akwamuhene had already opened up. The JPC had already strongly urged the Asanteman Council and the NLM to abandon their boycott of Bourne's mission. The JPC had openly met Bourne and in February 1956 were to attend the Achimota conference.[36] That opinion was further advanced at the Dodowa meeting. There was widespread unease that the insecurity of life and property in the Ashanti Region could spread to the Colony, and the uneasy times following the riots of 1948 were raised as ghastly warnings about history repeating itself. Their eventual resolution on events in Ashanti condemned political violence. Throughout the discussions it was clear that many Colony chiefs, either through fear or out of principle, felt that the Asanteman Council had painted itself into a corner.[37] There was a discernible unwillingness to join the chiefs of Asante in that particularly hazardous corner. There is no doubt that the government was well aware of these divisions and happy to capitalize upon them.

[36] With the Brong Kyempem Federation along with representatives of the CPP, the Moslem Council the Trans Volta Togoland Chiefs' Council amongst others.

[37] There were attempts at reconciliation. For example two joint provincial paramounts, Nene Azu Mate Kole, *konor* of Manya Krobo, and Nana Otu IX, Omanhene of Abura, had a meeting with the Asanteman Council and the NLM executive on 7 March 1956.

7

Independence & the Chiefs

While the chiefs of the Colony were clearly divided over their relationship to the National Liberation Council, the extreme position adopted by the Okyenhene of Akyem Abuakwa and most members of his state council remained unequivocally hostile to the government. In the interwar period Akyem Abuakwa had been widely regarded as a model of good 'native government'. But by the mid-1950s things were falling apart very rapidly because of the extreme tension between traditional authority and national government. As a result neither local government nor local justice was working in the Akyem Abuakwa state and, as usual, the victims were ordinary men and women. The journalist Bankole Timothy, visiting the kingdom in April 1956, was appalled at 'the childish level to which ... politics had deteriorated ... where a Local Council ... is CPP dominated and a town or village in the area has a strong NLM following, projects designed for such a village or town are shelved by the District Council...'.[1] The kinds of project he referred to included crucial matters affecting local health and education like the provision of pipeborne water and the building of local clinics. While things were particularly bad in Akyem Abuakwa, other parts of the south were no less troubled. Timothy's investigation of local government throughout the Gold Coast in the following weeks took him to Shama and then finally to Sekondi. His observations there led him to the depressing conclusion that 'politics is destroying the future of Local Government and impeding progress'.[2]

In Akyem Abuakwa this bleak picture was complemented by a wretched and deteriorating political stand-off which was routinely delaying the delivery of local justice. As noted above, CPP branches in Akyem Abuakwa had persuaded the minister of local government that the Akyem native court, which had traditionally sat in the kingdom's capital, Kyebi, was biased; it was, they claimed, dominated by the Okyenhene and his clients. As we have seen, in May 1954 the government

---

[1] *Daily Graphic*, 11 April 1956.
[2] *Daily Graphic*, 27 and 28 April 1956.

made an order which moved the site of the native court to New Tafo. This was a controversial political decision. The town of New Tafo was one of the heartlands of the CPP in the kingdom; it was also the home-town of Akyem Abuakwa's most prominent CPP activist, Aaron Ofori Atta. The ostensible reason for this, and other changes in the Akyem Abuakwa courts system, was that it was now deemed necessary for courts to correspond more closely to the areas of authority exercised by the new local councils.[3] There were, however, political reasons for moving the court away from the Okyenhene's capital and, it was hoped, his influence. The minister of local government expressed this in a neat circumlocution for his Cabinet colleagues. The court must move to New Tafo so that it would 'be more widely representative of the people in the area'.[4]

The move had been hotly contested by the traditional state council and the minister had been forced to hold a stormy meeting with a deputation which included his uncle, Dr J.B. Danquah, and his half-brother Willie Ofori Atta. They argued that the move had been instigated by partisan politics and would 'increase greatly the discord which already existed in Akim'.[5] That discord was to become an even more painful reality. The number of 'incidents' between CPP and NLM supporters increased to the point where the chief regional officer sought, and received, the minister of the interior's permission to impose the restrictive clauses of the Public Meetings and Processions Regulations on 'certain larger towns and villages'.[6] Meetings of any sort now required the giving of advance notice to and the getting of permission from the appropriate government agent, as district commissioners were now called.

The government's attempts to govern in Akyem Abuakwa were endlessly frustrated. Despite its illegality, the Okyenhene and the Akyem State Council continued to conduct a local court of sorts in Kyebi. This was a clear, aggressive and provocative attempt to flout the authority of government in the area. Towards the end of 1955 the minister of local government moved against the prime movers of this defiance and removed their names from the formal panel of those entitled to sit in court. The most significant member of that now proscribed group was the Okyenhene himself, Nana Ofori Atta II.[7] The other 17 removed from the list included virtually the entirety of the Okyeman Council and many close kin of the Okyenhene.

The disorder in local government and local justice was not limited to the

---

[3] The old Native Authority had been dismembered and divided into 11 new local councils: Asamankese, Kade, Kraboa Coaltar, Suhum, Kwabeng, Begoro, Kukurantumi, Kyebi, Nsawam, North Birim and South Birim. In some of these council areas like North and South Birim and Begoro, *akyemfo* – Akyem people – were in a distinct minority.

[4] Memorandum by the Minister of local government, 21 December 1954, NAG ADM 13/2/18.

[5] The deputation's representations were quoted *in extenso* by the minister in a memorandum, 20 May 1954, NAG ADM 13/2/16.

[6] These were Kibi, Suhum, Asamankese, Akwatia, Adeiso, Kade, Asiakwa, Anyinam, Osiem, Old Tafo, New Tafo, Kukurantumi, Osino and Oda. Paper by minister of the interior, Cabinet, 24 May 1955, NAG ADM 13/2/22.

[7] Discussion paper by minister of local government, Cabinet, 11 October 1955, NAG ADM 13/2/25.

Akyem Abuakwa area, even if it was particularly intractable there. Throughout the southern Gold Coast it proved hard to resolve any situation in which the untidy contentious relationship between traditional and elected representatives, inherited from the 1951 constitution and the consequent reforms of local government, still held sway. It was made even more difficult now that this untidiness had been deeply embittered by the violent politics of mutual frustration and by developments in national politics.

Not all of the problems in local government derived from this fraught relationship. The advent of elected rather than ascribed local government councils had been reasonably expected to deliver more transparent and honest administration than before. In many cases it had not done so. Frequent and flagrant abuses of authority came to light and were naturally exploited to the full by the opposition press. Despite the fact that the CPP dominated most local councils, the minister of local government now lamented in Cabinet the frequency of 'nepotism, party-political manoeuvrings or petty local squabbles' and it is clear that he was evenhandedly referring to the conduct of councils dominated by his own party as well as those very few which they did not control. Progressive and decent local government was being undermined 'by arbitrary dismissals and unwarranted promotions or appointments'. The government accordingly moved to control the 'appointment, promotion, interdiction and dismissal of the senior officers of Local, Urban and District Councils'. The resulting Staff (Local Government Council) Regulations of 1955 effectively gave the central government something close to absolute control of the manning of local government. It was a matter of political perspective which determined whether this contributed to the eradication of graft or simply ensured that abuses were henceforward to be only those sanctioned by central government. Opposition politicians naturally believed in the latter.

There was, however, an even more serious struggle for power taking place in Akyem Abuakwa. The Okyenhene had firmly nailed his colours to the mast not merely as a supporter of the NLM but increasingly as one of its leading members. He, for example, chaired a number of meetings celebrating the opening of new branches of the NLM outside Akyem Abuakwa. It was an impressive act and, for the CPP, a very disconcerting one. Aaron Ofori Atta, speaking at a meeting of the pro-CPP Akyem Abuakwa Youth Association on 20 April 1956, acknowledged that 'there have been country-wide rumours that the NLM dominated the State' (by 'State' he meant Akyem Abuakwa) even if he also somewhat perversely argued at the same time that 'the NLM has no footing in Akyem Abuakwa'.[8] National politics now permeated everything in the kingdom. In the large town of Osiem, the wrangle over who should become the next chief resulted in the pro-CPP and pro-NLM factions electing different candidates. The former was supported by the divisional chief, the pro-CPP Adontenhene, the latter was supported by the Okyenhene. In many parts of the kingdom, these struggles felt dangerously close to small but no less bitter civil wars.

Although the stark, all-or-nothing quality of rural politics in this period is

---

[8] Quoted in *Daily Graphic*, 25 April 1956.

particularly notable in Ashanti and Akyem Abuakwa, there were virtually no areas of southern Ghana where contemporary reports painted a dramatically different picture. The image presented by most of the secondary literature suggests that the conflict was largely confined to Ashanti, not least because the hub of the NLM's activities was undoubtedly the Ashanti Region. Partisan politics, however, seem to have dominated most of southern Ghana in the period. And this was seldom a gentle matter. It frequently involved intolerance, exclusion and, at worst, violence. For example the Adansi-Banka District Council was forced to move its headquarters from Fomena because 'some people were afraid to come to Fomena bcause they were molested by others with different political views ... the threatening and dangerous attitude exhibited at Fomena towards [CPP] councillors and employees'.[9] People were afraid and in many cases they were afraid for very good reasons. There were murders, beatings and woundings on all sides and the scale of the mayhem was such that many were forced to move their homes. In discussing raising penalties for law and order offences, the minister of the interior conceded that 'a state of sporadic unrest has existed in certain areas of the Gold Coast for some time ... over the past months there have been large numbers of cases varying in severity from threatening and minor assaults to small riots, murder, arson and the use of explosives ... such incidents continue to occur and have not markedly decreased ... and have at certain periods ... markedly increased'.[10] There was, it seemed, no possibility of compromise, no opportunity to be in two minds about events, no room to be liberal.

It is tempting to regard the extreme and uncompromising nature of rural politics in southern Ghana in the mid-1950s as the straightforward result of the politicization of older disputes. But the situation could also be read as the localization of national politics. Dunn and Robertson noted that ' major clashes of 1956/8 were still fought out in Ahafo in terms of the control of traditional office and the amendment of the traditional constitution'.[11] There is no doubt that such politicization, the result of the often over-enthusiastic activities of both the CPP and the NLM, increased the scale of individual, local wrangles. Protagonists in stool disputes or wrangles over land rights now could and did turn to the wider, national constituency in pressing their causes. The whole point of invoking national party politics in local contretemps was that it permitted antagonists to use the pages of the partisan press and the reasonably well-organized local machinery of either party, and in some cases to call upon the gangs of bully-boys both sides paid to intimidate their opponents. Both the NLM and the CPP used gangs who were usually paid on a daily basis. Conversations with some of the veterans of these local affairs have suggested that some individuals who served in the militias of both parties were often understandably more concerned with the payment than the underlying ideological issues.

It is, however, an equally plausible argument to suggest that the extreme nature

[9] See *Daily Graphic*, 2 May 1956
[10] Memorandum to Cabinet, 14 August 1956, NAG ADM 13/2/31.
[11] *Dependence and opportunity*, p. 94.

of party struggle in rural areas in this period owed much more to a longer tradition of obduracy in chieftaincy disputes. These were very frequent in the colonial period; this is, however, the only period for which we have detailed records. This has led some scholars to automatically invoke an innovative and causative role for colonial rule in such disputes; this is certainly an appealing argument in some cases, but the close relationship is seldom proved. It is entirely reasonable to argue that such disputes had been bitter and uncompromising well before the spread of colonial influence. There is little evidence to suggest that there had ever been a tradition of compromise and reconciliation in the Akan areas of the southern Gold Coast before the colonial era. There is a strong suspicion that stool disputes and succession crises had always been the cause of robust, confrontational politics.

Irrespective of their origins, the numerous cases covered in the archives of the period *before* the advent of seriously adversarial national politics almost always exhibit the same lack of compromise. Losers appear to have been only rarely reconciled to the outcome; instead, losing factions simply bided their time to re-assert their cases and then exact revenge upon their enemies if successful. Victors punished their opponents both formally and informally by exclusion from proximity to the limited pork-barrels of chiefly patronage. In many of the disputes of the 1950s it is clear that the cases made by individual factions had their roots in antique competitions for power and were based on apparently irreconcilable regional or family disputes.

The language of such politics constantly invoked the deep past, a time where truth, inevitably a convenient truth, prevailed. It frequently cited past wrongs, recensions of this or that partisan reading of local history and insistence upon the time-hallowed rectitude of one position or another. These conflicts were, more-over, extremely difficult to stand apart from. Rural areas are almost definitionally classic 'face-to-face societies' where everybody knows a great deal about their neighbours, many of whom are also kinsmen and women. In such claustrophobic circumstances, any pretension to neutrality could be read as shocking antipathy. As in any society, there were many people who were not much interested in politics and whose inner life was more dominated by the day-to-day struggle for survival, by strategies for self-improvement, with family concerns, the local church, or more prosaic pursuits. But there, and then, few adults and especially adult men[12] could enjoy the luxury of distance from events and the peace within which to simply get on with their lives. The pressures of neighbours, of family and chiefly obligation were considerable and membership of one or another faction was very frequently a matter of ascription rather than free choice. If you lived here or there, were a member of this or that branch of the lineage, were a member of this or that clan, you were expected to be appropriately, loyally aligned. People's memories and the archives reinforce one another in producing an image of entire communities caught up in disruptive, inter-party rivalry. Much of this caused a great deal of bitterly remembered personal misery.

---

[12] The records are sadly entirely silent about women who were undoubtedly significant players in politics in the 1950s.

Yet the registration and polling figures suggest an entirely different kind of picture. In all three of the colonial general elections these figures were low. Neither registration nor voting was compulsory. In the much-contested Colony Region, the southern Gold Coast with which this book is largely concerned, only 48 per cent of the eligible electorate registered to vote in the final bitterly contested colonial election of 1956. The census of 1948 gives the population aged 21 or over in the Colony as 1,067,358. Only 514,065 bothered to register to vote. Of these, only 221,626 actually voted. While there can be no satisfactory explanation of these data, it is entirely possible that evidence of fervent attachment to this or that party was frequently more of a necessary public performance in the close quarters of the village or small town environment, a performance which avoided local recrimination or worse. Free from the press of neighbours or close kin, southern Ghanaians often revealed the very human, universal response of indifference or even antipathy to all politics and even more understandably towards all politicians. This at any rate is the impression given by many of those who lived through these uncertain times.

They were uncertain times because by the mid-1950s the outcome of the struggle between the CPP government and the NLM was harder and harder to read. Support for the CPP was perceived by many chiefs, or their opponents, as wise alignment with the winning side and hence as the best guarantee of receiving much-needed development funding for the locality. For example at a huge CPP rally in Kwawu on 28 May, the Omanhene of Kwawu said that the 'chiefs and the people of Kwahu will ever support the Government'. He went on to ask for amenities such as a pipeborne water supply, radios and a secondary school.[13] But such allegiance seemed to be becoming more of a gamble; by 1955 the NLM gave every appearance of being a potentially successful challenger. If the NLM were to prevail, then having been an outspoken CPP stalwart and thus on the losing side might have serious repercussions for personal and communal futures. While there is no doubt that rural politics in southern Ghana were increasingly inflected by national politics in the 1950s, the implicit assumption that this meant that rural politics were being modernized by this trend is much more questionable. While the style of local politics was undoubtedly altered by being brought into the national arena, the obdurate, no-surrender quality of older chieftaincy disputes continued to haunt local process. The CPP's frequently invoked expectation of 'the dawn of the era of the common man', in which something close to a universal, patriotic national class identity would destroy older family or cultural affiliations, is difficult to discern both in the memories of the old and in the press of the period.

The obduracy of local politics was especially difficult to comprehend from the commanding heights of government. It was, of course, even more difficult to deal with. To the dismay of the CPP government, combatants were not, it seemed, amenable to reason; getting people round a table seemed to stoke the fires of local antipathies rather than dampening them down. Local political support had been

---

[13] Reported in the *Daily Graphic*, 30 May 1956. Such juxtapositions were very commonly reported in this period. The quotation uses the older orthography for the toponym.

tested throughout the country in the form of local council elections. Mirroring the results of national elections, CPP candidates had come to dominate most local councils. For modern politicians on the national scene, such as those who comprised Cabinet, the most elementary reasoning suggested that these victories were legal, democratically arrived at mandates to govern. Neither the laws of the land nor such political evidence of democratic choice, however, appeared to convince opponents of the government that their best chances for change would arrive through successful challenge at the next electoral opportunity. Despite its overt legitimacy both nationally and locally, the government was apparently regarded as illegitimate in opposition enclaves. Non-compliance in the form of failure to pay local taxes was widespread even if it was illegal; whether such resistance was opportunistic, political or simply criminal ultimately mattered very little. So turbulent was the countryside that in early 1956 the government had been forced to postpone the imminently scheduled local government elections, first to October 1957; and by October 1956 this delayed election date had been further advanced to September 1958.[14]

To some extent the national government and local opposition did not share a political language, the language of Western democracy, and this was to prove immensely damaging to both, and ultimately to all of Ghana.[15] In some respects this could be presented as a clash of political cultures. Defiant opposition areas were not necessarily turned or pacified by the usually persuasive generosity of government; in some cases, such as Bekwai which got a much needed water supply in November 1954, the NLM continued to be strongly supported. Punishment and the threat of punishment was no more successful in bringing recalcitrant areas to heel. In many areas of the southern half of the Gold Coast, government was being quite simply defied. In these circumstances it is not difficult to understand why a deeply frustrated CPP government was tempted towards the short cut of more and more authoritarian measures, even if it is also entirely reasonable to deplore this drift.

That frustration was brought to boiling-point in 1956. Arguably the most skilful element of the NLM's extra-parliamentary campaign was its ability to suggest that it was a great, new force in the Gold Coast which had appeared since the elections of 1954. There were still some opponents of Nkrumah and the CPP amongst the British officials and the expatriate business community in the Gold Coast who were more than happy to insist that this was indeed the case. The Conservative government in London, while formally committed to the completion of the transfer of power, were susceptible to criticism of the CPP regime mounted by their own backbenchers in the Lords and the Commons and less openly by the business houses. The CPP – and the British governor – argued, however, that the 1954

---

[14] By the Local Government Councils (Extension of Tenure of Office) Ordinance. The bill was taken through the House by Aaron Ofori Atta. Cabinet discussed the necessity to postpone local government elections on 12 May 1956, NAG ADM 13/2/80.

[15] Dunn and Robertson also write of 'the discontinuity ... between the central and the local political institutions in Ghana', *Dependence and opportunity*, p.197.

elections, which had seen the CPP win over 70 per cent of the seats in the Legislative Assembly, remained the most tangible endorsement of the people of the Gold Coast imaginable. But the NLM and its supporters insisted that political reality had changed very dramatically since that election. To counter this dangerous drift of influential opinion, the CPP had attempted to bring the opposition into the final stages of the transfer of power, whose most significant element was the drafting of the independence constitution. It had failed to do so because the NLM had boycotted the select committee, the mission of the constitutional advisor and the round-table meetings at Achimota which followed.

The NLM had been successful in convincing the secretary of state for the colonies that it was now unclear whether the CPP enjoyed widespread national support and hence whether it had the authority to draft a new constitution and to take the country into independence. Although desperately unwilling to concede that there was any such doubt, the CPP was eventually forced to call a further unscheduled election in June 1956.[16] This resulted in as comprehensive a clean sweep for the CPP as they had enjoyed in 1954. The government again took about 70 per cent of the seats. The NLM secured 12 of the 21 seats in what was still the Ashanti Region but captured none in any other region. Its allies in the scatter of other regional and ethnic parties won just 20 seats. This is not an exact figure; which parties did or did not see themselves as NLM allies was never entirely clear. What really mattered was that the CPP had won 71 out of 104 seats. One of the two independents was to join the CPP soon after the election. Even without this defection the CPP had secured 57 per cent of the votes cast and just short of 400,000 votes, while its opponents had won nearly 300,000 votes. In any 'first-past-the-post' system, this was unequivocally an extremely handsome victory.[17]

The sheer magnitude of this victory, coming as it did only two years after an equally unambiguous triumph, should have settled matters once and for all. In particular, the CPP looked to the result to answer the old and always pertinent question of who governs. They believed that no one could look at the results and continue to believe that chieftaincy and its supporters could claim to be above the law or beyond the command of a popularly elected government. One of the questions asked in the CPP manifesto for the 1956 election was 'Do I want to revert to the days of imperialism, colonialism and tribal feudalism?' and there is no doubt that 'tribal feudalism' now served as a pejorative soubriquet for chieftaincy. But the huge victory of the CPP sent a strong message. Many chiefs now had the political sensitivity to see that the CPP was the government that would take the Gold Coast into independence and that now their best interests and those of their localities would be served by at least recognizing that fact. At the meeting of the Joint Provincial Council on 11 September 1956, the Omanhene of Ahanta was widely supported when, despite the strong opposition of Dr J.B. Danquah, he suggested that as the country was shortly to be independent 'chiefs should not delay in associating themselves with the government'.

[16] For more on this see R. Rathbone (ed.), *Ghana: British documents ...*, Vol. II.
[17] For a full schedule of the results see D. Austin, *Politics in Ghana*, p. 354.

Some chiefs still found this course utterly unacceptable. On 5 August, the Okyenhene told a large crowd of NLM supporters who had come to pay him respect at his palace in Kyebi that he and his elders would 'continue to fight until a better government of responsible leaders was set up'. There can be little argument that this was a strange comment from a king who had just seen all of the five NLM nominees of his state council, including his uncle J.B. Danquah and his cousin Willie Ofori Atta, soundly defeated at the polls by CPP candidates only weeks before. At the same meeting one of the royal family added: 'the CPP won the recent elections but it was not a clear victory'. Most dispassionate readers regarding an election result in which the winning party secures 57 per cent of the vote might be unpersuaded by such an absurd argument. He might have replied that this was fair comment about his own home territory, for in Akyem Abuakwa the result was far closer than it was in the rest of the Colony. There the CPP polled just under 20,000 votes to the NLM's 13,500. In the Colony overall, however, the CPP polled nearly 160,000 votes and the opposition just under 20,000, a huge margin.

The embattled Okyenhene began to embark on a course which was to lead to his own tragic downfall. In October, at his instigation, the Okyeman Council finally suspended Nana Kwabena Kena II, the Adontenhene and the CPP's most senior chiefly ally in Akyem Abuakwa. His suspension was publicly justified by allegations that he had failed to discharge his duties and that he had refused to appear before the Okyeman Council. He was now replaced as Adontenhene by Nana Ofabi II, the Asuomhene. This was an odd and almost certainly desperate substitution; the Asuomhene was, in the traditional hierarchy, junior to the Tafohene who might have been regarded as the Adontenhene's understudy. Tafohene was, however, like Kena, a CPP supporter. Kena insisted that no destoolment charges had been preferred by the Elders, *asafoma*, or people of Kukurantumi, the town of which he was chief; most readings of tradition would suggest that this would have been necessary if his suspension was to have been legal in terms of customary law. The Okyeman Council was, said Kena, 'constituted by members and supporters of the NLM who are hostile to CPP members'.[18]

The Okyenhene, despite the serious reverses of the recent general election, was now attempting to mark out Akyem Abuakwa as something close to a sovereign state in which he and his state council held unchallengeable authority. This drift was not engineered in isolation. The NLM was now beginning to talk publicly about secession. At a large meeting in Abbey Park, Kumase, Joe Appiah told the crowd that they had now designed a 'separate national flag and coat of arms for Ashanti and the Northern Territories'. At the same meeting another NLM leader, Cobina Kessie, was reported to have said: 'what now remained for the Ashanti to do was to secede. [We will] demand federation and nothing else ... whether Britain likes it or not we will carry out our decisions to the full.'[19] For the tacticians of the

---

[18] *Daily Graphic*, 16 October, 1956.
[19] *Daily Graphic*, 6 November 1956.

NLM the argument for secession was almost certainly a bargaining exercise rather than a genuine bid for separate independence. The Ashanti Region is, after all, landlocked and would have had to rely on its southern, CPP-dominated neighbour for infrastructural linkages with its export markets which, in the circumstances, they almost certainly would have obstructed. Only the less reflective and more extreme NLM members really believed in the viability of a separate state. But it is more than likely that the Okyenhene's reckless behaviour both nationally and within Akyem Abuakwa was predicated on the success of the NLM's last-ditch manoeuvring.

Such ploys were, however, doomed. Towards the end of the year the CPP government was in constant debate with the secretary of state for the colonies on the final draft of the independence constitution and the date for Ghana's independence, 6 March 1957, had been announced. That constitutional drafting was a subtle if hectic exercise. The CPP Cabinet was forced to incorporate much that played to the sensitivities of the opposition and which was being fussily insisted upon by the British. The need for reconciliation in the run-up to the celebration of independence was, however, widely understood. In large measure this involved accepting much of the substance of the report of the constitutional advisor, Sir Frederick Bourne. Although some of Bourne's recommendations were decidedly unwelcome to the CPP,[20] his drafting had provided them with a number of useful tools. The eventual constitutional draft's insistence that 'the office of a Chief of Ghana as existing by customary law and usage is guaranteed' capitalized upon the vagueness of Bourne's own views of chieftaincy.[21]

At this juncture it is worth recalling how far chieftaincy had been altered in the six years in which the CPP had dominated domestic policy. In short order chiefs had lost most of their local government and local judicial functions. Their command of patronage had been profoundly undermined by their loss of control of stool revenues. Their access to traditional tribute was limited by the widespread evasion of such payments.[22] They had been left with some control over traditional matters but even here the amendment of the States Council Ordinance now allowed junior chiefs to appeal over the heads of their paramounts to, in effect, Cabinet. Chiefs were to be even further divorced from past powers by the creation of a stool lands tribunal;[23] this was to adjudicate where a local council and a traditional state council could not agree on how to divide local revenue. The future of chiefs in terms of national politics was to be reduced to their marginal role in the regional Houses of Chiefs, for these Houses could consider only matters referred to them by ministers or the national Assembly; and even then they could only proffer advice to government. The regional assemblies' powers were to be

[20] Most especially those which devolved even limited powers to regional assemblies.

[21] 'It would be undesirable', he wrote, 'to endeavour in detail to define the functions and privileges in the Constitution', Report (para. 3).

[22] See, for example, Dunn and Robertson, *Dependence and opportunity*, p. 54.

[23] First mooted in Cabinet in a memorandum by the minister of local government on 24 April 1956. The Puisne Judge, John Jackson, who was serving as land boundary settlement commissioner, was to be the one-man tribunal.

severely limited to consideration of those matters deemed to be their concerns by Parliament. As the drafting exercise gathered pace,[24] it is clear that the politicians' subtlety was being translated into a clever text by the newly appointed constitutional advisor to the prime minister, Geoffrey Bing, QC, who was formally appointed by Cabinet on 8 October 1956 partly because Nkrumah insisted that it was 'undesirable to over-burden the Law Officers' department'.[25] It is more than likely that his unusually skilful drafting set one of the major constitutional traps that both the British and the opposition blithely walked into, namely the extreme fragility of the regional assemblies.

Sadly the politics of constitution-making are not easy to reconstruct from the Ghanaian Cabinet record. There are some peculiarities about that record which merit a brief diversion. First, it is clear that between 1954 and 1957 Cabinet agendas more than doubled in size. Although Cabinet was doing twice as much business at the end of the colonial period as it managed to complete in 1954, the meetings appear to have been no longer than they had been in 1954. That suggests that more proposals were going through on the nod, an inference somewhat confirmed by the minutes of those meetings; these show that there was less and less discussion in Cabinet. Secondly, there is little recorded discussion of political strategy *per se*. Political concerns can sometimes only be deduced from subsequent actions noted in these records. Lastly and much more mysteriously there are a number of meetings, beginning on 16 July 1956, for which there was no agenda and no working papers. It is entirely possible that these meetings were occasions when political strategy rather than legislation was discussed. Agenda-less and minute-less meetings appear to have no precedent in the British Cabinet system upon which the Ghanaian system was based.[26]

On the eve of independence, the disruption of rural areas had not abated. But the government was biding its time, by now a very short time, before it had total control of the post-colonial state. Within a few months following independence government was to transform chieftaincy rather than destroying it by a mixture of coercion and inducement.

[24] See especially Cabinet meeting of 27 September 1956, NAG ADM 13/2/32.

[25] See prime minister's Memorandum to Cabinet, 8 October 1956, NAG ADM 13/2/33.

[26] According to the expert opinion of Professor Peter Hennessy of Queen Mary and Westfield College, University of London (personal communication).

8

Crushing the Chiefs

Within weeks of independence the government was demonstrating that it was in firm command. In mid-April it suspended the Accra Municipal Council and only days later also suspended that of Kumasi. This was, as J.B. Danquah said, 'a show of where power lies'.[1] The government was now, however, considering much stronger measures to control rural affairs. Three weeks after independence day, the prime minister presented a paper to Cabinet. As this concerned local government, the fact that the proposal was steered through Cabinet by the prime minister rather than the minister of local government suggests that this was perceived as a matter of considerable importance. In brief, Nkrumah suggested that the chief regional officers had had their day. They had, the prime minister claimed, 'found themselves at times in the difficult position of a civil servant endeavouring to carry out duties which are really appropriate to a member of the Government ... it is necessary to abolish the posts of CRO and RO. At the same time, there must be in each Region a political representative of the Government and a Chief Executive Officer of the Government'.[2] The memorandum goes on to stipulate that the first of these posts should be called a regional commissioner, 'a political appointment at the pleasure of the Government', and the second should be called a permanent secretary to the regional commissioner. By May 1957, it had been decided that the old chief regional officers, all of whom were still expatriate civil servants, should be redesignated as secretaries to the regional commissioners. Nkrumah argued: 'I consider that the regional commissioners should be fully responsible for what goes on in their Regions ... the ultimate responsibility for the conduct of affairs ... is vested in Ministers.'[3] The new regional commissioners were to be drawn from the ranks of the elected CPP Members of the Legislative Assembly and were to be of Cabinet rank. Because of their status they were to be

[1] Quoted in the *Daily Graphic*, 27 April 1957.
[2] Prime minister's memorandum to Cabinet, 2 April 1957, NAG ADM 13/2/37.
[3] Prime minister's memorandum to Cabinet, 31 May 1957, NAG ADM 13/2/38.

given police motorcycle escorts when on official business; and when involved in ceremonies, they were to be welcomed by 'all primary and middle school children [who] should line both sides of the road' as well as a guard of honour of the Ghana police.[4]

The context of these changes is complex. It could be argued that this initiative constituted a somewhat bizarre, even ironic, recreation of the deeper – and darker-colonial past by sub-Saharan Africa's first post-colonial government. It was inescapably *dirigiste* but it was only partially innovative. There is no doubt whatever that the old colonial structure had flown in the face of any idealistic notion of the separation of powers – let alone accountability. Provincial commissioners, the forerunners of chief regional officers and the old district and later regional commissioners, had for many years of the colonial regime been appropriately and honestly called 'political officers' in British official documents. For decades before the inauguration of the 1946 constitution, provincial commissioners had been ex-officio members of the Executive Council as well as the senior civil servants in their regions. They were thus members of both the legislature and the executive. That fusion, even confusion, of powers was augmented by their powerful roles as adjudicators as magistrates in the colonial legal system. The newly independent government of Ghana seemed intent on restoring a somewhat similar system despite the unfortunate disquieting echoes.

There was an immediate reason for the timing of this development. The new government had been deeply irritated, and not without good cause, by the support given to the Asantehene and thus indirectly to the NLM by the chief regional officer of Ashanti, Colin Russell. He had undoubtedly become involved in what was formally by the mid-1950s the orbit of African domestic politics; if there was any force in the notion of internal self-government which came into effect after the 1954 general election, he could be regarded as having interfered in the business of government. This had caused considerable friction not only with the CPP government but also between Russell and the governor.[5] The governor's exasperation was personal and not just official; it was not pressed upon him by Nkrumah and the Cabinet even if they must have welcomed Arden-Clarke's shared annoyance. By the end of 1957, Colin Russell's intransigence, which he certainly regarded as a principled stand against the encroachment of authoritarianism, was to result in an early end to his career in Ghana. He was summoned before Cabinet on 9 May 1957 where he was 'informed that it was considered that it would be in everyone's best interests if he proceeded on leave prior to his retirement as soon as possible'.[6]

Lastly, and much more importantly, the formal decision to politicize regional administration was the product of six years of painful frustration and governmental impotence in the face of intractable chiefs and their allies in rural areas.[7] As

---

[4] See Cabinet Committee, 22 October 1957, NAG ADM 13/2/41.

[5] The tension was not eased by the fact that Russell was a cousin of the governor's wife.

[6] Cabinet, NAG ADM 13/2/42.

[7] This might explain the rather anodyne treatment B. Amonoo gives to this issue in his *Ghana 1957–1966*, pp. 66–99.

we have seen, many rural areas were in chaos. The appointment of the regional commissioners was intended to remedy that, for it was a large step towards direct rule; they were, in effect, to be *intendants* or, as the opposition would have insisted, commissars. The first appointments were made in October 1957.[8] All of them were senior CPP Members of the Assembly who enjoyed the trust of the prime minister; some of them, such as J.E. Hagan, had well-known track records of considerable public hostility towards chieftaincy.

If any Ghanaian still entertained any serious belief that either regional assemblies or Houses of Chiefs were to exercise any serious authority in their respective regions, this major development at least suggested that they were to enjoy very limited powers. Unsurprisingly if curiously guardedly, the leader of the opposition, Professor K.A. Busia, considered that the creation of regional commissioners could 'have quite serious repercussions'. Five days later, the Joint Provincial Council formally 'disapproved' of the impending change. 'It is', they wrote to the minister of local government, 'an insidious attempt on the part of government to subvert the office of the heads of the regions and place them under an effective control of party interest.'[9] It is difficult to argue with that contemporary analysis of the government's intentions.

The whiff of centralization and authoritarianism became unmistakable in the months following independence. The archival evidence for this is overwhelming. The Special Branch of the police force was expanded 'to ensure that a more vigorous watch is kept on the political pulse and that prompt intelligence is received of subversive activities'.[10] Harsh and almost certainly economically necessary measures were taken against farmers. As the minister of finance, Komla Gbedemah, had predicted to Cabinet in mid-1954, the world cocoa price was falling and looked set to continue to do so. As it fell, so did government revenue, thus putting in hazard much of the government's cherished developmental project. In May 1957 the statutory Cocoa Marketing Board reduced the farm-gate price paid to farmers for cocoa. The price was precisely the same sum as that fixed in mid-1954; and it had been the huge discrepancy between that sum and the world price for cocoa which had so incensed farmers that it was to be one of the most significant causes of the formation of the NLM in late 1954. The price was reduced from £4.00 per load of 60lb to £3.60. Had it remained at £4.00, the minister of trade and labour estimated that the loss to the Cocoa Marketing Board, from whose surpluses government derived revenue, would have amounted to between £6 million and £8 million.[11] A month later, Cabinet decided to reduce the value of replanting grants to those farmers who had been forced to cut out cocoa trees infected with the still incurable and devastating swollen shoot disease. The reduction was massive. In the past, trees of more than 7 inches in height were

[8] C.H. Chapman for Trans Volta Togoland, W.H.T. Korboe for Eastern Region, J.E. Hagan for Western Region, C. de Graft Dickson for Ashanti and L.R. Abavana for Northern Region.

[9] Reported in *Daily Graphic*, 12 June 1957.

[10] Minister of the interior's memorandum to Cabinet, 24 September 1957, NAG ADM 13/2/40.

[11] Cabinet, 14 May 1957, NAG ADM 13/2/38.

valued for compensation at 4 shillings (20p); that was now reduced to 6d (2.5p). Smaller trees which had attracted replanting grants of 1 shilling (5p) in the past were now valued at 1d (about 0.25p). 'I am sure', an emollient prime minister told the House, 'that these farmers will be willing to accept these new rates in the interest of Ghana's economy.' To minimize the impact of the farmers' potential opposition, government moved to recognize only the CPP-sponsored farmers organization, the United Ghana Farmers' Council, an organization which could be expected to toe the government line, and not the independent National Farmers' Union. 'Considerable difficulty has been experienced in attempting to deal with farmers,' the Cabinet noted in a notable understatement. 'It would be convenient to be able to deal with one organisation which is fully representative of the general body of farmers.'[12]

By a combination of such major and minor steps[13] Ghana's government began to tighten its control over the state. Within eight months of independence Cabinet was discussing a memorandum on the 'removal and detention of Ghana citizens' by the minister of the interior, a discussion which was ultimately to lead to the Preventive Detention Act.[14] In his memorandum the minister proposed to create powers to 'remove or detain ... [those] who indulged in unconstitutional and subversive actions against the Government'. Such powers were necessary, it was argued, because 'there may ... arise a situation in which seditious activities are carried out which it may not be possible or desirable in the public interest to deal with through the ordinary machinery of the Courts'. The discussion of these proposals shows that Cabinet was prepared to draft along these lines in the full awareness that it might give the impression of a permanent state of emergency which in turn might inhibit much needed inward investment. Cabinet also made clear its appreciation that such a bill would be strongly opposed in Ghana and, if it became law, would also be deplored by free-world opinion.[15]

At exactly the same time, the minister of the interior began to move against the NLM. This began with 'picking off' its most vulnerable allies, the Moslem Association Party,[16] using his deportation powers. A long sequence of deportation proposals begin to figure in Cabinet business from October 1957.[17] The grounds for such deportations became somewhat formulaic. The continued presence of this

---

[12] Cabinet, 1 November 1957, NAG ADM 13/2/42. The entire question of the government's relationship with cocoa farmers is examined in great detail in B. Beckman's invaluable *Organizing the farmers*.

[13] Minor shifts included the decision to 'inculcate patriotism' in schools taken by Cabinet on 12 December 1957. Cabinet agreed that 'the history of Ghana during the period of foreign rule or at least those sections which did no credit to Ghana should be glossed over in the elementary and secondary schools'. NAG ADM 13/2/44.

[14] The full first draft of that act came before Cabinet on 21 January 1958. See NAG ADM 13/2/44.

[15] Cabinet, 15 October 1957, NAG ADM 13/2/41.

[16] The MAP was a numerically small party whose support was drawn from the large 'strangers' quarters' or Zongos of many of Ghana's bigger southern towns.

[17] The first deportations with a political flavour occurred before independence in November 1956. Nine men from Gao (in what was then French West Africa) were deported as part of their sentence following their successful prosecution, in May 1956, for assault. Ironically in view of what was to happen after independence, they were all members of a CPP 'Action Troopers' gang.

or that MAP/NLM activist was held to be 'not conducive to the public good', or that he or she had been 'responsible for much of the trouble' in this or that town. The exact extent of the number of those deported over the following two years is hard to ascertain. Well over 200 cases were, however, discussed and approved in Cabinet in those years. Almost without exception the grounds for deportation were basically political.

The right to deport undesirable aliens is a normal and reasonable aspect of sovereignty in most, if not all, nation states. The nature of these deportations from Ghana was not, however, the routine business of returning criminals, illegal immigrants or indigents to the states of which they were citizens. Before independence the government had naturally discussed its policy on citizenship. Those who were eligible to enjoy the rights and obligations of citizenship of the new state were specified in the independence constitution. But who was and who was not to be regarded as a Ghanaian citizen with full rights, including those of holding a Ghanaian passport, was in practice a somewhat politicized matter. In harmony with the pan-African aspirations of the party and the country, Ghanaian citizenship could be acquired by people of African descent or by anyone married to a Ghanaian. The operation of this clear racial bias was covert. It bore most heavily, almost certainly intentionally, upon the Lebanese community, many of whom had been born in Ghana. The records show that their frequent applications for citizenship were routinely refused. The interests of an international trading community, like that of the West African Lebanese, who were regularly denied citizenship and hence passports, were manifestly being seriously hindered by this unofficial policy. Conspiracy theorists might conclude that such restraint of trade might provide an artificial advantage to African traders. There is, however, no evidence of which I am aware which suggests that this was the intention of the policy.

It was, however, an unofficial policy not least because it could be pragmatically breached. In 1960, the first non-African to be granted citizenship was a Lebanese merchant called G.B. Moukarzel. The grounds for bypassing the covert racial criterion were that 'it is beneficial to Ghana if deserving persons are allowed to enjoy ... Ghanaian citizenship provided that they have shown that they are truly loyal to the Government. Mr Moukarzel has been a strong supporter of the Convention Peoples' Party for some years and ... were he to become a citizen of Ghana, he would vote for the CPP.'[18] There can be no doubt that citizenship for those born outside Ghana demanded the demonstration of an appropriate and particular political affiliation and enthusiasm.

But as far as the wider aspects of citizenship were concerned, the open-handed attitude to people of African descent was now also subjected to unofficial policy which was manifestly politically biased. Many of those who were deported in the three years following independence had not only lived in Ghana for many years but in many cases had been born in Ghana.[19] Musa Derikikyi, against whom

---

[18] Cabinet, 18 November 1960, NAG ADM 13/2/76.

[19] The Deportation Act, No. 14 of 1957 stipulated in Sections 3(1) and 4 (c) that the only defence against a deportation order was possession of citizenship. Deportation was entirely within the powers of the

Krobo Edusei, by then the minister of the interior, moved in January 1958, was born 'of foreign parents' in Cape Coast in 1905. Alhaji Baba, whose case was considered in October 1957, was born in Kumasi in 1914 of Nigerian parents, while another deportee, Idris Braimah, was born in Accra in 1904. Other victims of the policy included Aliu Allao, permanently resident in Ghana since 1919 and Sam Moshie who had lived in Berekum since 1911. The partisan quality of Cabinet's view of who was or was not eligible for citizenship[20] is to be found in the Cabinet papers for 28 January 1958. At this meeting Cabinet agreed with the minister that Musa Derikikyi, a member of the NLM and, as we have seen, born in Cape Coast in 1905, should be deported. At the same meeting, Cabinet bestowed citizenship upon the CPP Secretary General Cecil Forde, a Sierra Leonean who had not been born in Ghana.

Government discussions over deportations are revealing. The policy, whose intimidatory intent is beyond doubt, was enthusiastically pressed by the minister of the interior, Krobo Edusei, whose exuberant, 'man of the people' populism had made him a firm favourite of the CPP press and a man much feared by his enemies. In government the record suggests that his ebullient, disrespectful style acquired a far more sinister and Robespierrian cast.[21] In many of these deportation cases, the evidence produced by the police was fair and judicious. Musa Derikikyi, they reported, was 'quiet, unassuming, respectful and an Arabic scholar of the highest order'. The regional commissioner, J.E. Hagan, however, decided that he was 'the most dangerous, staunch member and financier of the Cape Coast Branch of the NLM and directly connected with all the diabolical activities of the Parent Body (NLM) at Kumasi ... a close associate of ... the arch leaders of all the atrocities in Ghana since the inception of the NLM'.[22] Interestingly Hagan's use of language closely mirrored the habitual and occasionally chilling hyperbole of the journalism in the party's newspaper the *Accra Evening News*.

Regional commissioner Hagan was, as we have seen, a CPP MP and enjoyed Cabinet rank. Edusei supported his view[23] of Derikikyi rather than that of the police,[24] as did Cabinet. And they did so despite the fact that Hagan's denunciation was in almost every respect verbally identical with his report on another deportee, Alhaji Hausa, against whom the police report had absolutely nothing negative to say, who was another Cape Coast resident, a devout Moslem and a rich man.[25] Hagan, however, wrote that he was 'instrumental for the violence, with all its horrors, in Ashanti, Southern Ghana and Togoland ... a close associate of ... the

---

[19] (cont.) governor-general and could not be questioned if the deportee was an alien. The acting governor-general at this time was Sir Arku Korsah.

[20] Deportation is a pretty final rejection of a claim to citizenship, after all.

[21] Given that he was privy to much that is recorded in these Cabinet records it is hard to understand how Geoffrey Bing could conclude that Edusei 'was a sincere egalitarian, and liberty, equality and fraternity summed up his political philosophy'. See *Reap the Whirlwind*, p. 122.

[22] Cabinet, 28 January 1958, NAG ADM 13/2/44.

[23] Which conceivably could have been Edusei's view *ab initio*.

[24] The police reports were presented by the Police commissioner but were prepared by the Special Branch.

[25] A lorry-owner and cattle dealer.

arch leaders of all the atrocities'.[26] Hagan's formulaic if grammatically idiosyncratic denunciations and Edusei's agreement with them against the calmer advice of the police suggest some of the growth of a political climate in which the fear of a knock on the door in the middle of the night began to loom large.

As disconcerting is the apparent contentment of the whole CPP Cabinet with these extreme actions, which affected the livelihoods and families of so many people, including old people who had spent their entire lives in Ghana. Cabinet members were without exception highly intelligent, sophisticated men and experienced politicians who seem to have allowed old grudges and party imperatives to overcome any doubts they might and perhaps should have entertained, as it is clear that many of the cases were based upon palpably bizarre and even contradictory evidence. There is no doubt whatever that the party had resolved to destroy the MAP wing of the NLM by using deportation wherever it had even the merest excuse so to do.[27] That merest evidence included having parents born outside the old colonial boundaries of the new state. Evidence, moreover, of good behaviour or local social integration could not, it seems, temper the government's resolve to rid itself wherever possible of opponents. Madam Mamarema Wangara, whose case was considered in October 1957, was judged by the police to be a 'well-behaved and reserved elderly lady, an impartial leader and very straightforward in all her undertakings. It is said that her 3 children are all members of the CPP.' Edusei's judgement which apparently commended itself to his Cabinet colleagues, follows this almost saintly depiction and reads: 'In my opinion the continued presence of Mamerema Wangara in Ghana is not conducive to the public good.' No grounds other than her membership of the MAP and its small women's section were cited in favour of her deportation.[28]

A similar dissonance between hard evidence and harder action is to be found in the more famous case of Alhaji Baba. Born in Kumasi in 1914 of Nigerian parents, the police report on the Alhaji suggested that 'nothing adverse is known against him ... he is respected by Muslims for his knowledge ... if ... he is deported the Muslims of Kumasi will lose a learned Arabic scholar and healer'. His fatal flaw was being an 'early supporter of the NLM'. In the same vein, although the police concluded that Salami Lagos was a registered member of the MAP '[there is] no evidence that he has been involved in the rioting ... [he is] considered to be a very quiet Yoruba', nonetheless, Edusei argued that his 'continued presence in Ghana ... is not conducive to the public good'.[29] Aliu Allao, who had lived in Ghana since 1919, was not even a MAP member but was merely alleged to be a supporter. 'He has no criminal record', the police report insisted, 'and although it has been alleged that he was instrumental in organising the NLM Action Groupers the allegations

---

[26] Cabinet, 28 January 1958, NAG ADM 13/2/44

[27] The MAP was to dissolve itself in October 1957. Partly because of the harassment members had endured, the party had split. Some members called in by the minister of information on 2 October were now reported to have said that it was the duty of Muslims as a community to 'support the Government of the day.'

[28] Cabinet, Memorandum by the minister of the interior, 29 October 1957, NAG ADM 13/2/41.

[29] Ibid.

have not been substantiated with a single fact. He is regarded as an honest Yoruba gentleman and wields a great deal of influence over his fellow Nigerians.' Krobo Edusei nonetheless insisted, and Cabinet agreed, on what must have become a wearying, boring formula, that 'his continued presence ... is not conducive to the public good'.[30]

These blows were accompanied by the beginnings of a clamp-down on the activities of the press. At the same time as deporting many MAP supporters, the government also deported Bankole Timothy. Timothy, a Sierra Leonean, was Deputy Editor of the *Daily Graphic* and an articulate critic, but not an especially fierce one, of the government. This followed hard upon the heels of the announcement on 31 July that Kofi Baako had been appointed minister of information and broadcasting. On appointment he said that he had no intention of banning any newspapers. All he wanted from the press, he said, was 'a sense of co-operation and respect for the authority of the Government'. He went on to say that he would not allow the Ghana Broadcasting Service to 'fan tribalism in the country'. Journalists were free to 'write what they think right. It is only when they write what is wrong that the law will deal with them.'[31] What was and was not 'right' was, it seems, self-evident rather than something for discussion in the courts – and in the press.

There was undoubtedly an atmosphere of strained apprehension throughout 1957. At a CPP rally in Accra in early August, Kofi Baako hinted darkly that 'events calculated to overthrow the present CPP Government have been happening in Ghana'. At the same meeting Cecil Forde argued that Ghana was the only independent country where the government was not allowed to rule. 'There is if anything', he said, 'too much democracy in this country.'[32] There can be little doubt that these hints referred directly to the state of affairs in the countryside and the continuing defiance of some chiefs.

On 5 April, a month after independence day, Ako Adjei made a broadcast as the minister of justice. In this he claimed that he had learnt that intimidation and extortion were being 'perpetrated especially in some villages in the Ashanti Region'. He suggested that some of this activity was being stirred up by 'some of our friends from neighbouring French territories'. This was almost certainly a reference to another ally of the NLM, the irredentist Togoland Congress whose largely Ewe membership straddled the Ghana–Togo border. He went on to say that the government was to set up an enquiry into the allegations. That enquiry was set up under the chairmanship of C.W Quist on 29 June 1957[33] and its report was before Cabinet by 3 December 1957. It was the government of independent Ghana's first use of a commission of enquiry to achieve manifestly political ends.

[30] Cabinet, 29 October 1957, NAG ADM 13/2/41.
[31] *Daily Graphic*, 2 August 1957.
[32] *Daily Graphic*, 3 August 1957.
[33] Committee of enquiry into allegations of intimidation, threatening and extortion in Ashanti. The other members were the barrister George Lassey and the superintendent of police, Kumasi, J.P. Tyrie. The secretary was the rather appropriately named P.E. Pentsil. The full text can be read in NAG ADM 13/2/43.

As will become obvious in the following chapter, it was not to be the last.

The committee's report is a very strange document. The grounds for setting up the enquiry had been laid down clearly by the minister. He had suggested that there was much to be worried about. But there was a clear subtext to his radio broadcast. The implication was that the disorder was being caused solely by the NLM, the chiefs and their supporters. If the enquiry could substantiate the allegations, it would criminalize a variety of local forms of dissent, 'acts of lawlessness' as the minister put it in his broadcast. In the light of the conclusions of the report, there are several possible interpretations of the minister's intentions. Firstly he and his colleagues might well have believed that there was a seriously destabilized situation in Ashanti. It is, however, equally probable that this was intended to be the first shot in a campaign of intimidation designed to take the wind out of the opposition's sails.

If there was genuine and serious apprehension of unrest in Ashanti, then the CPP government's intelligence sources appear to have been in error. These sources would have been the local branches of the party and of course the regional commissioner and his staff.[34] It is entirely possible that local party branches exaggerated the extent of NLM activism to encourage a heavier, more energetic government response against their opponents. But the enquiry report indicated that 'acts involving intimidation, threatening and extortion appear to have been at their height from December 1955 to February 1956'. Thereafter, they were satisfied that there had been a marked decrease in such activity and that such acts 'became practically negligible'. Their concluding paragraph records that 'there are at present very few cases ... and ... from the evidence we have gathered there has been little violence within the last six months'. There is no particular reason to dispute that judgement, not least because the committee took evidence very widely[35] and even extended their survey for an additional two months to ensure that no stone was left unturned. Those facts must have been known to the government *before* the enquiry was set on foot as they obviously had access to police information throughout this period. Yet the minister had begun his broadcast by saying: 'During the past few weeks ... I have been receiving information from different sources that some people have been ... threatening and intimidating peaceful citizens'.

It is this gap between rhetoric and documented events which leads to a strengthening of the argument that it was part of a more elaborated, longer-term campaign to extinguish the opposition. The report, however, yielded little of value to the government. In its historical sections, the report honestly and carefully drew attention to the evidence showing that the criminal acts it was set up to examine were committed by both the CPP and NLM, even if those of 'the Convention People's Party outnumbered those of the National Liberation Movement'. It devoted six paragraphs to indicting those chiefs who had entered national politics

[34] The sources which might illuminate what kinds of information the government was getting from the regions are still not available in the National Archives of Ghana.
[35] They took evidence from 548 witnesses in 15 different towns in Ashanti.

but carefully avoided any suggestion that such chiefs were active only on the NLM's behalf.[36]

The report did, however, provide a good deal of support for the contention that chiefs were heavily involved in national politics in the region. That was hardly surprising news to anyone in Ghana. But such further confirmation bedded in with other moves the government was making to circumscribe both the opposition and the chiefs. Firstly the government returned in August 1957 to discuss the bill they had earlier set aside, the bill which was to become the Freedom from Discrimination Act. Its intention was to illegalize any political party based upon tribal, racial or religious criteria. While few enthusiasts for national integration could argue with the sentiment, the immediate concern was to make illegal the NLM. Cabinet was forced to recognize that it would be difficult to outlaw any such party so long as its membership rules were not explicitly exclusive. That is to say that any party pressing the interests of a regional, ethnic or religious group could only be in breach if it formally restricted its membership to such a group. There was also worry expressed that 'legislation such as that proposed may ... be regarded by certain members of the UN as a breach of the spirit ... of the Universal Declaration of Human Rights'.[37] That latter concern was not to inhibit the later drafting of just such an act in November 1957.[38] But for the meantime the minister sought Cabinet approval of an amendment of the Public Meetings and Processions Regulations[39] which would have allowed the minister rather than the police to sanction or to ban public meetings.[40] He was only dissuaded from this course by the attorney-general, who pointed out that such powers would probably be *ultra vires* and would in any case make it possible for the minister to be sued in the courts.

Such discussions were not limited to the Cabinet room. Party branches were already discussing ways of curtailing opposition based upon ethnicity. A month before the matter came to Cabinet, the executive of the CPP in the Trans Volta Togoland Region met in Ho on 20 July. Here they called upon the national party to 'guard against the revival of tribalism in politics'.[41] In pushing this issue to the fore they were almost certainly guided by Komla Gbedemah, a member of Cabinet, who played a prominent part in that meeting.

The foregoing is intended to set the scene and to suggest the atmosphere in which the CPP's final struggle with the chiefs was to be conducted in the remaining years of the 1950s. The storm clouds were ever more obviously gathering over chieftaincy. The commitment to create Houses of Chiefs alongside regional

[36] Paras 41–6. The last reads: 'It is a pity that chiefs who are traditional heads of states should have taken active part in party politics thereby laying themselves open to accusations of intimidation, threatening and extortion.'

[37] Cabinet memorandum on the prohibition of organizations restricted to tribal, racial or religious groups, 23 August 1957, NAG ADM 13/2/40.

[38] It was finally drafted on 5 November 1957 and published on 19 November.

[39] Regulation 2.

[40] He singled out the growing Ga movement in Accra, Ga Shifimo Kpee, for special mention in this context.

[41] Reported in the *Daily Graphic*, 22 July 1957.

assemblies was seen by few chiefs as evidence of an enhancement of their positions. At the same time most of them were well aware that continuing to oppose government had become a seriously risky undertaking. The Joint Provincial Council, meeting in August 1957, mulled over the prospects and decided that it would 'accept no inferior role ... or tolerate anything that has the tendency to belittle or cripple chieftaincy' while agreeing that they should 'put aside their particular personal aspirations and co-operate in the spirit proper to the national cause'.[42] That conclusion was reached in an atmosphere soured by recent 'unpleasant events', according to the JPC president. These events included the ominous creation of regional commissioners, the reduction of financial aid given to traditional authorities from central funds and a much reported speech by the minister of local government at Kade. This speech had included the sentence: 'We are only accountable to God and the people and not to those who continue to classify themselves as occupants of this or that Stool.' These 'unpleasant events', the JPC concluded, made it hard to escape the conclusion that the CPP government's ultimate aim was the final liquidation of chieftaincy.

The minister of local government immediately denied the inference drawn by the JPC from his speech. But he did so in such a way as to greatly heighten chiefly apprehension. Chieftaincy was regarded by the CPP, he said, as 'an arm of government'. He went on to stress the increasingly dependent nature of chieftaincy. 'What the Chiefs forget', he told a journalist, 'is the fact that a Chief is a Chief partly because the government recognizes him as such.'[43] The JPC met again on 14 August. Here they decided that it was time for a joint meeting of all the chiefs' councils in the country, as 'the stage has now been reached ... when the united voice of the chiefs should be heard in the councils of state'. They also passed a vote of no confidence in the minister of local government and asked Nkrumah to 'change his attitude towards the chiefs in the interests of effective co-operation'.[44]

The minister of information, Kofi Baako, now attempted to cool things down. Speaking at the JPC meeting with dignity (and respectfully wearing traditional cloth) he insisted that the government sincerely wished to uphold the dignity of chieftaincy. But he also said that the government hoped that chiefs 'would adapt themselves to the progressive changes now prevalent all over the world. Chieftaincy must be progressive and not static. The times are changing and all of us must change with the times progressively.'[45] With no little courage, the president of the JPC replied by saying: 'Chiefs are honestly against some of the present aims and policies of the Government which we consider to be inimical to the interests and well-being of the nation as a whole and Chieftaincy in particular.' He went on to warn the government against being 'over zealous and unduly hasty'.

Despite such feisty performances, the net was tightening around chieftaincy. On 30 August the prime minister announced a Cabinet reshuffle in which Krobo

[42]Reported in the *Daily Graphic*, 9 August 1957. The main speaker was the president of the council, Nana Annorkwei.

[43] Reported in the *Daily Graphic*, 12 August 1957.

[44] Reported in the *Daily Graphic*, 15 August 1957.

[45] *Ibid.*

Edusei emerged as the minister of the interior whose responsibilities included the police and internal security matters. In his new capacity he began to visit paramount chiefs and their councils. On 10 October he visited the distinctly hostile territory of Akyem Abuakwa where he held talks, *in camera*, with the Okyenhene and the Okyeman Council. Intriguingly the opposition newspaper, the *Ashanti Pioneer*, suggested that there were two variants of Edusei's address. 'The minister's vernacular interpretation of his address was ... different in several respects from his official address. In his Twi translation there were a number of threats. The Minister made the translation himself.'[46] Whatever was or was not said behind closed doors, it was sufficiently frightening for the usually robust Okyenhene to issue a most extraordinary recantation. In this he agreed that he 'could not give support to one political party as against another'. He went on to say that 'it will be the constant care of the Okyeman Council and myself to see to it that the Government of Ghana as by law established receives our co-operation'. The Okyeman Council would now go about 'forgetting their party affiliations to take part in a re-dedication of ourselves to service in the interests of our land and people'.

There can be little doubt that Edusei, whose well-earned reputation as a 'hard man' was now enhanced by his command of the state's law enforcement machinery, had worried the Okyenhene and his councillors greatly. This had prompted the Okyenhene's long statement and the burden of that was considerably and notably at odds with his long-standing, outspoken and even reckless opposition to the CPP. The actual words and phrases used in the statement do not read like the usual style of the Okyenhene and it is possible that it was drafted for him. For example the sentences 'The new nation has arisen out of the long and arduous struggle of the chiefs and the people. We are committed to make it a success and a shining light in Africa' read very much like the standard 'CPP-speak' which is so apparent in the CPP press of those times.

The Okyenhene was, however, not the only paramount to be visited. The Asantehene was also to host a discussion with Krobo Edusei, and he received a personal letter from the prime minister asking him to clearly set out his position towards political parties. Under this pressure he too issued an emollient statement suggesting that he was above party politics and that it was 'inconsistent with the traditional role of the Asantehene as the elected constitutional head and father of his people to join or pledge his support to any one political party'.[47]

Both of these public recantations were almost certainly secured under duress. In the process both monarchs had been seriously and publicly humiliated; and it cannot be sufficiently stressed that humiliation is not part of an Akan king's job description. It was a major feather in the government's cap to have forced the two most important traditional leaders and chiefly supporters of the NLM in the country to abase themselves in this way. If any chiefs in Ghana had entertained any doubts about the determination of the government to control chieftaincy, they

[46] *Ashanti Pioneer*, 11 October 1957.
[47] Reported in the *Daily Graphic*, 9 October 1957.

could no longer do so. The government was not, however, to let matters rest here. Although both kings had been forced to eat humble pie in public, the CPP executives in both Akyem Abuakwa and Ashanti were now to insist that neither of these performances had gone far enough. The Akyem Abuakwa CPP executive described the Okyenhene's statement as 'amusing, cowardly and ridiculous'. The Ashanti regional CPP executive described the Asantehene's public statement as 'running away from hard facts' and recalled, quite accurately, that the Asantehene had supported the NLM for the past three years; he had, they said, 'been no other than the president of the National Liberation Movement'.[48] There can be little doubt that the CPP wanted more than just emollient, concessive statements from these obdurate chiefs. It was now out to destroy them.

[48] The source for both these statements is an announcement by the minister of information and broadcasting, Kofi Baako.

9

Controlling the Chiefs

Although the government had forced both the Asantehene and the Okyenhene to make public statements which were humiliating climb-downs, it had not finished with them. On 16 October 1957, only days after the Okyenhene's public statement, the government announced that it had withdrawn its official recognition of the Okyenhene. This withdrawal of recognition was to remain in force while a commission of enquiry into the administration of the state of Akyem Abuakwa was sitting. There is no doubt whatever that this dramatic move was intended to be seen as exemplary. It was to be a lesson for any chief who chose to maintain public opposition to the government. The memorandum prepared for Cabinet on this matter by the minister of local government[1] concerned a much wider constituency than that of Akyem Abuakwa. Its preamble mentions 'the present attitude of many Paramount Chiefs whose actions indicate that they deliberately intend to impede the Government ... and prevent minor chiefs from securing justice'. The generalization about intransigent chieftaincy continued as the minister's memorandum accused 'some Paramount Chiefs' of ignoring legal decisions and of using 'their traditional influence to ... bring into disrepute the statutory machinery'.[2]

The minister's Cabinet paper went on to spell out the specific case against the Okyenhene and a significant amount of it was certainly justified. Some of the matters concerned the Okyenhene's refusal to accept the judgements of the legally appointed appeals commissioner in traditional constitutional disputes. He was further accused of tampering with witnesses and hence evidence in such cases. All of these things, argued the minister, added up to a 'determination to impede the Government in the execution of its lawful duties'. There can be little doubt that

---

[1] Who was by now Aaron Ofori Atta, a cousin of the Okyenhene and the son of the Okyenhene's predecessor on the Akyem Abuakwa stool.

[2] Cabinet memorandum by the minister of local government on the withdrawal of recognition of the Okyenhene of Akyem Abuakwa, 15 October 1957, NAG ADM 13/2/41.

much of this was a reasonable, even balanced summary of the Okyenhene's political behaviour. The minister's belief, however, that by acting in these ways the Okyenhene had 'failed in his duty as a Paramount Chief' was a much more arguable proposition. A commission was set up under a single Commissioner, the judge John Jackson who was currently serving as the stool lands boundary settlement commissioner.[3]

This was a very bold step indeed. Whether the government actually had these powers under the independence constitution was never entirely clear.[4] The reaction of other chiefs was understandably muted by considerable confusion and fear. The Joint Provincial Council met in Dodowa on 18 October in discernibly subdued mood in order to discuss 'the position of the chiefs in the country'.[5] The debate was cautious and its president reminded the 34 chiefs who attended that the future of chieftaincy was ' at present in the balance'. In view of the frightening context, it took some courage for him to stress that, despite the slight constitutional safeguards for chiefs, 'there has been no evidence that the future of the chiefs is assured. That unfortunate position has been accentuated in recent times.'[6] The JPC knew that every word uttered there would be noted by the regional commissioner and then discussed by a hostile government. Either to remind them of that fact or as an attempt to bring them round, the prime minister sent a despatch rider to the hall in Dodowa where the JPC met with a jaunty message which did no more than ask the chiefs to 'a cocktail party' at Christiansborg Castle that evening.

Many chiefs and not just southern chiefs were seriously alarmed by the turn of events even if many of them accepted the invitation to the drinks party. A good deal of hard work was now being put into closer liaison between the various regional councils of chiefs. The councils of chiefs arrived at an agreed line and, armed with this, a strong delegation representing the councils of the Northern Territories, Trans Volta Togoland and Ashanti as well as the JPC was received by Nkrumah at the castle.[7] The meeting, which was reported as being cordial,[8] asked the prime minister to reconsider the position of the Okyenhene. Nkrumah promised to raise the points they had made with Cabinet at the earliest opportunity.

The derecognition of the Okyenhehe was, however, seen by the government at least as a final showdown leading to his complete removal. Things were now moving very fast and the government now contemplated the possibility of violence. A crowded gathering of Akyem Abuakwa people, *akyemfo*, had massed outside the royal palace in Kyebi in the pouring rain on 18 October. There followed

---

[3] Jackson had been a judge of the Nigerian High Court, 1935–45, and from 1945 was a judge of the Gold Coast's Supreme Court. He had acted as chief justice on two occasions in 1951 and 1952.

[4] It would, however, certainly have had these powers under the 1946 and 1954 constitutions.

[5] *Ashanti Pioneer*, 18 October 1957 suggested that the derecognition had been timed to occur just before the JPC met, so that the chiefs might together ponder the serious implications of continuing to defy the government.

[6] Reported in the *Daily Graphic*, 18 October 1957.

[7] There were 17 chiefs from each of the four councils.

[8] All such meetings were routinely described as 'cordial'.

drumming and the singing of war songs throughout the night. The Eastern Region mobile police reserve was now on stand-by and the police strength in Akyem Abuakwa had been reinforced 'as a precautionary measure'.[9] Fortunately no violence ensued.

Nkrumah followed up his earlier meeting with chiefs with another with a JPC delegation. That group did not include the Okyenhene. The prime minister again said that Cabinet would discuss the recognition issue 'as soon as possible'. On this occasion this promise was purely political and entirely cynical; it was made in the full knowledge that he had just emerged from a Cabinet meeting that very morning, before his meeting with the JPC delegation. While mention was made in that Cabinet meeting of a 'number of representations from the chiefs', the minister of local government insisted that there could be and would be no change of heart. 'No step should be taken ... to restore recognition ... until I am satisfied that he is prepared to abide by his recent public statement. A restoration of recognition at this stage will be misinterpreted as a misuse of a statutory power by the Executive in order to threaten an individual.' His recommendation, to which the Cabinet agreed, was that the protesting parties should be told that there was no question of the restoration of recognition of the Okyenhene until the commission of enquiry had completed its work.[10] That decision was made public shortly afterwards.

The Okyeman Council also met in emergency session on 21 October and the meeting lasted for a draining five hours. It was estimated that at least 100 chiefs and sub-chiefs had converged on the small town of Kyebi for this occasion. Eventually the Okyenhene appeared at 4.00 pm before a crowd in front of his palace holding two eggs; one was an ancient one brought from the stool room, the other a misshapen freak. The ancient egg signified, the Okyenhene said, that he was the protector of the people of Akyem Abuakwa; he did not specify the meaning of the distorted egg. Earlier, at 2.30, and less mystically, a telegram had been sent to the prime minister requesting an urgent meeting. The meeting of the Okyeman Council had mandated a delegation to ask the government to abandon its intention to revoke its recognition of the Okyenhene and to tell the prime minister that Okyeman was anxious to resolve matters between them in a peaceful and constitutional manner. Somewhat disingenuously,[11] the Okyenhene claimed in the course of the discussion that he had in fact withdrawn his support from the NLM when it became a political party at the end of 1954. He also urged the people of Akyem to desist from violence.

The impact of all of this upon vulnerable chiefs was predictable. The Omanhene of Abura, speaking at an emergency meeting of the Abura State Council on 29 October, declared that it was now his 'civic duty to support the Government in power'. Only days later the Omanhene of Assin Attandasu also said that 'it is ... my duty to support the Government in power'. There were others who came out in the same formulaic vein. Many of the pledges of loyalty by chiefs made during

---

[9] By 4 November the police detachment numbered about 300.

[10] Cabinet memorandum by the minister of local government, 22 October 1957, NAG ADM 13/2/41.

[11] And dishonestly. He had done no such thing.

these fraught moments repeated the phrases 'civic duty' and 'government in power', which might suggest that regional commissioners were putting pressure upon chiefs to make specific points in such announcements.

Those who did not so submit were now increasingly open to harassment, for failure to publicly align themselves with government was seen as overt hostility. For example the CPP branch in Agogo sent a strong letter to the Agogohene demanding that he declare publicly where he stood in political terms. The pressure on wavering and frightened chiefs was not only mounted by CPP branches. It was also maintained from the centre. Kofi Baako spoke at a press conference on 11 November, resplendent in *kente* cloth. Here he said that it was not appropriate for chiefs to concern themselves with party political matters; they 'must not attempt to influence voters ... Chieftaincy will flourish as long as it is not used to stem the tide of parliamentary and democratic development in Ghana.'[12]

On 7 November, the Jackson commission of enquiry had begun its work, although its report was not to be delivered to the minister of local government until May 1958. Its establishment and the revocation of recognition of the Okyenhene had more immediate effects. On 25 November, the Joint Council of Chiefs met again at Dodowa. After some discussion they sent a telegram to the prime minister asking somewhat presumptuously and hence unsuccessfully for him to come to Dodowa to discuss their anxieties. Foremost amongst these were the now powerful rumours that Ghana would soon be declared a republic and that in the process the institution of chieftaincy would be abolished. These rumours were obviously widely believed and only one chief of the JPC, the Omanhene of Western Nzima,[13] the area of Nkrumah's birth, dissented by arguing that they were no more than tittle-tattle 'carried about by some people who were opposed to the Prime Minister'.[14]

The JPC were annoyed but could hardly have been surprised that Nkrumah did not respond to their invitation and come to them in person. That annoyance was, perhaps, a symptom of their failure to understand just how powerful elected government was and how hollow their beliefs in their own powers were becoming. But the prime minister sent three of his Cabinet ministers in his stead. What was said by them to the JPC is not recorded but it was almost certainly forceful and left the JPC in no doubt about who held the whip-hand. That must be a reasonable inference, for their intervention resulted in a remarkably anodyne resolution that greatly strengthened the government's position. The JPC called upon all chiefs to refrain from party politics and to refuse to preside at political rallies. The country, they said, 'had accepted the party system of Government based on the principles of Western Parliamentary democracy ... it was therefore the duty of the Chiefs now to see that the ship of state sails smoothly on calm waters'. Chiefs, they

[12] Reported in the *Daily Graphic*, 12 November 1957. Baako made clear at that meeting that there would be no national House of Chiefs, as the issue of a Second Chamber, a cherished ambition of the NLM, was 'a dead one'.

[13] Nana Kwasi Amankye III.

[14] Reported in the *Daily Graphic*, 26 November 1957.

argued, should be above party politics and it was 'wrong for chiefs ... to support one political party where there is more than one party in a state'. As it was common knowledge that the Okyenhene, whose recent career was now being raked over by the Jackson commission, had supported the NLM, the only inference that could be drawn was that the JPC now regarded his previous actions as 'wrong'. Salt was rubbed in that bloody wound as the JPC continued: 'it is common knowledge that some chiefs were open supporters of one party ... and ... occupied chairs at public rallies at which they declared their open support for one party and condemned the other. That naturally engendered ill-feelings ... and led to a great deal of unrest.'[15] Fearful that they might be next in line for derecognition by the government, the Okyenhene's old allies and colleagues in the JPC were melting away.

There can be little doubt that the southern chiefs were now on the run. The protests against the withdrawal of recognition of the Okyenhene were silenced and in public at least, the chiefs of the JPC not only agreed that they should play no part in national politics but also that such involvement was both wrong and likely to lead to disorder. Building on this success, Krobo Edusei again visited the Asantehene.[16] Edusei was an old and fearless antagonist of the Asante monarch and his very presence in the royal palace at Manhyia was always decidedly provocative. He is reported to have urged the Asantehene to call a meeting of the Asanteman Council which, once convened, would then denounce violence. But he also said to the Asantehene that there were 'some people in Ashanti who advised him badly[17] and that such people would be dealt with according to the law'. That this was intended to sound threatening is beyond doubt. Edusei's tone, however, grew even more threatening and authoritarian. There were, he said, 'other chiefs and politicians whose presence in Ashanti was not conducive to the public good[18] and as Minister of the Interior I will see to it that they are deported from Ashanti forthwith'.[19] This was the first public airing of the alarming possibility of the use by government of internal exile for vexatious chiefs and politicians. Although his audience was duly shocked, the Asantehene retained his composure. Asked by a journalist afterwards if he was worried by Edusei's threats, the Asantehene replied: 'I do not regard the many things said by Mr. Edusei as official.' This was a mistake; Edusei, the minister of the interior, was 'official' in every sense of the word.

In his very official capacity as a Cabinet minister, Edusei was involved in a complex government strategy which aimed at ending the fissiparousness of regionalism

---

[15] Reported in the *Daily Graphic*, 28 November 1957.

[16] On 29 October 1957.

[17] One of those implicitly 'fingered' in this wording was Bafuor Akoto, one of the Asantehene's senior linguists and *quondam* Chairman of the NLM. It is an interesting coincidence that Akoto had resigned, on medical advice, as the Ashanti Chairman of the newly formed successor to the NLM, the United Party, only two days before this exchange.

[18] A phrase used again and again in his case-making in Cabinet in the many deportations which had taken place since independence.

[19] This exchange is reported in the *Daily Grapic*, 2 December 1957.

and at relegating chiefs to marginality, dependence and impotence. The independence constitution had promised the creation of regional assemblies. This was the eleventh-hour price paid to silence British doubts about regional disquiet, even if few members of the Ghanaian opposition regarded the concessions as coming anywhere close to their aspirations for greater regional devolution.[20] 'Shadow' regional assemblies had been established which comprised the sitting members of the national Legislative Assembly sitting additionally in their regional assemblies. The precise shape of these assemblies was under discussion after independence. As we shall see, they were not destined to survive. Alongside these bodies, the government proposed to create regional Houses of Chiefs to replace the old chiefs' councils. While the powers of these Houses were, as we have seen, to be extremely limited, the government was now manifestly keen on closely controlling and subordinating chiefs.

Part of the general strategy was clearly the complete humbling of the most significant oppositional chiefly voices, most notably those of the paramounts of Akyem Abuakwa and the Asante. Steps were already being taken to remove the Okyenhene completely, for few were in much doubt that his suspended recognition would become substantive once the Jackson report was submitted. Such a manoeuvre was, however, far too dangerous in the case of Ashanti. Any attempt to derecognize and then remove the Asantehene would almost certainly have unleashed a massive wave of violence in Ashanti. He could, however, be, and was, to be further harassed by the aggressive agency of commissions of enquiry. Another enquiry, to be conducted by a single jurist, Mr Justice Sarkodee Addo, and this time into the affairs of the Kumasi State Council, had been publicly announced by the minister of local government on 8 February 1958.[21] But an attempt to remove the Asantehene, as the Okyenhene had been removed, was out of the question. Accordingly, the government turned towards a two-pronged approach which aimed at the dilution of the authority of the Asantehene.

One of the limbs of this attack had been in the pipeline for some time. This involved the cultivation of those parts of the Ashanti Confederacy which had railed against the control of the Asantehene and the Asanteman Council since the creation of the modern confederacy in 1936. This principally involved a large number of the so-called Brong states lying in the western part of the region. Although those states were yet to enjoy full regional status,[22] it was clear that it would be only a matter of time before this was granted. In the light of that, they were at liberty to ignore the rulings of the Asantehene and his council. But another tactic emerged early in 1958. It involved a calculated manoeuvre whereby the

---

[20] For more on this see R. Rathbone (ed.), *Ghana; British documents ...*, Vol. II.

[21] This was a very sensitive area indeed. The Asantehene is the paramount of not only a federation of states but is also himself the paramount of one of those states, Kumase. The state council's affairs were accordingly very close to his interests.

[22] It is probable that the late establishment of a Brong-Ahafo Region owed everything to the fact that dissident Brong chiefs served as a useful wooden horse on the Asanteman Council. To have removed them from the Asanteman Council by creating a new region would have reduced their capacity to undermine the notion of Asante unity at this juncture.

political nature of the Asanteman Council could be fundamentally altered by the statutory drafting on to that council of a number of pro–CPP chiefs.

Eligibility for membership of the Asanteman Council was a complex matter touching on traditional protocol and hierarchy as ordained by the Asanteman Council itself. By right and custom all the paramount chiefs of constituent states of the Asante Confederacy were amongst its members. In January 1958, the minister of local government brought a quite remarkable memorandum to Cabinet on the subject of 'the Creation of Paramount Chiefs in Ashanti'. The document makes clear that the scheme was jointly crafted by the minister and the regional commissioner. It proposed that eight new states[23] should be recognized by the government while removing recognition of the paramount status of the chief of Duayaw Nkwanta.[24] As recognized states, their chiefs would now hold the coveted status of being paramounts and were thus full members of the Asanteman Council. The process was simple enough. All the government needed to do was to make an order amending the official schedule which listed the constituent states of the Ashanti Confederacy. Then the government could formally recognize their chiefs as paramounts. All that the law then required was that the Asanteman Council was informed of these changes and notice of these changes was published in the *Government Gazette*.[25]

This might be seen as a somewhat crude mathematical and even gerrymandering approach to politics.[26] What had been done, however, was an immediate, brutal affront to any reading of customary law and hence to the sensibility of Asante chiefs and many Asante. For decades chiefs and their people had confronted colonial authority when it attempted even minor infringements of what was widely felt to be the autonomy of traditional ways of doing things. What was now proposed was very much more than a minor infringement. The amount of public rage these decisions raised was, however, remarkably slight. That above all suggests the very low morale of a cowed and frightened chieftaincy in the country. The Asanteman Council met in emergency session on 17 February. Its members wore 'mourning cloth',[27] the robes usually worn at funerals. Irate as its members were, and some were reported to have kola nuts protruding from their lips, a traditional sign of defiance, their most radical action was the passing of a decidedly mild resolution calling upon the government to reconsider their decision.

Any notion that the CPP had delivered a massive cultural as well as political insult to the Asante people as a whole would have been very wide of the mark. That the Asante were divided and not merely along the older Asante-Brong fault-line was becoming even more obvious than it had been in the 1956 elections. Shortly after the government had, in effect, deconstructed the Ashanti Confederacy

---

[23] Akrokerri, Bechem, Beposo, Bompata, Domiabra, Kukuom, Manso Nkwanta and Obogu.

[24] Although it was not discussed at this meeting, the government also withdrew its recognition of Offinso as a constituent state and thus reduced the Offinsohene from the status of being a paramount chief. The Offinsohene was a long-term opponent of the CPP, Wiafe Akenten.

[25] Cabinet, Memorandum by the minister of local government, 28 January 1958, NAG ADM 13/2/44.

[26] By April 1958 it seems that 17 Asante Paramount Chiefs had declared for the CPP openly.

[27] *Kuntunkuni.*

at the stroke of a pen, the people of the region took part in the frequently post-poned elections for local councils. Of the 82 contests, the CPP won 48 and the successor to the National Liberation Movement, the United Party, only 24.[28] The elections to the Kumasi Municipal Council gave the CPP 17 out of 24 Council seats.[29] It would be reasonable to conclude that the CPP government by fair means and foul had proved to a wide constituency that chiefs were no longer reliable rallying points of opposition because of their proven fragility. It was a lesson that was not lost on chiefs either. Only days after the final local council election results were announced, the Kumasi State Council, the council of Kumasi chiefs headed by the Asantehene in his role as Kumasihene, resolved not to support any particular political party but would instead 'support the Government in the administration'. For reasons which no informants could remember the Asantehene was not present at the meeting; it is possible that his absence had no political overtones but it is unlikely. He was, however, dutifully sent a copy of the resolution which he duly and almost certainly unhappily signed.[30]

Only two weeks later, the Asantehene, sitting in a meeting of the Asanteman Council, suggested that chiefs should henceforward emulate the role of the British queen 'who supported no party but ruled with the party which came to power'. But any notion that the chiefs had simply capitulated would be mistaken. The Asanteman Council had not accepted the government's derecognition of some paramounts and they continued to be invited to attend. At the same meeting of the council, a strong letter from the regional commissioner was read out which said: 'It is in the Government's view highly undesirable that the 5 Chiefs[31] should be invited or permitted to attend meetings of the Asanteman Council.' That view was supported by the presence of three platoons of police, 80 men in all, who cordoned off the Manhyia palace in Kumase where the meeting was held and refused entry to the derecognized chiefs and their entourages.

A further wave of declarations of chiefly support for government followed this show of force and not only in Ashanti. Kotoku State Council, for example, made such a declaration on the same day as did that of Nsuta, a long-time NLM strong-hold. Many such declarations were prompted by direct pressure not only from local CPP activists and regional commissioners but also from clearly frightened subchiefs sitting in council. By 29 April this rush towards conformity ended with the deeply worried Asanteman Council formally deciding that they too would now support the government. The meeting was told that the Asantehene was 'indisposed' and could not attend.

---

[28] Independents controlled three Councils and a further seven were hung.

[29] Of the 60,904 registered voters of Kumasi, only 41,487 voted. 22,673 cast their votes for the CPP.

[30] This incensed the leader of the United Party, Kofi Busia. The *Daily Graphic* of 1 April 1958 reported him as having said that the Council had 'not appreciated the change that had come over the political life of the country ... whether that is the best way to serve the course [sic] of chieftaincy time alone will tell'. The only possible interpretation of the council's resolution is that they had very precisely appreciated the change that had come over the country.

[31] The two derecognized chiefs and three others, Berekumhene, Ejisuhene and Bompatahene, whose destool-ment by government enquiry was not endorsed by the Asanteman Council.

Throughout the course of these grim events, the enquiry into Akyem Abuakwa's recent political history was being carried out, in public.[32] It was reported *in extenso* in the press. Although partisans on either side were unlikely to be persuaded that their reading of events was controverted by the evidence, the entire proceedings revealed just how wretched the stand-off in Akyem Abuakwa had been. Witnesses supporting the CPP and hence its major chiefly figure, Nana Kwabena Kena, the Adontenhene, or the NLM and hence the Okyenhene, gave long detailed accounts of mutual intolerance, violence and threats of violence. Neither side comes well out of the assembled evidence.

The enquiry's terms of reference suggested that it should concern itself with two matters. Was there serious evidence of an 'abuse of power' by the Okyenhene and his councillors? And had the Okyeman Council made payments 'for purposes other than those properly connected with traditional matters'? Any dispassionate reading of the conduct of the enquiry and its subsequent report leaves little doubt that the enquiry revealed unequivocal evidence that the Okyenhene and his councillors had threatened, victimized and excluded those who would not support them and thus the NLM. The evidence is equally clear that the Okyeman Council made payments to the NLM.[33] The enquiry was, however, of much greater interest. Throughout its long days of taking meandering testimony, what was gradually revealed was much more than just a party conflict. It revealed instead the heart of a conflict between chieftaincy and the modern state, a conflict in which the definition of where the boundaries of authority could and should be drawn was central.

That conflict came out at its clearest during the several days of cross-examination which began on 2 February 1958, of Dr J.B. Danquah. He challenged the government's right to insist that chiefs should play no part in national politics. Such participation had been 'accepted customary practice from the days of the Aborigines Rights Protection Society until today'. As we have seen, what was or was not customary was consistently the object of contestation. But history was on his side. Chiefs, not least his late half-brother Nana Sir Ofori Atta I, had, without criticism, been open supporters and patrons of earlier political movements.[34] These movements, like the ARPS mentioned by Danquah, were now being constructed as part of the genealogy of the modern nationalist movement which had liberated the Gold Coast in 1957. The most recent and most successful heir of that linear if selective account was of course the CPP. Danquah's implication was, with

---

[32] The state council was represented by the British barrister, E.L. Mallalieu, QC, MP, as senior counsel. The senior counsel for the commission was G.L. Scott, the solicitor-general. After the commission ended Scott was raised to the High Court Bench as Puisne Judge. Ironically most of its sessions were held in Guggisberg Hall in Dodowa where for years Ofori Atta II had presided over meetings of the Joint Provincial Council of Chiefs.

[33] Much of this is contested in H.K. Akyeampong's book *The Akim Abuakwa crisis*, which was published very shortly after the Jackson Report was submitted. The rebuttals are, however, insubstantial for the most part.

[34] Ofori Atta I had been a patron of Danquah's Youth Conference in the 1930s. His successor, Ofori Atta II, had, as we have seen, supported the UGCC and had even written for Nkrumah's *Accra Evening News* in happier days.

considerable justification, that the insistence upon the removal of chiefs from national politics was not an ancient Ghanaian tradition; it was, rather, an entirely novel tradition only invoked by the government party when chiefs had the temerity to espouse parties opposed to the CPP.[35] As the Akyem Abuakwa State Council's counsel pointed out in his summing-up: 'Other State Councils have spent their money on the 'right' political party; but no Commission of Enquiry has been placed on them.' The very concept of 'involvement in national politics' disguised the more precise meaning of 'involvement in national opposition politics'.

More importantly Danquah, the most articulate voice of the Okyeman Council, maintained the claim to something close to the autonomy of the Akyem Abuakwa state. This repeated, in essence, the conviction of many paramount chiefs during the colonial era that, as they were bound into the wider Gold Coast/Ghana state by treaty, they were in some fashion insulated from the demands of the national legislature. These ancient states were older than the modern state of Ghana and the lives of their subjects were regulated by custom and not solely by national laws and regulations. It followed, Danquah argued, that the Okyeman Council, 'the parliament of the government of the Akim Abuakwa State', had an absolute right to control its own expenditure. Neither the governor-general nor the national government enjoyed the right to regulate that expenditure. This reasoning sought to question the validity of the enquiry's second limb. But its force was also to challenge the constitutionality of the full incorporation of pre-colonial states in the modern state of Ghana.[36]

In many respects this virtually secessionist posture was politically futile just as it was almost certainly legally weak.[37] Upon independence, the 19th-century treaties between the British and myriad African states were formally abrogated. The tenuous ambiguities relating to the relationship of such states to the colonial power had been overtaken by events and resolved by the everyday reality of an independent government with a massive national majority. Danquah, however, went further in rejecting the authority of the government. This was most pointed in his rejection of the right of the newly created local councils to collect stool land revenue. Local councils were, he claimed, 'foreign institutions', whilst Akyem Abuakwa remained 'a sovereign state'. The CPP's longer-term plan was, he added, that 'Chieftaincy should be absorbed or destroyed with the state's [Akyem Abuakwa's] sovereignty left without a protector'. The Okyenhene had been resolved to fight against this; and in so doing he had, rather than 'failed in his duty as a Paramount Chief', as the government's case had alleged, actually carried out his customary duties to the letter. It was, Danquah said, no surprise that he was 'only the first victim of the party in power in the furtherance of its long-standing

---

[35] Report of the Akim Abuakwa enquiry and verbatim reports of the evidence in the *Daily Graphic*, 3 February 1958.

[36] 'The Akim Abuakwa State has never sacrificed any aspect of its independence by any such treaty...The several instruments which brought about the independence of Ghana did not alter that picture', Danquah said in chief. His speech is found as an appendix in H.K. Akyeampong, *The Akim Abuakwa Crisis*, p. 52.

[37] The state council's counsel, E. L. Mallalieu, conceded as much in his summing-up: 'the State Councils', he said, 'are of course subject to the laws of the country without any doubt at all.'

policy'. The government by withdrawing its recognition of the Okyenhene had 'hit one of the party's strongest opponents ... [in order] to make an example of him among chiefs'.[38]

The compelling force of Danquah's testimony was undermined by his frequent flashes of ill-temper, his descent into palpable dishonesty and his innumerable contradictions. For example, when asked whether he knew that the majority of *akyemfo* supported the CPP, he replied 'Yes, and so what?', a curmudgeonly response from a *soi-disant* democrat. Despite the huge weight of evidence to the contrary, he consistently denied that the NLM had shown any violence to CPP supporters. And in the dying moments of his cross-examination, he agreed that Akyem Abuakwa was subject to the laws of Ghana, an admission that considerably weakened the foundations of his earlier arguments about sovereignty. Although there was much in his evidence, as there is much in his writing, of overstatement, of internal contradiction and of bombast, at the heart of his arguments lay the problems created by the still unresolved relationships between the Ghanaian state and many of its component 'traditional' states.

In terms of its conduct this was not a partisan enquiry even if the reasons for its inception were undoubtedly political, as Danquah suggested. Jackson, sitting alone, was no more sympathetic to CPP than to NLM witnesses. Indeed on 24 February he showed an unusual degree of considerably impatient hostility towards the CPP's most significant witness, the Adontenhene. 'Your manner as a witness is as bad as it can be. You are dodging all the questions. I am not interested in your speeches.' He exempted only one of the many witnesses who spoke about organized gang violence from the harsh generalization: 'All witnesses other than one ... were evasive when answering questions relating to the duties of the Action Groupers.' Although there were strong partisan reactions to the commission's negative findings about the Okyenhene's and his councillors' political conduct and fiscal probity, the evidence for coming to those conclusions reads very convincingly.

The wider context within which these events should be read was one of a tottering system of local government which was seriously frustrating central government. As well as intervening in more and more disputes concerning chieftaincy, government was also suspending local councils in large numbers, replacing them with *de facto* direct rule. In many cases it is apparent that such suspensions of elected councils were prompted by complaints by local CPP branches and regional commissioners. Akpini Local Council was suspended because 'the Council has been used on too many occasions for political purposes' and because there was 'a growing lack of confidence and unwillingness to co-operate by the majority of the ratepayers.'[39] In the same month the minister sought the suspension of Manya Krobo Local Council following 'repeated petitions and deputations from the Ratepayers Asociation [a CPP organ] enumerating many irregularities committed by the Council'.[40] The Atwima Mponua Local Council was suspended after the

[38] Evidence given on 6 February 1958 in the *Daily Graphic*, 22 February 1958.
[39] Cabinet, Memorandum by the minister of local government, 14 January 1958, NAG ADM 13/2/44.
[40] *Ibid.*

minister had received 'several petitions from the Ratepayers Association and from the Atwima Mponua area CPP which draw attention to irregularities'.[41] Ekuoma Local Council was suspended 'in view of the resolution submitted by the Ekuoma Youth Association [a CPP organ]'.[42] Western Tongu Local Council was suspended because it was 'bedevilled by internal strife arising from traditional jealousies ... and ... deliberately flouted my instructions'.[43] In these and numerous other cases,[44] the frequent invocation by the minister of councils 'forfeiting the confidence of the ratepayers' is obviously formulaic. There can be little doubt that where the local CPP had failed to capture a local council, it could achieve such a council's suspension by submitting complaints to the regional commissioner which were then conveyed to the minister. It appears to have been remarkably effective.

The crudeness of these procedures was, however, planned only as a temporary expedient. The government was planning to reform the palpably unsatisfactory local government system. The old system initiated by the Local Government Ordinance of 1951[45] would need considerable reform; this was argued by the minister and agreed by his Cabinet colleagues ostensibly because of the needs created by the eventual creation of regional assemblies.[46] The new plans included 'the abolition of traditional and special members of Local Councils' and the assumption of the responsibility for the collection of stool revenues by central government. The proposed removal of all traditional figures from the local government system was matched by the unabating removal, by variation orders, of unreliable traditional members from the still unreformed system of local justice.

The partisan quality of the tinkering with the membership of local court panels is very evident in a sweeping set of changes in Ashanti in February 1958. In the course of a single Cabinet meeting, the composition of the local courts[47] of Obuasi, Banka, Bekwai, Wenchi, Bompata-Juaso, Kintampo and Kumasi East Districts were drastically altered by the removal of traditional figures and the nomination of non-traditional members at the suggestion of the regional commissioner. Where, however, there was chiefly support for the government party, traditional figures' names were *inserted*. This appears to have been the case in Nkoranza where the Krontihene, the Adontenhene, Akyeamehene, Benkumhene and Gyaasehene were all empanelled. The same pattern is visible in the reform of the Amansie and the

---

[41] Cabinet, Memorandum by the minister of local government, 28 January 1958, NAG ADM 13/2/44.

[42] Cabinet, Memorandum by the minister of local government, 25 February 1958, NAG ADM 13/2/45.

[43] Cabinet, Memorandum by the minister of local government, 17 February 1958, NAG.ADM 13/2/45.

[44] Other local councils suspended in the first four months of 1958 included those at Tumu, Drobo, Suma and Osudoku.

[45] Which interestingly appears to have been borrowed in large measure from the Nigerian (Eastern Region) Local Government Ordinance of 1950.

[46] The discussion on this is particularly interesting in that it suggests that by as late as May 1958, the government was still toying with the possibility of *not* establishing regional assemblies. The minister's memorandum begins with the conditional 'Should regional Assemblies be established'. Cabinet, NAG ADM 13/2/48.

[47] Still anachronistically if utterly accurately described by the minister of justice in his memorandum as 'Native Courts'.

Denyase courts where several traditional leaders were now nominated to serve.[48]

The frustration which led government to combine active interventionist policies with palpable intimidation was real enough. The newly independent state's local government structure, its capacity to collect revenue and to promote rural development remained in disarray. While some of these deficiencies were almost certainly systemic, much of the mess could be attributed to the clumsy statutory linkages between modern local government and the remnants of the old Native Authority system which rested upon chieftaincy. Few in the CPP and no one in Cabinet would have dissented from a view that enough was enough; the time had now come when chiefs should be directly controlled by the elected government. In the initial drafting stages of what would become the act setting up houses of chiefs, ministers carefully wrote in clauses which empowered government to recognize and derecognize chiefs, to control chiefly finance and even to force destooled chiefs into internal exile.[49] The tenor of the times is strongly suggested by the fact that, at the same Cabinet meeting, the final form of the notorious Preventive Detention Act took shape.[50] There is little doubt that radical reform and intimidation were combined elements in the government's approach to its political enemies and to the diminishing number of chiefs who were incautious enough to maintain their hostility.

[48] Cabinet, Memorandum by the minister of justice on the Native Courts (Ashanti) Variation Order 1958, 17 February 1958, NAG ADM 13/2/45.

[49] Cabinet, Memorandum by the minister of local government, 27 May 1958. NAG ADM 13/2/48.

[50] The act provided for detention without trial for those deemed to be risks to state security. Edusei explained it as being necessary at a CPP rally at Ntonso in Ashanti on 19 May 'because it is the business of any good politician to uproot his opponent whose actions are likely to be detrimental to his progress'.

10

Making & Unmaking the Chiefs

The sheer extent of government power over chiefs was to be emphatically demonstrated in mid-1958. Having received the report of the Jackson commission of enquiry into Akyem Abuakwa affairs, which in harmony with the evidence had concluded that the Okyenhene had abused his powers, the government immediately and permanently removed its recognition from the Okyenhene. So far as the independent state of Ghana was concerned, Okyenhene Ofori Atta II was no longer the paramount chief of Akyem Abuakwa. When the Okyeman Council gathered on 27 May 1958 to consider its reaction to the report, it was met by the regional commissioner and, outside the palace walls, a deputy super-intendent of police with a small detachment of both armed and unarmed constables. The government officials insisted that the council should act 'in the interests of peace' and thus with restraint. Okyeman had little choice but to comply. Eventually on 9 June the council put out a 1,800-word statement, clearly written by Dr J. B. Danquah, which fundamentally argued that the Okyenhene had been convicted without being allowed to defend himself.[1]

The Okyenhene's enemies in Akyem Abuakwa now acted very quickly. On 13 June over 60 people rather loosely described as chiefs of Akyem Abuakwa met at Kukurantumi, the stool town of the pro-CPP Adontenhene. After state drums had been beaten and 12 sheep had been sacrificed, the meeting destooled the Okyenhene and installed the Adontenhene, Nana Kwabena Kena II, as regent until a new Okyenhene could be enstooled. This, however, was not a meeting of the vast majority of the members of the Okyeman Council and the destoolment was undoubtedly highly irregular within any reading of customary law. Just how one went about destooling an Okyenhene was not, however, exactly a practised art in the area. The first and only Okyenhene in a long regnal list to be destooled was Amoako Atta III who was removed in very different circumstances in 1912. But

---

[1] This case and other objections are spelled out in the much longer work, *The Akim Abuakwa Crisis* by H.K. Akyeampong. It includes a long foreword by Danquah.

126

the government was happy to accept this as the formal destoolment. Even though the formal *Gazette* notice of Ofori Atta II's destoolment was not to be published until 8 August, that notice says that his destoolment took effect from 13 June 'in accordance with the State Council Regulations of 1954'. The legality of this was hotly contested by the king-makers of Akyem Abuakwa at an understandably angry meeting in Kyebi on 11 August. There is no question that they were entirely correct in seeing the destoolment at Kukurantumi as highly irregular. The Joint Provincial Council routinely met on 14 June, a day after the meeting at Kukurantumi, and rather remarkably made no recorded comment whatever about these events even though the deposed Okyenhene had for years served not only as a member of the JPC but as its president. By 20 June the government had rushed a bill through the House which appointed an official receiver to handle Okyeman stool revenues.

The government's increased control over chieftaincy was evident in other cases and in other ways. It endorsed the destoolment of the Offinsohene, the anti-CPP Nana Wiafe Akenten II, and his immediate replacement by the more compliant Nana Wiafe Abatgio by *Gazette* notice; despite this, all of those customarily entitled to hear destoolment charges and to elect a new Omanhene denied that destoolment charges had been preferred and insisted, somewhat convincingly, that the Omanhene had not been destooled customarily but only by the government.[2] Their protest achieved nothing more than limited newspaper coverage. It was obvious that where the destoolment of contrary chiefs was concerned, government was content to regard the procedures which brought about the desired end as proper even when they ran against custom. But traditional propriety demanded the participation of traditional office-holders, and if they refused to assist, a further stand-off ensued. The government had no more patience with recalcitrant chiefs and elders.

In fact no protest from any quarter was making much headway. In the Legislative Assembly debate on the governor-general's speech from the throne,[3] chieftaincy and its future figured prominently. The United Party MLA R.B. Otchere,[4] referring to the draft House of Chiefs Bill, said that it was 'designed merely to take powers from the chiefs and to make them poor. Yet unfortunately we have some chiefs who are following the CPP.' Victor Owusu, another UP member,[5] said that regional commissioners 'have been threatening chiefs with withdrawal of recognition and dismemberment of States and promising others promotion as paramount chiefs. They go round … telling people that if they vote for the United Party there will be no development in their areas.' J.D. Wireko[6]

---

[2] There was one exception, the pro-CPP Krontihene of Offinso, Nana Yaw Boamah. This case is examined in fascinating detail in R.C. Crook, 'Local elites and national politics in Ghana'.

[3] The formal speech outlining future legislative intentions, written by government but given by the governor-general at the beginning of the parliamentary session, was a routine borrowed from British parliamentary practice.

[4] For Amansie-West.

[5] For Agona Kwabre.

[6] UP member for Amansie East.

said that the chiefs were 'going to be made *simpampanyinfo* [mere figureheads] ...
Government is trying to destroy an institution that enriches our culture and
tradition.' But the House was dominated by CPP members and the small squall
initiated by the handful of opposition members was successfully ridden out by
government. The opposition's failure to make headway was further underlined by
the departure of its leader, Professor K.A. Busia, who left Ghana for medical
treatment in the US on 22 July. Ironically he shared the same flight with Komla
Gbedemah. Gbedemah was, it was reported, 'carried shoulder high' to the aircraft.
Busia was 'booed, hit, pushed and kicked by a large crowd'.[7] The sense that the
battle for chieftaincy was finally lost was further underlined when the long-term
secretary of the Joint Provincial Council, the distinguished scholar Magnus
Sampson, died at the age of 58 on 27 July.[8] And then on 15 August the Asantehene
announced that he would take a holiday in Las Palmas.

The Asantehene's holiday plans were, however, disrupted by the government's
legislative reaction to the Sarkodee Addo report on the alleged misgovernance of
Kumase. The Ashanti Lands Bill, drafted in anticipation of the Sarkodee Addo
Commission's findings, repeated, in essence, the measures taken in the wake of the
deposition of the Okyenhene of Akyem Abuakwa. It placed the Kumase stool
lands, the intimate heritage of the Asante of Kumase and their rulers for centuries,
and their revenue under the direct control of central government.[9] Although the
bill again excited vigorous if ineffective debate, B.D. Addai, the UP MLA, arguing
that it was 'contrary to Ashanti custom, tradition and usage which from time
immemorial invest the land in the stools for the benefit of the people', this
measure, the Stool Lands Act, became law on 5 September.[10] The Kumasi State
Council, again wearing *kuntukuni*, the cloth worn by mourners at funerals,
apparently received this news in silence. 'A catastrophe has befallen the chiefs of
Ashanti', the Asantehene told the Kumasi State Council on 2 October. He had
actually been forced to swallow the bitter pill on 2 September when the minister
of local government and the attorney-general had 'received the Asantehene in
Kumasi' to explain what happened next, according to Cabinet record.[11] The use of
language here is remarkable, for it was the Asantehene who had for centuries done
the receiving in Kumase, as it were. The government's control over chieftaincy
was further enhanced on 8 September. At a brief court hearing before Mr Justice
Nii Amaa Ollennu, the Okyeman Council attempted to obtain an injunction which
would have restrained the government from recognizing the contested destoolment
of the Okyenhene on the grounds that he had not been customarily destooled. The
judge, finding against the Okyeman Council, formally accepted that the *Gazette*
announcement of his destoolment was legally enough to mean that he was legally

---

[7] *Daily Graphic*, 23 July 1958.

[8] He had acted in that capacity since 1945.

[9] This did not have the effect of confiscating the lands by altering their ultimate ownership. But the receiver
now managed both the lands and their revenues. See Cabinet, 29 July 1958, NAG ADM 13/2/50.

[10] This attracted the rare attention of a London *Times* editorial which described the act as 'a serious material
blow' and a 'blow to prestige' for chiefs.

[11] Cabinet, 2 September 1958, NAG ADM 13/2/57.

no longer Okyenhene. This was an important decision in that the legal status of what amounted to government approval of an uncustomary destoolment had been tested in the courts and found to be legal.

Throughout the surviving historical material there is a pervading sense of a government increasingly using an iron grip on a softer and softer target. In mid-July a Cabinet reshuffle abolished the ministry of justice, remitting all the issues relating to law and order to the ministry of the interior whilst announcing that the attorney-general was now 'directly responsible to the prime minister'. As minister of the interior, Krobo Edusei had initiated the large number of deportations which had broken the Moslem Association Party and was proud of his reputation as the 'hammer of the Asantehene'.[12] This was further bad news for the chiefs. Less openly, Cabinet discussed internal security. The prime minister worried that 'certain parts of the country would be ideal for guerrilla operations by opponents of the Government'. The answer to this bizarre possibility was quite literally 'the smack of firm government'. In an extraordinary, essentialist vision of his country-men and women, Nkrumah argued that 'the psychological outlook of most Ghanaians is such that opposition by force to the Government could be stamped out quite early if nipped in the bud by strong, immediate punitive measures which could not be appropriately administered by the police'.[13] It was a judgement of which only the harshest of the old-style colonial officials might have been the author. In October, the minister of the interior announced his intention to increase the national police force from 7,000 to 10,000 men at a CPP rally in Bukom Square in Accra. In the same speech he suggested: 'Nsawam [the site of Ghana's high security prison] was now too good for opposition leaders ... I will arrest them and damn the world press ... the world press has no vote ... we will impound all their passports.'[14]

This atmosphere of menace was real enough. Reacting to what the government at least regarded as the 'successful' introduction of regional commissioners, the prime minister now suggested that political commissioners should be created 'in each District in each Region ... they would be personal assistants to Ministers ... and their appointments would be ... made by me in consultation with Regional Commissioners ... There is a need for the political aspects of the day to day administration to be provided for in Ghana ... [they] would be the Regional Commissioners' political "eyes" in the District.'[15] Thus political commissioners would not form part of the public service, would not be civil servants, but, rather, political appointees. There were direct implications for the countryside in that this

[12] The *Ashanti Pioneer* of 17 April 1958 claimed that Edusei had told a rally in Cape Coast that he 'had forever broken the pride of the Ashanti because the Asantehene is now in my pocket'. Edusei's later denial of this was followed by a flurry of letters to the editor from people who claimed to have heard him and said that the paper's account was mild in comparison with his words on the occasion.

[13] Prime Minister's memorandum to Cabinet, 27 May 1958, NAG ADM 13/2/48. The same meeting noted that the Ghanaian police were receiving training with the Indian Intelligence Service in Delhi at the time.

[14] While the opposition *Ashanti Pioneer* (Edusei had ironically worked for the paper in the 1940s) of 1 October 1958 carries the longest account, other newspapers reported much the same text.

[15] Prime Minister's memorandum to Cabinet, 9 September 1958, NAG ADM 13/2/52.

revealing memorandum went on to recommend that 'Political Commissioners should work closely with the Administrative Officer serving in the District who would continue to receive his instructions from the Regional Commissioner'. It is hard to avoid the conclusion that the frequent invocation of 'democratic local government' by the national government was becoming, in large measure, decidedly empty rhetoric. The government's remaining commitment to devolution and local accountability was ordered by constitutional requirements and most assuredly not by conviction.

The independence constitution obliged the government to move rapidly to create both regional assemblies and Houses of Chiefs for all regions of the country. The government's intentions were, from the beginning, quite clearly to dispense with the former and to marginalize the latter. That it was the government's wish to get rid of the regional assemblies at the earliest opportunity is clear from a Cabinet memorandum written by the minister of local government and discussed on 2 December 1958; here the minister wrote of the impending fact of the 'abolition of the Regional Assemblies' because 'their continued existence will be unnecessary' and did so several months before the deed was done[16] in March 1959.[17] In their discussions of the bill creating Houses of Chiefs, Cabinet proposed that there should be no formal definition of 'paramount' or 'divisional' chiefs and that all chiefs would be, by law, henceforward either recognized or have recognition withdrawn by government. The histories of the pre-colonial states, the traditions which ordained matters like precedence were secondary to the all-important matter of government approval or disapproval. By implication, government and neither custom nor history would now ordain the hierarchy between chiefs. The bill required all state councils to notify the government formally of their membership; failure to do so within a month of any request would lead to such Councils being 'deemed to have ceased to exist'. The minister for local government now had the right to control the finances of state councils. It is worth remembering that these councils were not recent bureaucratic creations but in many cases centuries-old representations of local constitutional understandings. Chiefs who lost government recognition could be forced to leave their towns and could be subjected to 'exclusion from any specified area'.[18]

The contemplation of, in effect, internal exile was the direct result of several destooled chiefs, the Okyenhene being the most prominent, refusing to leave their palaces and refusing to relinquish the guardianship of their stool treasures following what they regarded as untraditional deposition.[19] Ofori Atta II was taken to court on 24 September for refusing to hand over stool property after being forcibly ejected, provocatively if rather pathetically wearing traditional battledress,[20] from the palace.

[16] By the Constitution Amendment Act.

[17] Cabinet, 2 December 1958, NAG ADM 13/2/55.

[18] Cabinet, Memorandum by the minister of local government, 27 May 1958, NAG ADM 13/2/48.

[19] Cases of such rearguard actions include Obomeng, Aduasi, Wenchi (where the younger brother of Kofi Busia, Nana Kusi Apea I, had been destooled), Otwereso, Akuapem and Akyem Abuakwa.

[20] A smock and hat with numerous protective charms, *gris gris*, sewn over them.

Outside the palace gates a crowd had gathered, many of them wearing mourning cloth. Ironically the removal order[21] was signed by his close kinsman, the minister for local government, Aaron Ofori Atta. No less ironically, the prosecution case was eventually presented at Koforidua Magistrates Court by Senior Superintendent H.A. Nuamah, the police officer who 14 years before had been a key figure in the investigation of the case of 'ritual murder' which had resulted from the funeral of the Okyenhene's predecessor, Ofori Atta I.[22] The present case was to be referred to the Supreme Court and amongst the Okyenhene's bail conditions was his exclusion from the entire state of Akyem Abuakwa. This was enough to convince a number of other chiefs[23] who had dug in in similar fashion to immediately surrender the stool regalia they had retained and to leave their palaces in a hurry.

The earlier suggestion that government regarded the Houses of Chiefs as nuisances is borne out in a number of ways. Members of some Houses at least were for example not even informed of the date of the first meeting[24] of the newly constituted Houses and members of the JPC[25] claimed that they only knew of this through newspaper coverage. The marginalization of the Houses of Chiefs was further emphasized when on 3 November the prime minister told the Legislative Assembly that he had the 'gravest misgivings' about the country's constitution and that he intended to review and repeal elements of it. Amongst his objections was Section 35 which was 'inserted' he said:

> to make certain that Chiefs were consulted on matters directly affecting them.[26] Unfortunately the wording of this section is so obscure that it is difficult to determine the Bills which should in law be referred ... There is ... an even more important reason why this section is not in the interests of the chiefs ... This process will definitely lead to considerable delays ... I am sure that the Houses of Chiefs will realise that this amendment is designed in their interest and in order to facilitate closer co-operation between chiefs and the government.

When the prime minister had originally flagged this intention in Cabinet on 14 October he wrote: 'Once the Bill has been passed ... it will *never* [my emphasis] be necessary on any future occasions to have to consult the Houses of Chiefs.' As constitutional change required a two-thirds majority in the Assembly, Nkrumah insisted that all CPP members must be present and that 'this might require ... the recalling of delegates from the United Nations'.[27]

The records of the first meetings of Houses of Chiefs suggest that they met as

---

[21] The Akyem Abuakwa Paramount Stool Order 1958.

[22] He was also author of *An account of the Kibi ritual murder case*, Accra 1985 and rose to be deputy commissioner of police. For more on him see also R. Rathbone, *Murder and politics*.

[23] Such as the Aduasihene, who was quoted by the *Daily Graphic* of 22 October 1958 as having said 'It's never been my intention to flout government authority'.

[24] On 5 November 1954.

[25] Amongst other things, the inauguration of the Houses of Chiefs led to the dissolution of the old Provincial Councils.

[26] This was certainly a reference to the eleventh-hour addition of clauses in the independence constitution designed to pacify the NLM. For more on this see R. Rathbone (ed.) *Ghana; British documents on the end of Empire*, Vol II.

[27] Cabinet, NAG ADM 13/2/53.

thoroughly cowed, fearful institutions. Although their advice rather than consent was required, they all approved this amendment to the constitution which meant that chiefs need not even be consulted over proposed legislation dealing with chieftaincy itself. Chiefs were now formally recognizing that they were inescapably clients of the government.

The remnants of independent chiefly power were being consistently eroded throughout this period. With considerable frequency chiefs were being derecognized and others being recognized by government. Any chief who was or was suspected of being an NLM sympathizer lived under the immediate threat of destoolment.[28] In most cases there was a discernible pattern to these events. Almost without exception, the minister of local government reported to Cabinet that considerable local disaffection had resulted in the destoolment of an incumbent from whom government should now withdraw recognition. These reported expressions of disaffection appear to have uniformly been voiced by local CPP branches and the destoolment was frequently carried out either by uncustomary means or by the customarily entitled members of state councils under pressure from vociferous claques of 'youngmen'. Again, almost without exception it was 'youngmen' who preferred the destoolment charges.[29] While it is rumour rather than fact, The Ashanti Pioneer reported that the Ashanti CPP, at an all-night meeting at its Kimberley Avenue headquarters in late October 1957, resolved that 'destoolment committees [should] be set up in the whole country by the Party in order to uproot all the Chiefs who are against the government'.[30]

That there was more to this kind of event than the simple anger of this or that local group leading to low-level spontaneous jacqueries is suggested by a mass of evidence. Political allegiance was at least believed by some to be the key to the funding by the central government of local development; an oppositional chief could, conversely, constitute a barrier to local improvement. The relationship between loyalty to the government and the expectation of the good life was spelled out by Nkrumah at a CPP rally in Agona Nyakrom on New Year's Day 1958. Here he freely admitted that the district had not enjoyed the advantage of development projects because the Agona people 'went the other way round'. The opposition had established itself in some towns and thus the CPP had 'experienced difficulties in its organization in the State'. In the 1956 election, Agona had supported the CPP and 'if you continue to be loyal to me, I will consider extending amenities to you. I will extend electricity and pipe-borne water to all the towns and villages[31] ... a secondary school will be built at Swedru.'[32] This kind of blandishment was gentle

---

[28] This was clearly the case in Anyinam, Apapam, Asamama, Kwabeng and Osino in Akyem Abuakwa alone. The chiefs of Tafo, Jejeti and the Mankrado of Asamama abdicated early in the year owing to intimidation, they alleged.

[29] While there are many examples, the destoolment of the Kofiasehene of Agona on 11 March 1957, the Offinsohene on 1 February 1958, the Agogohene on 28 January 1958 and the Edwesohene on 23 November 1957 all conform to this pattern.

[30] 26 October 1957.

[31] A promise which remains unfulfilled in many towns and villages in the area.

[32] This is most fully reported in The Ashanti Pioneer for 2 January 1958, but is also quoted in other papers. No denial was ever made about this reported speech.

compared with the approach adopted by Krobo Edusei in a speech made in Aflao in the run-up to a by-election there. 'You think I am a fool to give you water to drink and vote against me? After the election if you vote CPP, I will give you water to drink.'[33]

This somewhat brutal theme is echoed by the reports of those 'religious leaders' attempting a reconciliation between factions in Agogo. They informed reporters that the CPP 'youngmen' had said that the Ashanti regional commissioner, C. de Graft Dickson, had told them that 'the Chief had not supported the government party. Because of that, progress and development in the area was at a standstill.' Accordingly, 'Unless the Chief declared his stand as a CPP member, CPP youngmen were determined to destool him so that the development which they wanted could be undertaken by the government.'[34] This perception was almost certainly responsible for the drift across the floor of the House by UP MLAs such as the Northern Territories members Mumuni Bawumia and M. Tampuri.[35] Even more alarmingly, Krobo Edusei was widely reported as having told a CPP rally at Ejisu that the local CPP must 'elect their own Edwesohene to be recognized by the government ... What the government wants at Ejisu is a full-blooded CPP Ejisuhene ... the government wants every chief to be a hundred per cent CPP – or perish!'[36]

While there is evidence here of direct ministerial involvement, this is less common than the frequency with which the hands of regional commissioners can be seen in matters which less than a decade beforehand had been widely viewed as being firmly within the bailiwick of tradition and custom. Regional and district administration was increasingly politicized. The few British government agents who remained, under contract, with the Ghanaian civil service were now to be withdrawn from the district administrations 'as early as possible';[37] their Ghanaian successors, answerable to regional commissioners, were to 'deal directly with all matters concerning chieftaincy'.[38] In these circumstances, regional commissioners enjoyed considerable powers both as administrators but also as local party functionaries.

In case after case it is clear that it was local party opinion, or that which was presented as local party opinion, which was conveyed to the ministers of local

---

[33] Speech made on 13 October quoted in the *Ashanti Pioneer* of 14 October 1958. In the event the voters of Aflao did not elect the CPP candidate and instead returned an Independent candidate. The piped water supply was not forthcoming.

[34] *Daily Graphic*, 31 January 1958.

[35] Members for Mamprusi East and Mamprusi West and South respectively. Their move, in May 1958, reduced UP membership in a House of 104 members to a mere 25.

[36] While *The Ashanti Pioneer*, an opposition newspaper, was the only paper to carry this story (on 7 February 1958), the disturbing allegation was never denied by the minister or his civil servants.

[37] They had been retained because of manpower shortages at the higher levels of the civil service. Their removal was, it seems, slow. As late as 6 November, the prime minister was to write a memorandum on Africanizing regional administration in which he wrote 'all overseas Administrative officers should be transferred from the Regions ... immediately after the visit of the Duke of Edinburgh'. Cabinet, 6 November 1959, NAG ADM 13/2/66.

[38] Prime Minister's memorandum to Cabinet on regional administrative organisation, 2 December 1958, NAG ADM 13/2/55.

government and the interior or even the prime minister. Whether such opinion was 'massaged' by regional commissioners is unclear, as contemporary opponents of the CPP today credit commissioners with virtually demonic powers whilst old CPP stalwarts have somewhat gentler recollections. Their activities lay, presumably, somewhere in between these two poles. There is, however, something almost formulaic in the ways in which regional commissioners impress upon the ministers the need for frequently draconian central government interventions in their regions. This affected chiefs, but it was also visible in the extended control over 'democratic local government'.

Independence had brought with it no enhancement of the efficiency or smooth running of local government. Part of the blame for this lay with the messy nature of the local government structure for which CPP government was not responsible and for its over-rapid implementation, for which it was. Some local councils were responsible for at least twice as many people as others. 'There was no time for detailed consideration of the factors to be taken into account in determining the optimum size of councils and accordingly they were based ... on existing native authority areas.'[39] Throughout the terminal colonial period and during the early years of independence the income from local taxation, rates, always fell far short of estimates. Rates were assessed on the basis of estimates of local incomes, and were not progressive; everyone, irrespective of income, paid the same rate and the levy was gendered. The guiding assumption was that rates constituted something close to the amount of 3 days' pay per year. The highest rates levied annually were £3 for men and £1.50 for women. The lowest were 4 shillings for men and 2 shillings for women. The differences between rates account for a deal of physical relocation from high-rate council areas to low-rate areas. It was also the case that the central government grant was consistently well above 50 per cent of the regional estimates of necessary expenditure.[40] Almost without exception the real costs of the most basic services, which included the police, road maintenance, health clinics, education and the running costs of local courts[41] exceeded the revenue from rates and stool lands income. Unsurprisingly the Greenwood Report recorded that in many areas the commissioner had 'received vigorous protests about the inadequacy of the services'.[42] In so far as local councils were charged with development, and it was the lack of such development which had been the nail in the coffin of the old chief-dominated Native Authorities, it was clear that 'the amount of development

---

[39] From the report of the commissioner for local government enquiries, June 1957, p. 1. The commissioner was Arthur Greenwood.

[40] See NAG ADM 15/2 series. Local council estimates were consistently low, being based, it seems, on the previous year's revenue. As the ratepayer rolls were old and inaccurate it is clear that many councils had no idea of the total number of those who should have paid rates. The amount of stool land revenue was a further factor and amounted to a total of £181,391 for the entire Gold Coast in 1954–5, but it was, naturally, very unevenly distributed, there being no such funding in the Northern Territories and very little in Trans Volta Togoland.

[41] Courts, however, also provided revenue in the form of fines and licence fees. The total revenue from this source was about £100,000 per year by the early post-independence period.

[42] Greenwood Report, para. 10, p. 7.

financed from councils' own revenues was comparatively insignificant'.[43] As the evidence suggests that many of the smaller councils[44] were incapable of managing without government and Cocoa Marketing Board grants, it is not surprising that the government's control of their financing was translated into political terms. At the same time government's private, accurate and gloomy assessments of the probable continuing fall of the cocoa price and its heavy commitments to capital projects made it vital to drive down the amounts being spent on local government services by central government. The logic seemed to point in the direction of fewer but larger and hence, it was believed, more efficient local government units.

The suspension of maladministering local councils continued unabated after independence. Among the reasons for suspension were venality and inefficiency, the two being frequently intimately related to the relative and entirely pardonable inexperience of councillors and officials. This was especially notable in the issuing of local council contracts where open tendering was rare, where 'improper advances', bribes, were given by contractors, and close-focused audit was a rarity.[45] But suspending local councils, which brought them under something close to direct rule from Accra, was more frequently justified in Cabinet by the minister of local government citing the regional commissioners' reports of public unhappiness. As we have seen, that this or that council had 'forfeited the confidence of the rate-payers' had become a mantra. On closer examination the ratepayers usually turn out to be the area's CPP branch who 'drew attention to the irregularities'.[46] In some cases the tone both of the minister and of the regional commissioners is inescapably colonial, the irascible paternalism of a weary administrator dealing with recalcitrant children.[47]

Part of the explanation for this lies within the generic government hostility to chiefs who were frequently blamed for obstructing the objectives of local good government. But part of it lay within the new imperative of creating larger local government units. The administratively rational step of amalgamating councils was hotly contested by many chiefs who stood to lose even more authority by such reform. The evidence also suggests that it was not only chiefs who felt threatened by the loss of fit between the new local councils and the old, in some cases

---

[43] Greenwood Report, para. 14, p. 10. Greenwood estimated that the government development grant to such non-municipal local projects as 'schools, markets, roads, bridges, water supplies and clinics' amounted annually to £700,000 in 1955–6. Central government also made a block grant of nearly £1,170,000, and gave a subvention for the maintenance of traditional states of £125,000. Additionally, Cocoa Marketing Board funds gave grants of nearly £400,000 to council projects. Municipal councils received grants amounting to £276,310 in the same period.

[44] There were four municipal councils, 26 district councils and 252 local and urban councils. Of the local and urban councils, the census suggests that 31 council areas had populations of under 5,000 people.

[45] Councils were empowered to make contracts of up to £2,000, a very great deal of money at the time, without the approval of the minister.

[46] See for example the minister of local government's memoranda on Atwima Mponua Local Council (28 January 1958, NAG ADM 13/2/44) and Tumu District Council (18 March 1958. NAG ADM 13/2/46).

[47] The minister suspended Western Tongu Council for 'deliberately flouting my instructions ... and refusing to accept my rulings', for example. Cabinet, 17 February 1958, NAG ADM 13/2/45.

traditional state councils.[48] What is beyond doubt, however, is that regional administration was increasingly direct and, if the poor revenue collection rates are to be believed, no more efficient than it had been in the days of ramshackle colonial indirect rule.

In tandem with these trends and events, the future of the regional assemblies was being sealed. On 23 October the results of the regional elections, which were to return members to the regional assemblies, were announced. CPP candidates had won 213 out of the 221 seats. Almost without exception they had been returned without contest, as the UP had decided to boycott these elections as a protest.[49] The constitution stipulated that any regional assembly could assent to the national government's proposals to amend the constitution, including measures dissolving itself, if such a motion commanded a two-thirds majority. The way was now open for the government to dispose of what they regarded as the constitutional encumbrance of even so limited a degree of regional devolution. Given that the UP was the direct descendant of the old NLM which had struggled for regional devolution, it remains difficult to understand the political reasoning which suggested that it would be a good idea to surrender to government in such a self-defeating fashion; by boycotting the elections the UP had assured that even the minimalist amount of devolution involved in regional assemblies would be lost.[50] Although the British had packed their bags and departed long before, the opposition appears to have continued to play to that particular gallery in the hope of some consequent sanction against the CPP government. It was a hopeless misreading of the post-colonial situation.

This is a confusing period in hindsight. It was a bewildering mixture of very positive achievements and heavy-handed policy. The second half of 1958 witnessed the laying of the foundations of Ghana's first and only deepwater port at Tema, a massive, ambitious and imaginative project. At much the same time the government gave notice to the world that even a small country like Ghana was to be a significant international player by the establishment of firstly a national airline, Ghana Airways, and then a national merchant shipping fleet, the Black Star Line.[51] The final surveying work for Ghana's, and one of the world's, greatest capital works, the Volta River hydro-electricity project, was being conducted prior to the grant of contracts and the commencement of the work. In international

---

[48] Greenwood Report, para. 17, pp 12–13. Greenwood also reported that many chiefs, especially in Ashanti, also believed that the resultant pooling of stool revenues would deny chiefs 'their fair share of the revenue'. Chiefs' salaries, Greenwood recommended and the government agreed, should henceforward be taken from the control of local councils and remitted to 'the Regional Authorities'; in reality this was to lie with the regional commissioners. Paramount chiefs received £600 per year.

[49] The boycott prompted the government to ban all UP rallies in all regions until after the election to the regional assemblies. The boycott resulted in a tiny poll. In Kyebi which had 2,708 registered electors, only 67 votes were cast.

[50] Boycotting as practised by the NLM in the case of the Bourne Mission and the Achimota conference and by the UP in the case of the regional assembly elections was a risky policy. It was to be repeated by the opposition, in some ways the ideological descendant of these parties, in the aftermath of Ghana's general election of 1992 and with similar self-damaging effects.

[51] Named after Marcus Garvey's 'Back to Africa' fleet.

terms Ghana's diplomatic offensive ensured that Accra was the site of the first meeting of the All-African Peoples' Organization and that Nkrumah was internationally regarded as the voice of the new Africa. Ghana was certainly punching above its weight. But domestically things were very different. Not only was the constitution being slowly torn up and the future of chieftaincy more than ever in doubt, but members of the opposition were beginning to endure increasing harassment and worse.

Deportations continued throughout the year. Some continued the work of removing the last traces of the Moslem Association Party. The intended victims continued to include people with ostensibly good claims to be Ghanaian like Idris Braimah whose father was Nigerian but whose mother was Ghanaian, a member of the distinguished Accra Brazilian family, the Peregrinos, who had been born in Accra in 1904. His offence was that he 'was Political secretary of the … MAP. He is now reported to sympathise with the UP.'[52] The same Cabinet meeting decided to deport Sam Moshie, an elder of the Berekum Zongo and someone who had lived in Ghana since 1911. The reasons given were that he was 'a staunch member of the … NLM and … a member of the UP'. On 7 November 1958, Cabinet expelled Adamu Dogo for being 'a staunch supporter of the UP'. Similarly political reasons were adduced in numerous cases throughout the course of 1958.[53]

Other deportation orders simply got rid of 'foreign' Africans, the vast majority of whom had no criminal antecedents. On one occasion Cabinet's discussion of over 20 such cases[54] gave as the proximate causes of ending long residence and the consequent breaking-up of families, a handful of mostly trivial allegations. The offences of deportees included 'is considered quarrelsome, greedy and dishonest and has been suspected of having taken part in burglaries', 'is considered to have a pugnacious and violent temperament and to be a heavy drinker' and 'a born troublemaker … is said to be dishonest'. Attempts to restrain government by the invocation of *habeas corpus* in the courts enjoyed a brief success when the minister and the chief of police were found to have been in contempt in the case of three deportees. Within three days the Assembly had passed, in only 35 minutes, a Deportation Indemnity Act which indemnified them.[55] All of this makes for uneasy reading today. That unease is underlined by the announcement that the deportee Kwadjo Aforna, aged 105, who was taken to Keta hospital after collapsing before he could be physically taken across the Togo border, had died there on 22 August. There is a whiff of what we would now call ethnic cleansing about some of this which marries uneasily with the pan-African pretensions of the government.

But things moved more notably against prominent members of the opposition in the course of 1958. House searches by the police extended to those of Members

[52] Cabinet, memorandum by the minister of the interior, 28 October 1958, NAG ADM 13/2/53.

[53] See for example Cabinet papers for: 28 January, NAG ADM 13/2/44; 29 August, NAG ADM 13/2/51; 16 September, 17 October, 29 October, NAG ADM 13/2/41, NAG ADM 13/2/53; 2 December, NAG ADM 13/2/55 .

[54] On 18 March and 1 April 1958, NAG ADM 13/2/45 and NAG ADM 13/2/46.

[55] The act was pushed through on Christmas Eve 1958.

of the Legislative Assembly by July.[56] As a result of things said at an opposition rally at Osu on 18 September, R.R. Amponsah, a stalwart of the NLM and now of the UP,[57] was arrested and charged with 'uttering seditious words', but was later released following his acquittal on 13 December. By the end of the year, the Preventive Detention Act[58] was used to arrest, without trial, 43 people including the entire executive committee of the Accra branch of the UP and prominent opposition politicians like Dzenkle Dzewu and Ashie Nikoi, all of whom were alleged to have been involved in an assassination plot against Nkrumah, Edusei and Kofi Baako.[59] Very shortly thereafter the act was used to 'nail' Amponsah (only days after he had been freed by the court) and Modesto Apaloo, a prominent Anlo Ewe member of the NLM and, after its abolition,[60] the UP. If justification was to sought, it could be found in Kojo Botsio's pugnacious address to the All-African Peoples' Organization on 11 December. 'Once independence is attained our duty is to consolidate that power ... our first obligation is the security of the state. When strong measures are taken to establish the authority of the state against any subversion – this is done to prove that Africans are capable of ruling themselves.'

The only good news so far as chiefs were concerned was that Edusei was moved sideways as minister of communications and on 16 November 1958 the prime minister took over the portfolio of the minister of the interior. This was almost certainly the result of an extraordinary speech of Edusei's on 13 November in which he was quoted as saying that all passports of opposition politicians would be impounded. 'So long as I am Minister of the Interior I will see to it that the movements of these Opposition members within Ghana is restricted by the police. What is coming is coming. I will arrest all opposition members and detain them.'[61] The prime minister's office was quick to deny that these ideas represented government policy. Edusei's voice was ultimately too extreme and harsh. But there is enough evidence to suggest that the domestic assertiveness of government was not the work of just one man.

Ghana's first full year of independence was, as we have seen, bittersweet. The great national and international achievements were matched by domestic politics increasingly dominated by rough justice, or worse – no justice. In Akyem Abuakwa

---

[56] On Sunday 6 July the houses of the UP MLAs R.R. Amponsah, Joe Appiah and B.F. Kusi were ransacked by police.

[57] He shared the platform with Daniel Cobblah, amongst the greatest of Ghana's modern potters, who was also arrested.

[58] This was finally drafted at a grim Cabinet meeting on 27 May 1958, when not only were the final touches to the PDA made but seven deportation orders of a plainly political sort were approved. Cabinet, NAG ADM 13/2/48.

[59] This was the Zenith 7 plot. The prime minister said that it was 'based upon a revival of a paramilitary organisation used in the past in a campaign of terrorism and violence ... a 'secret cell' system'. Cabinet, 7 November 1958, NAG ADM 13/2/54.

[60] By the Prevention of Discrimination Act which was finally drafted in August 1957. It was intended to outlaw, the minister of justice wrote, 'any organisation which has a name of national significance, even though in practice it is restricted to members of a particular tribe, race or religion'. Cabinet, NAG ADM 13/2/40.

[61] The fullest report is to be found in *The Ashanti Pioneer*, 15 November 1958.

today older people remember this as a terrible period not least because nature seemed to conspire with humankind. The short dry season, *openimaa*, during which farmers burnt their farms and did their second-season planting usually only lasted for two weeks or so. That of 1958 was unusually long and crops planted during the rains of April and May were drying out. Cocoa pods ripened prematurely and seedlings showed signs of withering. Rivers became streams and wells dried up. By the end of the year food was increasingly expensive. At the same time the world cocoa price again fell below £300 per ton at the turn of the year. By 31 January there were 37 members of the UP in preventive detention. For those on all sides of the political divide, these were dark days.

11

'Loyal Co-operation with the Government'

Considering the dangers of the two years immediately preceding independence, the speed with which the government had cowed intransigent chieftaincy was remarkable. The change was apparent in a symbolic but personally deeply tragic moment. In a grand, conciliatory gesture the government invited the Asantehene to Accra for the celebrations marking the second anniversary of the gaining of independence. This was to be his first visit to the capital since 1946. In the course of this he broadcast to the nation. 'It is my hope that all traces of bitterness shall fade away and give way to an atmosphere of amity and friendliness. Let us therefore all resolve to co-operate and support the Government to shape the destiny of our beloved country ... we must endeavour to cast away every mis-understanding ... I wish to thank Premier Nkrumah personally for his interest in me and my people and I assure him of my co-operation and support.'[1] The contrast between his earlier statements and these fulsome remarks could hardly be more striking. Less than two years previously he had warned that 'chiefs who supported the Government would suffer equally from the iniquitous laws the Government was passing'.[2] His presence in Accra and his remarks summon up the sad images of defeated kings in Roman triumphs. Even if the means might have been harsh, the CPP's campaign against chieftaincy was now beginning to pay serious dividends. The analogy with investment and profit is not mine. Speaking of the Asantehene's visit to Accra, the *Daily Graphic*'s leader of 7 March 1959 spoke of 'an understanding which is bound to yield the highest dividends'.

What had changed the Asantehene's mind? It is obvious that his position had not shifted because of any palpable softening of government attitudes, let alone policy, towards chieftaincy or towards his erstwhile allies in the old NLM. The only viable answer is that he, like many other senior traditional figures, was now

---

[1] *Daily Graphic*, 13 March 1959.
[2] This speech of 18 January 1956 was Exhibit 56 before the Sarkodee Addo Commission of 1958. It was not challenged by the Asantehene's lawyers and can thus be assumed to be authentic. NAG ADM 5/3/194.

both extremely frightened as well as finally aware that beyond doubt he had been politically defeated. He feared not only the hand of government. At an emergency meeting of the Kumasi State Council on 28 January, the Asantehene claimed that a plot to kill him had been uncovered. The plotters were not his old enemies in the CPP but Asante diehards motivated by the Asantehene's new expressions of support for government. But the defeat by government was complete. This was widely recognized and was underlined in a broadcast by Kofi Baako on 25 October 1958, when he was confident enough to say that it was 'obvious ... that the chiefs of Ghana have realised that the future of the Chiefs and Chieftaincy lies in loyal co-operation with the Government'.

Not every chief caved in without some measure of protest. In a letter to his people, which merits quotation *in extenso* for its dignified if tragic message, the 98-year-old chief of Ntonso[3] wrote: ' Ntonso has always been a peaceful place ... it would be unfortunate if you chose to propagate disunity ... Your main concern is to urge and get me to declare my unflinching and loyal support to the govern-ment within a week. You threaten that my failure to do your bidding may result in some unpleasant action being taken against me.'[4] His refusal to do as he was asked, to come out in support of the government, led to his destoolment shortly thereafter.

There was by now little fight left amongst the chiefs and that is very clear from the remarkably depressing recorded minutes of the regional Houses of Chiefs. What was remitted for their consideration tended to be unimportant and what they could and could not do was closely ordered by the minister of local government. They were also to meet very infrequently. The rules of engagement were spelt out in a somewhat courageous comment by the president of the Eastern House of Chiefs at its inaugural meeting on 17 December 1959. 'It is a plain fact', he said, 'that the chiefs are the same as the Government and automatically anyone who comes to power no doubt will make us experience an unexpected difficulty and even more than what we suffer now.' A few months later, the same House of Chiefs was discussing the government's plans for a republican constitution. One of the chiefs wisely suggested that 'our main duties are to advise the Government ... we are not in a position to openly criticize ... [we should] be more cautious in dealing with the present political trend ... [and] register our loyal support to the Government of the day'.[5] These debates and others in Houses of Chiefs seem to have fulfilled the United Party's MLA Victor Owusu's resigned prophecy during the earlier parliamentary debate on the Houses of Chiefs bill 'which', he said, 'plainly demonstrates the Government's gradual destruction of the institution of Chieftaincy ... the chiefs themselves appear to be quite satisfied with this gradual disintegration'.[6]

[3] Nana Kofi Dei.
[4] *Daily Graphic*, 14 February 1959.
[5] Eastern Region House of Chiefs, Minutes 30 March 1960.
[6] Legislative Assembly Debates, Vol. II, July 1958. p. 245. It was in this debate that Kofi Baako said that 'no good chief should think in terms of power; he should rather think in terms of dignity and respect'.

There was not much more activity amongst the dwindling opposition in the Assembly. The voice of the official opposition became fainter and fainter in the House as well as in the country. By November 1959, S.D. Dombo, a Northern chief, Duori Na, as well as a UP Member of the Legislative Assembly lamented: 'there are now no chiefs ... all the chiefs ran away and those who are remaining are merely stooges of the Government ... It will not be long when we shall hear the Minister of Local Government saying that all the chiefs have agreed that chieftaincy should be abolished.'[7] A month later another opposition member and by then almost the last of the UP members in the House, Jateo Kaleo, called the Constitution (Repeal of Restrictions) Bill 'the final funeral obsequies of chieftaincy in Ghana'.[8]

Although independent chieftaincy, as it had tried to present itself from the 1920s, was most assuredly defeated, chieftaincy itself was not dead. Instead a new kind of chieftaincy was being put in place; it was a kind of chieftaincy that government would tolerate and one which was in turn dependent upon government.[9] Only a chief and hence a chieftaincy sanctioned by government now stood any chance of survival. If this needed any further elaboration it was to come in March 1959 in the form of the Chiefs (Recognition) Bill. This bill was discussed in Cabinet in January. Here the minister of local government reminded colleagues that recent events had unleashed a spate of petitions which alleged that many destoolments and enstoolments had been carried out despite being contrary to custom. It would be difficult not to sympathize with his feelings that 'these cases represent a great waste of time and money ... in many cases it is virtually impossible to determine what the accepted custom is'. Such challenges meandered around the Ghanaian judicial system; those with some latent legal merit or those with the greatest amount of financial backing ended up in the High Court and risked thwarting government intentions. 'In my view', the minister wrote, 'this situation can only be met by drastic action', and that action now included legislation.[10]

The bill ensured that no enstoolment or destoolment could be effective unless it was formally recognized by the government. It went much further than that. It gave government, or more formally the governor-general as the head of state, considerable new powers: 'where ... he considers it to be in the public interest, a person may be ordered to cease to exercise all or certain functions of a Chief despite the fact that he has not been destooled'. By this law the government could now legally depose chiefs and could do so without any recourse to customary laws or practices as their perception of public interest was now to dominate decisions. The bill went even further in allowing government to stipulate that any chief so

---

[7] During the debate on the Stool Property (Recovery and Validation) Bill on 2 November 1959. Legislative Assembly Debates, Vol. 17, 131–4.

[8] Legislative Assembly Debates, 29 February 1960, Vol. 18, p. 113.

[9] Many of the issues addressed in subsequent paragraphs have been studied in great detail in the exceptionally good regional studies of Ahafo by Dunn and Robertson, *Dependence and opportunity*, and of Offinso by R.C. Crook, 'Local elites and national politics in Ghana'.

[10] Cabinet memorandum on chiefs and constitutional disputes by the minister of local government. 16 January 1959, NAG ADM 13/2/59.

deposed could be ordered into internal exile, to live outside the state over which he had been chief. Lastly it protected those chiefs recognized by government from the traditional sanction of destoolment. 'It shall be a criminal offence for anyone to treat as deposed any person the Governor General recognises as a chief and to treat as a chief any person whom the Governor General does not recognize as a chief.' The minister commended the bill to his Cabinet colleagues by stressing that it would 'overcome the many legal difficulties of the present situation and would simplify the work of my Ministry'. What was, however, left out of this persuasive argument was the inherent demolition of the entirety of those historical *raisons d'êtres* of the many forms which chieftaincy had taken in Ghana. The under-pinnings of chieftaincy – history, tradition, customary law – were brushed aside in favour of government convenience. The minister suggested that 'if a chief is prepared to co-operate with the Government, he has nothing to fear from the legislation'.[11] The bill as finally drafted on 13 February 1959[12] totally reconstructed the basis of chieftaincy in modern Ghana. Under the CPP government, chiefs were henceforward to be in very large measure the clients of the government of the day rather than the products of traditional processes. Now, as Dunn and Robertson wrote, 'tenure of chiefly office was undoubtedly dependent on political party affiliation'.[13]

In the light of the attenuated campaigns waged against chieftaincy by CPP governments, the minister's opening remarks when introducing the bill to the House were quite extraordinary. 'By this Bill', Aaron Ofori Atta said, 'the Govern-ment wants to keep Chiefs in the very forefront of the affairs of the country in furtherance of our avowed aim to cherish and uphold the institution of chief-taincy.' The bill was presented as the only solution to genuinely intractable situations in which the appointment and removal of chiefs rested upon an extremely messy mixture of various recensions of customary law with the statutory laws of the state of Ghana. The ensuing debate was, as others before had been, a lame affair and the bill became law. The post-colonial government had by now done enough in both the political and legislative arenas to be largely unafraid of chiefs. It had, moreover, exorcised the spirit of tradition which had haunted and frightened colonial governments for decades. And it had done so by cutting rather than untying the Gordian knot. The CPP government, unlike its more nervous and much less powerful colonial predecessors, could now override customary law and insist upon the primacy of the national government's view of the propriety of individual enstoolments and destoolments. Implicitly traditions regarded as inimical to the prevailing view of what was believed by the government to constitute good government could now be set aside.

Once the bill became law the government went ahead and comprehensively reviewed its recognition of the enstoolment and destoolment of all Ghanaian chiefs. In three remarkable and long Cabinet meetings[14] the government recognized

---

[11] This important Cabinet discussion is in Cabinet papers for 16 January 1959, NAG ADM 13/2/59.

[12] See Cabinet, 13 February 1959, NAG ADM 13/2/57.

[13] *Dependence and opportunity*, p. 204.

[14] On 4, 6 and 25 September 1959. See NAG ADM 13/2/64 and NAG ADM 13/2/66.

the enstoolment of no less than 84 chiefs and the destoolments of a further 32. Some of these were chiefs of considerable status, others were minor figures. Without exception they were chiefs who had been either enstooled or destooled in the months between December 1958 and July 1959. A very considerable degree of government-approved change over who was (and who was not) to be accorded the now much reduced dignity of chieftaincy was achieved in a very short period.[15] Local party activists and regional commissioners had clearly been very busy supporting potential incumbents and destooling those chiefs who were in their way. In many cases such action had engendered protest. But protest could be shrugged aside or suppressed. In Juaben for example the unusual enstoolment of a woman Omanhene[16] who was also a staunch CPP supporter attracted strong opposition from the local youth association, a normally strident pro-CPP group, who argued that it was 'in flagrant violation of custom'. The regional commissioner summoned the chairman of the association and successfully demanded that their protest be withdrawn.[17]

Government also ran roughshod over the previously all-important issues of hierarchy. Most chiefs in Ghana were and are in effect sub-chiefs, owing allegiance to a ranked succession of more and more important figures and ending with their ultimate loyalty to their paramount chief. These tiers of traditional authority were never absolute; seniority was a not infrequent cause of conflict and attempts at *de facto* secession from the authority of this or that state council had occurred before the advent of nationalist government. Such contests were often only the latest stage in age-old disputes. By the end of the 1950s, however, the government had actively inserted itself not merely as the arbiter of such disputes but was actually determining hierarchy.

In some respects this had begun with the countenancing of the separation of the Brong states from the control of the Asantehene and the Asanteman Council. As early as May 1956 the government had begun to draft legislation initially to allow the states of Dormaa and Tekyiman to terminate their allegiance to the Golden Stool and to remove the citizens of those states from the remaining authority of the Asantehene's jurisdiction.[18] The implementation of this was held up by the refusal of the British chief regional officer, Colin Russell, to implement it because 'he considered this Order was based on political rather than administrative arguments'. By the end of February 1957 Cabinet agreed that 'the CRO could not and should not pick and choose in respect of the powers delegated to him ... this delegation of powers should be withdrawn'.[19]

---

[15] Reduced dignity did not imply a lack of power. A chiefly informant of Dunn and Robertson's said: 'If as a CPP man I said that you should be removed now they would remove you'. *Dependence and opportunity*, p. 204.

[16] Nana Juaben Serwah II.

[17] This was reported in the *Daily Graphic*, 18 May 1959.

[18] Memorandum of minister of local government, 'The termination of the allegiance to the Golden Stool', Cabinet, 12 May 1956, NAG ADM 13/2/30.

[19] See Cabinet, 26 February 1957. NAG ADM 13/2/36.

The upshot of the gradual creation[20] of a new region, Brong Ahafo, was immediately political in that it reduced the number of traditional states owing obedience to the Asantehene and the Asanteman Council, thus weakening him and his council. It also demanded the creation of a new hierarchy of chiefs now that the supreme authority of the Asante paramount no longer applied to them. Chiefs previously subordinate to the Asantehene were now elevated to paramountcies and a new table of precedence was constructed for the incipient House of Chiefs for the new Brong-Ahafo Region. The creation of the new region was an inevitably messy affair, not least because in some areas Asante chieftaincies had ancient and legal claims to parcels of land and to the allegiance of clusters of villages within the states which were to constitute the new region. To resolve these problems the minister of local government initially created these anomalous areas as five new states[21] and proposed that their chiefs should all be recognized as paramount chiefs.[22] These government-constructed states and the elevated status of their chiefs had no serious historical or customary justification.

Such elevations were not confined to the possibly necessary readjustments in the wake of creating a new administrative region. For example in mid-1959 government decided that the chief of Effiduase in Ashanti, a reliable pro-CPP figure, should be recognized as a paramount. This was strongly objected to by the chief of Mampong who was, arguably, only second to the Asantehene in terms of hierarchical authority among Asante states. Effiduase traditionally owed its allegiance to the Silver Stool of Mampong and its incumbent as well as to the Asantehene. The government, confident in its authority, overrode the objections of the Mamponghene and his councillors and duly recognized the Effiduasehene as a paramount; now he was formally equal in status to his traditional overlord, the Mamponghene, 'in the best interests of the area and the need to ensure harmony and peace within the Mampong Division'.[23] The recasting of stool allegiances and the restructuring of hierarchies is perversely but strongly reminiscent of the colonial government's restructuring of Asante after 1900 following the arrest of the Asantehene.[24]

The primacy of national government was sometimes more apparent in the detail than it was in big events. By the beginning of 1959, for example, there were several instances where the Asantehene was reported to be routinely and formally accepting the oaths of allegiance from new chiefs whose enstoolments, by most understandings of traditional propriety, had been improperly carried out. The Asantehene was in effect now participating in rubber-stamping government policy, however personally painful it must have been for him and his councillors. As we have seen, there were great pressures imposed upon him and it is unlikely that he

[20] Its final shape was not proclaimed in the *Government Gazette* until 14 March 1959.

[21] By January 1960 two further new states had been created.

[22] See Cabinet, memorandum on the issue by the minister of local government, 4 December 1959. NAG ADM 13/2/67.

[23] See Cabinet for 20 October 1959, NAG ADM 13/2/65.

[24] I owe this point to the acuity of the anonymous reader of this manuscript. For more on the British reconfiguration of Asante see William Tordoff, *Ashanti under the Prempehs*.

145

had any alternative beyond the unthinkable final humiliation of resignation.

The government not only had the power to make or break individual chiefs, it had now given itself powers to act as the ultimate arbiter in chiefly affairs. Although intractable stool disputes were formally brought before a judicial body, the appeals commissioners, their decisions were not binding upon government. The Houses of Chiefs (Amendment) Act now empowered the governor-general in council, a synonym for the minister of local government, to reject the decisions of appeals commissioners. In March 1959 seven such cases were under review.[25] In five of these cases the minister, with Cabinet approval, rejected the reports of the commissioners[26] and resolved these disputes in ways which were more acceptable to the government. It is worth remembering that one of the charges brought against the Okyenhene was that he had flouted decisions made by the appeals commissioners. That government's rejections or acceptances of such decisions were politically motivated is beyond question. In January 1959, a committee of enquiry was established by the minister into a stool dispute in Nsuatre. Its terms of reference included the request that it report on whether 'it was *politically sound* to recognize the reported destoolment of the Ohene of Nsuatre'.[27] The two commissioners charged with this enquiry were senior CPP parliamentarians. Although of minor importance, the Nsuatre case usefully illustrates the politicization of local affairs. The destoolment charges against the chief included the accusation that he had 'contrary to the wishes of the people of Nsuatre identified yourself with forces which are deadly opposed to the Government of Ghana from which you as a chief derive your powers'. The three elders who brought these charges were local CPP activists.[28]

Both the general political climate and the emerging legislative environment had turned rural Ghana into a turkey-shoot for local CPP supporters opposed to individual chiefs. The sheer scale of depositions of the chiefs in this period suggests that it was widely perceived that open season had begun. In Akyem Abuakwa over 100 traditional figures from the most minor of headmen, *adikro*, to the most senior chiefs, including five of the most senior figures under the paramount, the wing chiefs, were destooled in the six months following the final withdrawal of recognition of the Okyenhene. In many cases both the destoolments and the subsequent enstoolments of others fell foul of the usual requirements of custom. But the sheer scale of the depositions probably ensured that tradition could hardly be adhered to; in many ancient states, those traditionally charged with the proper conduct of either of these processes had themselves been either deposed or were facing deposition. A good example of this was the enstoolment of the new Odikro of Apapam.[29] Only two of the seven men regarded by custom as king-makers were in office and hence at the ceremony.

[25] Those of the disputes in Ahanta, Krachi, Attebubu, Kumawu, Mampong, Ada and Ga.
[26] Cabinet, 24 March 1959, NAG ADM 13/2/58.
[27] My emphasis.
[28] See Cabinet papers, 24 February 1959, NAG ADM 13/2/57.
[29] Apapam was part of the Adonten division, the bailiwick of the pro-CPP chief, Kena.

In many areas stools remained vacant as chieftaincy looked more and more fragile. Becoming a chief was less and less regarded as desirable by well-qualified candidates who often surrendered their candidacy in favour of much less interesting kinsmen. Unresolved disputes threw chieftaincy into even further disrepute. As the post of secretary to state councils was frequently in the gift of the chief, many such councils were now without an effective administrative centre and were no longer keeping decent records. Employees of state councils went for weeks and months without wages and little work was being done. Letters went unopened, bills remained unpaid. None of this did much to improve the local standing of traditional authority.

In Akyem Abuakwa, the pro-CPP Adontehene, now acting as regent and expecting to control the election of the new Okyenhene, set out his stall at a bewildering meeting of the Okyeman Council on 5 February. He and his supporters managed to offend custom once again by summoning the meeting on a Wednesday, a traditionally holy day on which meetings had never before been held. The queen-mother of Akyem Abuakwa,[30] an important figure in the state and a key figure in the selection of the next Okyenhene, refused to attend the meeting. For this reason as well as her continued allegiance to the derecognized Okyenhene, this 80-year-old woman was destooled *in absentia*. For similar offences several senior chiefs of Akyem Abuakwa were also banned from entering the palace. Such rulings were without traditional precedent.

The meeting went on to expel journalists from opposition newspapers, including the reporter of the *Ashanti Pioneer* who had the traditional right as a citizen of Akyem Abuakwa to be present. The Adontenhene presided, presumptuously and symbolically from the physical space where the Okyenhene traditionally sits. His pronouncements at the meeting were intensely political. He said that no one who was not a member of the CPP could now become a chief in Akyem Abuakwa. Those who resisted this included many of the Akyem Abuakwa state dignitaries.[31] At almost every turn the regent and his supporters overturned even the most liberal understandings of tradition and custom, words whose meanings were by 1959 more vague than at any previous time.

Stool politics in Akyem Abuakwa ebbed and flowed but always under the astute stage management of the Adontenhene and carefully watched by the man who was the most prominent, powerful member of the Akyem royal family, the minister of local government. By 13 April a new Okyenhene,[32] the 33rd in that kingdom's history, had emerged from the intricate dealings and debates behind closed doors that always characterizes Akan king-making. The enstoolment was a rushed affair and took place only 24 hours after the nomination was announced.[33] It was

---

[30] Nana Pomaa.

[31] Apart from the probably illegally destooled queen-mother, they included the Abontendomhene, the Gyaasehene, the Kyidomhene, Sanaahene, Asafoakiafo,and the Chief Farmer of the state.

[32] He was Kwame Manu, a royal who was to sit with the stool name of Nana Amoako Atta IV.

[33] Compare this with the far more attenuated processes which brought the deposed Okyenhene to the stool after the death of his predecessor in 1943. See R. Rathbone, *Murder and politics in colonial Ghana*.

rumoured that the rush was necessary because the Adontenhene, who had laboured so long and hard to see that the CPP prevailed in the kingdom, was on the point of leaving for London where he had been appointed as Ghana's deputy high commissioner. Like so many rumours in Ghana, this was only half right. It was correct that he was shortly to be leaving Ghana; his labours had instead been rewarded with the even more glittering office of being Ghana's high commissioner in India. There is little doubt that this reward had been contemplated for a while. Speaking at the last meeting of the Joint Provincial Council on 14 November 1958, Nkrumah said that he was prepared to consider the appointment of chiefs to serve on special missions abroad as ambassadors. 'This is a role for which our chiefs will be eminently suited.'[34]

Amoako Atta IV's enstoolment was followed by the predictable destoolment of all the chiefs in the kingdom who had supported his predecessor. A matter of weeks later the prime minister visited the kingdom's capital, Kyebi. For the first time in 10 years CPP flags now flew all over the town; a brave, solitary UP flag had been removed ostensibly because it flew on the spot where the prime minister was to have his official car parked. The new Okyenhene swore personal allegiance to the prime minister whom he would support until his death. 'If even all desert you, I will never desert you',[35] he is reported to have said before asking rather pointedly for government-funded development projects for the area. After being presented with a handsome gift, Nkrumah assured his audience that 'my government is equally determined to examine the existing position under which chieftaincy can be preserved'.[36]

Amoako Atta IV was a representative of a new kind of Ghanaian chief. Chieftaincy, as the prime minister had suggested, would be preserved under his government but it would be chieftaincy of the subservient sort typified by the new Okyenhene. The eminent Northern chief, Tolon Na, speaking at the University College at Legon near Accra repeated the message. 'Chieftaincy and all that it stands for must conform to the changing needs of the people.'[37] He had underlined the point of this comment most recently in his capacity as a Member of Parliament by crossing the floor from the opposition benches to join the CPP. During a visit to the Eastern Regional House of Chiefs in June 1959, Nkrumah was presented with a golden replica of the Akyem Abuakwa state sword, *bosomtwe*, by Amoako Atta IV. The symbolism of this act was not lost on a large audience which included a detachment of over 300 police.

Nkrumah's visit to Kyebi in June was only the first of a number of visits to the capitals of Akan-speaking states in southern Ghana. On each of these occasions he was greeted effusively; Ghanaians revere good manners and appropriate respect. But these visits were undoubtedly intended to be more than just showing the flag,

---

[34] Reported in the *Daily Graphic*, 15 November 1958. Kena was appointed on 10 June 1959 and served with great distinction in New Delhi.

[35] This form of words forms part of the traditional promise of fealty made by Akyem Abuakwa chiefs to their newly enstooled paramount. Few present on this occasion would have missed this meaning.

[36] Quoted in the *Daily Graphic*, 16 June 1959.

[37] *Daily Graphic*, 1 January 1959.

chances to press the flesh. On every occasion the local Omanhene literally paid obeisance to him in the same sort of language as that adopted by Amoako Atta IV. Nkrumah's primacy was being formally acknowledged and, slightly less obviously, so was his victory over them. Nkrumah shared the Ghanaian taste for politeness and none of these visits was made distasteful by any overt show of triumphalism on his part. On the contrary his message was consistently a prayer for putting past differences behind them and the making of new beginnings. But conciliatory as he was, this was implicitly a triumphant progress throughout the Akan kingdoms where he greeted either new incumbents or those who had once counted themselves amongst his enemies but who could no longer do so with impunity. Reading accounts of these visitations, one is uncomfortably reminded of the numerous accounts of earlier times when colonial governors gracefully accepted the expressions of loyalty to the British monarch from African kings. These modern recensions of such durbars were, like their predecessors, dignified but also very sad ceremonies.

A popular chant of the Builders' Brigade, established in 1958,[38] consisted of two lines, repeated over and over again. They caught the new political reality with brutal simplicity. '*Bafuor Akoto dwane o, Nkrumah eba o* / Bafuor Akoto [a founder and then leader of the NLM] ran away, Nkrumah is coming.' So far as obdurate chieftaincy was concerned, Nkrumah and his party, on the brink of going to the country to secure support for the declaration of a republic, was now the absolute master in what was unequivocally his own house.

The changes to the nature of chieftaincy in this brief period following independence were of great importance. At root, the entire basis of chiefly legitimacy and illegitimacy, however robustly contested they were, had been destroyed. It is difficult to dissent from one of the several unsuccessful legal pleas made by Dr J.B. Danquah to save his kinsman Ofori Atta II from being deposed. 'No chief in Ghana', he argued, 'was made a chief by the Queen, nor has the Queen, the sovereign of Ghana, power under the Ghana constitution to make or unmake a chief [a reference to the fact that Ghana was not yet a Republic and that government policy was enacted in the name of the head of state who remained the queen's viceroy, the British governor-general]. Everything about Chieftaincy existed by customary law and that alone.'[39] Although Danquah can often be criticized for spoiling decent arguments by exaggeration, this lean commentary rather precisely captures the harsh novelty of the situation. For the first time in its history Ghana had a government which was prepared not only to control chieftaincy but also one which was consistently to disregard the revered if confusing tangle of what was held to be customary law. What was now formally recognized as chieftaincy had been systematically altered in a relatively short time.

---

[38] A largely unsuccessful project aimed at reducing urban unemployment.

[39] He was before the Accra Divisional Court on 27 January 1959 seeking to quash the legitimacy of Ofori Atta II's removal by *Gazette* notice. The case was covered in the *Daily Graphic*, 28 January 1959.

12

Conclusions

Within the very short compass of less than two decades, the independent political influence of Ghanaian chieftaincy had been virtually extinguished. For many chiefs as well as for those who continued to believe that chieftaincy was one of the irreducible cornerstones of the cultures that together now comprised the modern state of Ghana, this was perceived as a period of tragedy and loss. Some of them undoubtedly had selfish reasons for this regret for, as we have seen, chieftaincy attracted clients and dependents as well as those whose enthusiasm for the institution was more obviously intellectual and moral. And historians are trained to be aware of the distortions that can arise when we 'pity the plumage and forget the dying bird'; it is important to remember that the evidence shows clearly that some sections of chieftaincy had warranted a considerable amount of the criticism which had led to extensive popular distaste in the late colonial period.

Some might argue that chiefs would have been better able to resist the roughness of enforced change had they initiated significant reform of the institution themselves. Others would argue that a modern state like Ghana, under a modernizing regime like that of the CPP, had little room for a system described by Kwame Nkrumah as 'largely feudal'.[1] By the 1950s it was difficult to deny that the mounting evidence suggested that unmodified traditional authority was a barrier against rather than a facilitator of the attractive modernizing, developmental agenda espoused by the CPP from its inception. The CPP shared with the later colonial regime a serious conviction that development required popular involvement and hence participation. Although the more politically sensitive chiefs claimed that they were traditionally obliged to accord with local popular opinion, and some of them certainly ruled in accordance with those values, chieftaincy was always vulnerable to the powerful case against oligarchy and ascription that has been pressed throughout the modern world. However skilful and persistent CPP

---

[1] He was reported to have said this at a press conference in New Delhi on 29 December 1958. See the *Daily Graphic*, 30 December 1958.

propaganda may have been, it alone did not create the negative image of chieftaincy standing for the past but had, rather, built upon that popular perception.

The reduction of chiefly significance was carried out roughly but it was carried out by a popularly elected government which had, by independence, won three fairly conducted general elections and had secured large parliamentary majorities in each of these. In the period between independence day and the inauguration of the First Republic in mid-1960, that parliamentary majority had steadily increased as members of the Assembly defensively or opportunistically crossed the floor of the House to the government benches. The reforms were, moreover, carried out under the evolving laws of the new state. However unwelcome some of that legislation might have been, these were properly drafted instruments, many of which had received the endorsement, after debate, of the legislature. If much of the fundamental structure of chieftaincy had been undermined, it had been undermined by a demonstrably popular government acting within its own laws. The legality of government actions could be and occasionally was tested by the country's courts.

If further proof of the government's popularity was necessary, it was soon to be in place. In April 1960, Ghana again went to the polls. The electorate was asked to approve the new republican constitution and to elect its first president of the Republic of Ghana. Although those who opposed Nkrumah and the CPP at the time, as well as some scholars, have doubted the overall honesty of that process,[2] nearly 90 per cent of those Ghanaians who voted endorsed the new constitution and then voted for Nkrumah as their president. Even if we choose to regard these numbers as, in part, the product of electoral fraud, there was other evidence to suggest that opposition to the CPP regime had dwindled significantly. The United Party, a legal and necessary recension of the National Liberation Movement since parties based on ethnicity were now outlawed, underwent a series of defeats in local council and parliamentary by-elections. These by-elections were necessary as a number of MPs were now disqualified for having been arrested under the Preventive Detention Act. That at Wenchi caused by Professor K.A. Busia's flight into exile was a violent affair and there were at least three deaths. Several UP activists were placed under preventive detention orders as a result of this. Some of the CPP's electoral success might be explained by the bandwagon effect of the CPP's victories in the previous years, amplified by the party's much greater access to campaigning resources. Some of it is explained, however, by the fact that overt opposition was increasingly viewed as a dangerous occupation.

These dangers were more substantial than mere threats. As we have already seen, the Preventive Detention Act had swept up and imprisoned many significant opposition figures. By March 1959 just under 50 people were detained, without trial, under the act. This number was to grow. Fifteen UP members were detained in November 1959, including one of the founders of the NLM, the Asantehene's chief *okyeame*, Bafour Akoto. The charge against him was that 'since 1954 he has consistently shown active opposition to Government decisions and policy'.[3] It had

---

[2] Most cogently by Dennis Austin in *Politics in Ghana*, pp 387–95.
[3] Cabinet, 6 November 1959, NAG ADM 13/2/66.

also removed many insignificant people; one did not have to be a national figure to be apprehensive. Samuel Codjoe, 'a supporter of the United Party and a regular attendant at its public rallies', had been incautious. He had read of the assassination of an MP in Ceylon in the *Daily Graphic* and allegedly had remarked that 'the same thing will happen to Dr. Kwame Nkrumah'. The accusation in the official papers which swept him off into confinement without trial read that 'you informed other persons that you favoured the assassination of the Prime Minister and said that you had information that such assassination would take place'. The same Cabinet meeting condemned Nana Kwadjo Darko, the chief of Nkonya Ahundwo. His offence was that ' [you] had pledged your support and used your influence as a chief to persuade others to support a movement [the Togoland Congress] whose object it is to transfer the allegiance of a part of Ghana to a neighbouring state'.[4]

Members of Parliament who were detained under the Preventive Detention Act now automatically lost their seats as the new National Assembly (Disqualification) Act of 1959 disqualified from sitting those who 'failed to carry out their parliamentary duties'; manifestly it was impossible to carry out those duties from prison. At a stroke prominent opposition politicians like Modesto Apaloo and R.R. Amponsah lost their seats and, as we have seen, the CPP went on to win most of the resulting by-elections. Others, like K.A. Busia, chose political exile rather than risking imprisonment without trial.[5] In June 1959 Cabinet was discussing what became the False Reports Act.[6] The original draft of this measure made it illegal to utter 'any false statement affecting the reputation or credit of Ghana or of the Government of Ghana'. This measure explicitly ruled out any defence based upon public interest arguments.

Shortly after the enactment of this law, a new and more restrictive Sedition Bill was discussed in Cabinet and subsequently approved. Under this law the definition of sedition now included bringing the government of Ghana into 'hatred, ridicule or contempt'[7] and exciting 'disaffection against the government of Ghana'. It was now a criminal offence to 'raise discontent or disaffection among the peoples of Ghana'.[8] It is hard to conceive of much useful criticism, let alone organized opposition, which could comfortably claim to be within the legal bounds of such a law.

The intimidatory use of deportation continued in this period. With some courage the National Union of Ghana Students had criticized this and the Preventive Detention Act at their annual general meeting on 24 January 1959. Cabinet's initial reaction was to consider seriously the withdrawal of scholarships

---

[4] Cabinet, 29 October 1959, NAG ADM 13/2/64.

[5] And of course J.B. Danquah was to die in Nsawam prison in 1964 during his second period of detention under the act. The record suggests that had he been given the medical attention he frequently requested this tragedy might have been averted. See Report of the Commission of Enquiry ... into the conditions prevailing in the Ghana Prisons Service. (Chairman Sir Edward Asafu-Adjaye), Accra 1967, NAG ADM 5/3/164.

[6] Cabinet, 16 June 1959, NAG ADM 13/2/61.

[7] A phrase borrowed from the English laws of libel and slander.

[8] Cabinet, 9 October 1959, NAG ADM 13/2/64.

from all members of the union's executive but they were persuaded to 'reprimand them rather than ruin them' by the minister for education.[9] In June 1959 Cabinet considered a list of 113 people the minister of the interior wished to deport. The charge against all but 13 of them was that they had been or were active members of the NLM or the UP.[10] At another meeting of Cabinet in September 1959, the deportation of 13 people who 'have interfered in Ghanaian politics, have flouted the authority of and have incited people against the Government' was considered. They were all accused, amongst other things, of a charge which was being increasingly used by the government, that of 'subversion'. In most modern states subversive foreigners are regularly deported. In these cases, however, there was no evidence beyond the word of the regional commissioner that the deportees had committed any offence whatever. As the minister of the interior, A.E.A. Inkumsah, wrote in his Cabinet memorandum: 'no police reports have been made of these people's nationalities or activities ... the information ... though not obtained through the normal official channels, is correct'.[11] Only two days later Cabinet approved the deportation of an 80-year-old man on the recommendation of the regional commissioner for the Volta Region.[12] His offences were membership of the Togoland Congress and the UP. He had lived in Ghana since the age of 10.[13] In his prorogation speech to the House on 19 June 1959 the prime minister said that ' it has been necessary to deal decisively with a comparatively small number of residents of foreign extraction who, while enjoying Ghana's hospitality, have sought to interfere in her domestic politics to the detriment of good government'.

Opposition, such as it was, was being closely monitored by the Special Branch of the police service. Its reports were discussed by Cabinet's National Defence Council, a body which included not only the elected ministers Nkrumah, Ako Adjei, Botsio, Gbedemah and the western regional commissioner, but also George Padmore[14] and a number of senior figures in the Ghanaian defence community, some of whom were expatriates on contract.[15] While the proceedings of this committee were probably little different from those in its equivalents in other democracies at the time, they are chilling to read. The Special Branch was, for example, being politically directed, presumably with the active consent of the commissioner of police,[16] to investigate 'dangerous sources of subversion such as ... the reliability of persons holding positions of trust in Government Service'.

Despite its overt sensitivity to the requirements of the law, the government was increasingly circumventing the legislature and public scrutiny in favour of more

---

[9] Cabinet, 16 June 1959, NAG ADM 13/2/61.

[10] *Ibid.*

[11] Cabinet, 16 September 1959, NAG ADM 13/2/64. In the event some of those the minister wished to deport were merely to suffer 'internal exile' by being banned from living in their home city of Kumasi, as he could not show that they were not Ghanaians.

[12] C.H. Chapman.

[13] Cabinet, 18 September 1959, NAG ADM 13/2/64.

[14] Then acting as Nkrumah's advisor on African affairs.

[15] See Cabinet, 4 March 1959, NAG ADM 13/2/58

[16] E.R.T. Madjitey.

direct governance. For example the Statutory Instruments Bill allowed the attorney-general to decide which orders made legally by government under current legislation needed to be published and thus open to scrutiny. Those which needed to be gazetted were to be regarded as legislative. The others were henceforward known as executive instruments and were not published. The prime minister, who brought the draft bill to Cabinet, concluded his remarks by saying: 'It may thus be possible to save the expense of publishing in the Gazette Instruments such as Deportation Orders which relate only to individuals'.[17] Executive Instruments, unpublished decrees made by Cabinet, were used to regulate chieftaincy and it is for this reason that Cabinet records are such valuable sources for this period of the history of Ghana's chieftaincies.

An even more direct form of government was being exercised by the regional and district commissioners. Without exception these officers were regulating regional affairs in considerable detail. Their roles were expanding and by the beginning of 1960 no less than 26 functions previously reserved to the minister of local government under the Local Government Ordinance had been delegated to regional commissioners. These powers enabled them to control in many senses of that word the workings of local councils. Regional commissioners were of course answerable directly to the minister of the interior and Cabinet but not to the House. All of them were CPP MPs and in terms of protocol enjoyed the rank of Cabinet ministers. The personnel changed from time to time, but by June 1959 there were seven of them: C.H. Chapman in Ho, C. de Graft Dickson in Kumase, J.E. Hagan in Cape Coast, L.R. Abavana in Tamale, E.H.T. Korbo in Koforidua and S.W. Yeboah in Sunyani. There was also a special duties regional commissioner, Yeboah Afari, who was not regionally based and was deployed as a trouble-shooter. That some regional commissioners tended to act as local potentates, masters of all they surveyed, without reference to the minister, is the stuff of some bitter local memories. It is also suggested by a Cabinet discussion which resulted in a strong letter from the prime minister to all regional commissioners which reminded them that 'they should always act in consultation with the Minister ... but also in accordance with directions issued by him'.[18]

Regional commissioners carried out executive instruments but they were also, as we have seen, immensely powerful in that it was their advice which influenced Cabinet to enstool or destool this or that chief, to deport individuals, to empanel or disempanel individuals from local courts and to suspend or support local councils. Examples abound of how this 'line management' worked. In November 1959, the minister of local government was able to secure Cabinet approval for an executive instrument which banished the destooled Omanhene of Otwereso, an old NLM supporter, from his home town. The minister wrote: 'My colleague the Regional Commissioner ... has advised that he has reason to believe that not only is the ex-chief engaged in activities calculated to hamper the general progress of

---

[17] Cabinet, 3 November 1959, NAG ADM 13/2/66.
[18] Cabinet, 2 February 1960, NAG ADM 13/2/69.

the area, but also that his conduct is a continual source of disunity and unrest.'[19] The role of district commissioners was, the prime minister said, 'vital ... in explaining Government policy ... but also ... in promoting an atmosphere of political tranquality [*sic*] throughout the country'. How some of that 'tranquality' was sometimes arrived at is suggested by an interesting memorandum by the prime minister following a meeting he held with regional and district commissioners in November 1959. They had asked for more co-operation with the police service as they had 'experienced difficulties when requests for assistance for police protection and backing are made'. DCs would, the prime minister noted, 'require wider powers over the police'. The prime minister added, approvingly, that regional and district commissioners wanted such powers 'in order to compare favourably with their counterparts in the neighbouring French Territories'. At the time this curious remark was drafted, the French territories were, of course, still formally under French colonial rule. Cabinet concluded that from now on the police should salute district commissioners and that the criminal code should now include the offences of insulting DCs, threatening DCs and 'refusal to attend the call of DCs'.[20] Dunn and Robertson's interviews a decade later revealed that 'for the majority of Ahafo citizens, the CPP District Commissioner seems to have epitomized the major vices of the government he represented – above all its bullying qualities'.[21] That such reflections and recommendations recall so much of what was most objectionable about the colonial mentality is perhaps a token of just how direct and unparticipatory rural governance had become.

The purpose of these paragraphs is not merely to underline the authoritarian nature of Ghana's government in the last half of the 1950s. This has been noted by previous scholars just as it was suffered by too many Ghanaians at the time. The point is rather to suggest that it is immensely difficult to assess the real feelings of Ghanaians when it comes to political changes in this period. With an increasingly hobbled press, a shrinking, silent or silenced parliamentary opposition, and government domination of virtually all recorded expression, quite what ordinary Ghanaians made of the radical transformation of chieftaincy, let alone any other processes in the years after independence, must remain something of a mystery.

By the time that the new republic was inaugurated, chiefs had lost virtually every element of their earlier autonomy. By 1959 the previous mandatory reservation of one-third of the membership of local councils to the nominees of traditional councils had been statutorily removed. Chiefs no longer had direct access to stool revenue. The collection of such revenue along with local taxation rested with local councils. The administration of stool lands lay ultimately with government in Ashanti, Brong-Ahafo and Akyem Abuakwa by mid-1959. After then central administrative control was extended to all other areas of the country. Such control was, the minister argued, 'beneficial to all concerned'.[22] Under the

[19] Cabinet, 17 November 1959, NAG ADM 13/2/66.
[20] Cabinet, 8 December 1959, NAG ADM 13/2/67.
[21] *Dependence and opportunity*, p. 125.
[22] Cabinet, 4 August 1959, NAG ADM 13/2/63.

Stool Lands Amendment Act of 1960, the president was now empowered to act as 'substitute[d] for the occupants of Stools as trustee of the Stool Lands' where there was conflict between stools, as there was in Brong-Ahafo and Ashanti. 'In my view', the minister of local government wrote, 'no useful purpose will be served by going into the historical or legal claims.'[23] The financing of chiefs and their traditional councils lay in the hands of local and municipal councils, most of which were dominated by members of the government party and whose policies and practices were frequently steered by regional and district commissioners. There was no legislation which laid down the duties, let alone the rights, of chiefs and thus rectitude and its opposite were matters which were judged by the minister of local government. Neither enstoolments nor destoolments had any effect unless they were recognized by the government and, after mid-1960, by the president.

Irrespective of history and custom, paramount chiefs were now paramounts only when government gazetted them as paramounts. Similarly erstwhile paramounts could find themselves reduced to more junior status by executive instrument. Chiefs could also be appointed and removed by executive instrument. Chiefs could be imposed on areas which had not previously had chiefs. Local failure to recognize a government-approved chief had become a criminal offence.[24] The government could and did pay no attention to the customary decisions of state councils; it was no more obliged by law to heed or follow the adjudications of its own appeals commissioners in chieftaincy matters when it chose not to do so, as we have already seen.[25] This tendency was to continue; in 1959 the state council of Ahanta refused to recognize the installation of Kojo Tah as Omanhene of Ahanta. The appeals commissioner supported their right to do so. The minister of local government informed his colleague that 'I am advised by the Minister of the Interior, within whose constituency ... [the matter] has arisen that the appellant is de facto Chief ... and commands the support of an overwhelming majority of his subjects ... I therefore recommend that Kojo Tah be recognized.'[26] Kojo Tah was a pro-CPP man who had supported his local member, the minister of the interior, Inkumsah. On 8 March 1960, Cabinet approved 'the recommendation by the Regional Commissioner, Ashanti' for the enstoolment of the Odikro of Chichiwere, even though the state council did not agree with this. Cabinet also overruled the appeals commissioners when they held that the Manso Nkwanta state council, a pro-CPP council, had been wrong to destool the Tetremhene.[27] The obvious lack of anything approaching due process and the importance of personal and party influence in the Ahanta case is striking, but it was far from unique. By March 1959

---

[23] Cabinet, 18 November 1960, NAG ADM 13/2/76.

[24] This seems to have happened first in Kwawu in December 1959 where an executive instrument made it an offence *not* to recognize the newly installed Bukuruwahene. This became national law under the Chieftaincy Act (No. 81) of 1961.

[25] The Houses of Chiefs (Amendment) Act gave the governor-general in council (the minister of local government) the power to reverse or agree to the decisions of the appeals commissioners.

[26] Cabinet, 31 July 1959, NAG ADM 13/2/62.

[27] Cabinet, 8 March 1960, NAG ADM 13/2/70.

the government had rejected five of the decisions of the appeals commissioners in the eight stool disputes recently considered by them.[28]

There was now no legal requirement for the government to listen to, let alone act upon, the advice proffered by the Houses of Chiefs and in any case some of these, especially that of Asante, were now to a large extent packed by government-appointed chiefs. Some met very infrequently. The Eastern Regional House literally fell down in 1964 and lay in ruins for nearly two years before the government provided £3,000 of the £10,000 needed for its rebuilding. Chiefs and their affairs were increasingly ordered by a combination of local councils which were for the most part hostile to traditional authority, regional commissioners who were answerable only to the minister of local government, and from 1960, by a president operating under a constitution which enabled him to 'give directions by legislative instrument' against which there were no appeals allowed. The legal role of chiefs had virtually disappeared and the residual function of state councils to hear cases seems to have been little used. Village development committees whose creation had been encouraged by government and which had been in many cases initially chaired by chiefs were taken over by local CPP branches and were sucked into local administration. The real value of chiefly salaries had sunk in real terms but they were frequently not paid as the paymasters were cash-strapped local councils which frequently retained hostility to individual chiefs and chieftaincy in general. The contrast with the powers enjoyed by chiefs less than 20 years previously is very stark indeed.

It is possible to argue that by the mid-1950s the CPP government was bent upon the destruction of chieftaincy by all means open to it. By denying chiefs access to real power through local government reform, judicial tinkering and then cutting them off from direct access to traditional revenues, they had become shadows of their predecessors of the 1930s. In material terms, the government could so starve chieftaincy of power and resources entirely constitutionally; but the prominent role of some chiefs, and most significantly those in the Akan-speaking world, as activists or symbols in opposition politics from the end of 1954 greatly complicated the process. Just as the CPP in its earliest manifestations had successfully sought rural support from those who felt alienated from specific chiefs, from 1954 opposition political rhetoric actively courted chiefs and their supporters. Chieftaincy was painted as the very essence of Ghanaian life which was being crushed by the CPP's centralism and its vision of a unitary, modernizing Ghanaian citizenry. This appeal was most potent amongst many in the already aggrieved Ashanti Region but it played reasonably well elsewhere.

Although there is no direct evidence to support this, CPP tacticians presumably learnt in time that the vast well of distaste for chieftaincy, from which they had drawn so successfully, was far from universal. Although individual chiefs had attracted opprobrium, and in many cases for very good reasons, chieftaincy retained a significant place in the hearts and minds of many Ghanaians. Where perceptions of regional deprivation were felt and most especially when a view of

[28] Cabinet, 24 March 1959, NAG ADM 13/2/58.

157

the CPP as an essentially self-serving southern party emerged, chiefs could be presented as potent symbols of locality and bruised particularity. The process in which a new counter-offensive was planned by the CPP is hidden from us as there are no available documentary records of the deliberations of the party's central committee. Logically, however, it seems likely that a new tactic of turning chiefs towards support for the government party first emerged in the successful attempt to split the Ashanti Region, and hence the power of the Asantehene and his Asanteman Council, by promising and eventually creating a new Brong-Ahafo Region out of Asante's western marches. By 1956 it seems clear that the CPP's earlier intentions to rid the country of what many of their activists regarded as the anachronism of chieftaincy had been replaced by an active campaign to bring as many chiefs as was possible within the CPP's fold.

The implicit advantages of supporting the government party were not, as we have seen, lost on many southern chiefs. Government ministers, parliamentarians and regional commissioners publicly as well as privately threatened that failure to support the government risked the denial by government of local development projects, with serious consequences for communities which hankered after decent water supplies, schools, clinics, infrastructural development and electrification. As the sanctions against opposition increased, the threat of regional deprivation was joined by a mounting sense that opposition was a dangerous occupation. At a material level then, it is relatively easy to understand why overt chiefly hostility to the government all but disappeared in the years immediately following independence.

Such explanations, however, marginalize the politics of chieftaincy itself. Although the assault upon chieftaincy had been sustained and extensive, chiefs had considerable difficulty in assembling anything that might appear to be, let alone act as, a united front. A partial explanation of that might be that they lacked the resources and modern political experience to develop organized resistance of that sort. But it is important to recognize that while we – and the CPP – might see chieftaincy as a singular institution with a raft of recent common experience, this did not reflect local political realities. In particular it ignores the fact that chiefs had always been in constant competition with one another, struggling for control over people and land.[29] Neighbouring chiefs both high and low always sought to maximize the extent of their command and inevitably this brought with it unending conflict. The late Dormaahene, an early convert to the CPP colours, commented: 'we were all at war with one another. We were all struggling for control of villages and rivers and markets. It was easy to play divide and rule with us.'[30]

The existence of legislation such as the Preventive Detention Act provided a new avenue for factions in stool disputes to denigrate their opponents by fingering them for being members of the opposition. An example of this is provided in Jamase at the end of 1960. The chairman of the local CPP branch, the Jamasehene and a subchief denounced seven local men agitating for the removal of the

[29] This is further elaborated for Akyem Abuakwa in R. Rathbone, 'Defining Akyemfo; the construction of citizenship in Akyem Abuakwa'.

[30] Interview with Nana Agyeman Baadu, Accra, 25 February 1996. This extremely important and highly educated figure in the history of the creation of the Brong-Ahafo Region sadly died in 1998.

Jamasehene because 'they have dedicated themselves to the United Party's policy of preaching false gospel against the Government'. The regional commissioner, in agreeing with the need to detain these opponents of the chief, added: 'I wish to stress the importance of protecting the interests of our supporters by way of proving to the rivals that we have the benefits ... the detention of these people will push some fear into the people who just adhere to whatever they are told to do.' In this case entire villages were indicted as 'hot beds for political unrest' by the regional commissioner.[31] Such competition was fought out not merely in wrangles over individual chieftaincies but also over inter-state issues like boundaries and jurisdictions, some of which had dragged on for decades in the courts. There were also frequent struggles over the all-important issue of who owed allegiance to whom.

The CPP government's ability to acknowledge or to debar individuals' rights to be regarded as chiefs necessarily courted the support of aspirants to chieftaincy. More importantly perhaps the government now exercised its legal right to create traditional states. While this is obviously an oxymoron, it was extremely important. Irrespective of history and tradition, it was now possible for any Omanhene or even town headman, *odikro*, to apply to the ministry of local government for recognition of his, and occasionally her, town as a state. Similarly it was open to chiefs to ask for the recognition of themselves as paramounts.

As we have seen, this conjoined policy was initially deployed in the case of the Brong chieftaincies where the recognition of new paramounts enabled some of these states to escape the traditional control of the Asantehene, their previous overlord. The political intentions of that are inescapable. It was a policy that was then to proceed to do signal service in breaking the power of the Asantehene within Asante itself. By the late 1950s, government recognition of new paramountcies had assured that the old Asanteman Council had been significantly diluted by a large influx of newly recognized paramount chiefs, all of whom were government supporters. This policy remained in force for some years. In June 1960 Cabinet considered the applications of no less than 19 *amanhene* for recognition of their towns as states and themselves as paramounts.[32] The minister of local government acknowledged 'the dangers inherent in a multiplicity of states' but went on to ask for Cabinet's 'more sympathetic consideration to applications from chiefs in Ashanti'. Accordingly, he asked them to now limit government recognition of new states 'to chiefs owing direct allegiance to the Asantehene'.[33] The near unity of Asante chieftaincy behind the NLM in the period 1954–7 was finally broken by this strategy.

What drove individual *amanhene* to seek paramount status for themselves and state status for their towns or villages was partly a matter of personal gain. Chiefs

---

[31] Cabinet, 16 December 1960, NAG ADM 13/2/77. A few months earlier an attempt to destool the Chief of Adansi state had been made. Amongst the destoolment charges is to be found the charge that he was 'feigning to be a supporter of the Convention Peoples' Party'. NAG ADM 13/2/74.

[32] This was a relatively small list of applicants. On 5 August 1960 Cabinet considered 49 applications, 34 of which 'have the strong endorsement of the Regional Commissioner concerned'. NAG ADM 13/2/74.

[33] Cabinet, 28 June and 5 August 1960, NAG ADM 13/2/72.

enjoying paramount rank, almost all of whom were in public at least staunch supporters of the CPP, received a government subsidy.[34] The number of newly recognized chiefs resulted in a mounting bill. In August 1960 Cabinet rewrote its rules on 'upgrading chiefs'. In future applications would only be considered 'on the strict understanding that no subsidy will be granted' and that 'in view of the increasing number of applications ... the Government will be unable in future to bear the burden of providing subsidies at the present rates to Paramount Chiefs ... and that this responsibility should be accepted by the Traditional Councils'.[35] Despite such worries, the government went on to endorse the creation of no fewer than 10 new states in the Brong-Ahafo Region only one week after signalling its fears about the proliferation of traditional states.

Having created a significant number of 'reliable' chiefs, the government was now faced not only with an increasing bill for their maintenance but a further problem for which they were not prepared. They had created a new and somewhat chaotic universe in which traditional hierarchies, however oppressive these might have been historically, had been dismantled or distorted. Endless new arguments about who owed allegiance to whom increased in arithmetic progression as the number of states and paramounts increased.

Obviously in previous years government had helped create that chaos not only by the sheer numbers of their upgradings but also by their earlier instrumental legislation. Some of that had been drafted with the clear political intention of making it easier for opponents of pro-NLM chiefs, especially in Asante, to defy their para-mounts. As we saw earlier, the politically provocative State Councils Amendment Bill of 1956 allowed sub-chiefs to appeal over the heads of their paramounts against decisions made by state councils dominated by those paramounts. The *post hoc* argu-ment for the drafting of this bill was that 'there were so many instances of Para-mount Chiefs using the State Councils as instruments of political terrorisation'.[36]

By the end of the 1950s, however, the rural political terrain had altered and the country had, in the words of the minister of local government, 'returned to more healthy political conditions'. By this he meant that Ghana now enjoyed or endured a situation in which, almost without exception, paramount chiefs had either swung their support behind the government or had actually been created by that govern-ment. But that earlier legislation had been designed to undermine the authority of paramount chiefs and it still lay on the statute books. It was, the minister now argued, a 'provision [which] reduces the status of a Paramount Chief in his own community and also weakens his authority'. The earlier legislation was designed to hurt pro-NLM paramounts; now the new breed of paramounts were CPP men and they needed protection. In further amending the Houses of Chiefs Bill the government returned to the original legal position whereby appeal against state council decisions was allowed to paramount chiefs alone.[37] Although a matter of

---

[34] Of £600 for paramount chiefs.
[35] Cabinet, 5 August 1960, NAG ADM 13/2/74.
[36] Cabinet memorandum by the minister of local government, 12 January 1960, NAG ADM 13/2/68.
[37] *Ibid.*

detail, this legal reversion suggests, entirely correctly, that chieftaincy was, by the dawn of the First Republic, seen by the government as under its control and as a part of its own extensive corporation.

This turbulent history suggests that the transformation of chieftaincy in Ghana was not the result of the kinds of organic change which result from the varied processes of modernization. It was in large measure the product of a battle for control of the countryside which was very clearly won by the governing political party. Although the CPP had been committed to something close to the destruction of chieftaincy, political expediency eventually suggested that it needed instead to create an entirely different kind of chieftaincy. This was to be a chieftaincy entirely dependent upon the government for its legitimacy, maintenance and survival and hence a chieftaincy that was to be a subset of the government itself.

Matters were not to rest there. As is well known, the president of Ghana and his government were removed from office in February 1966 by Ghana's first military coup d'etat. For three years direct military rule was imposed by the military's National Liberation Council (NLC). After June 1966 that body sought advice from the Political Committee, a formally constituted civilian body, many of whom had been NLM and later UP activists and some of whom had recently been released from long periods of detention or exile.[38] The NLC proscribed the CPP and began the issuing of a large number of decrees which, amongst other things, sought to reverse those CPP policies which it and its advisors found most repugnant.

NLC Decree No. 112 dealt with chieftaincy. It was an attempt to remove all those whose chieftaincy could be shown to have been the direct result of the CPP government's patronage. It also demoted all those sub-chiefs who had been promoted to paramount chief status by the ousted government. 'Chiefs at any time occupying stools specified in this ... decree, these stools, the Chiefs of which were contrary to customary law ... elevated ... to the status of paramount chiefs by the government of Kwame Nkrumah shall ... be deemed to have been reverted [sic] to the status enjoyed by the Chiefs of these stools immediately before the said elevation.'[39] Well over 100 chiefs were destooled as a result of this decision. The numbers are instructive. Something like 45 chiefs were destooled in the south and a slightly smaller figure in Ashanti. For those who like tidy endings to stories, the CPP-approved Okyenhene of Akyem Abuakwa was destooled and Nana Ofori Atta II was re-enstooled as a result of these changes. At a less exalted level, an even larger number of chiefs were stripped of their paramountcies and demoted to sub-chief status or destooled.[40] This redressive action demonstrated above all just how out of hand the process of creating traditional states and paramounts had become. This was obviously a moment to be enjoyed for those who had opposed the CPP government and had lost.

The damage to chieftaincy was, however, not repaired. It was in any case

[38] There were denials and counter-denials about whether the Political Committee and even the NLC might be regarded as the UP in another guise. On this heated debate see K. Danso-Boafo, *Political biography of Dr. Kofi Busia*, p. 75.

[39] NLC Decree No. 112. 5 December 1966. para. 1.

[40] Most notably in Ashanti (28), Brong Ahafo (25) and the Volta Region.

uneven damage. In the more remote and less politically contested areas, chieftaincy had in some cases simply bent with the wind rather than snapping. It is possible to argue that minor chiefs and village headmen who were less obviously in the firing-line had continued to perform their roles without undue interference at a time when their seniors were being attacked or replaced. The NLC period and the successor civilian regime under the chairmanship of Edward Akuffo-Addo, a founder member of the UGCC, and the deputy chairmanship of the old leader of the NLM, Dr Kofi Busia, were welcomed by many of those who had opposed the CPP's policies on chieftaincy. Chiefs and those who continued to regard chiefs as the cornerstones of Ghanaian civil society were mollified by policies such as those implicit in NLC Decree No. 112.

The NLC instituted a major commission of enquiry into electoral and local government reform which reported in 1968. It heard from many chiefs in the course of its deliberations and their views were heard sympathetically. But it was not to recommend that chiefs should once again administer and judge rural Ghanaians. Instead the commissioners addressed the chaotic mess that local government had become in recent years. Despite the clear evidence that many local councils were economically unviable, their numbers had proliferated from 70 in 1958[41] to 155 by 1962, and to 183 by 1965. The new recommended structure was, as might have been predicted from a report generated by a group dominated by those who had argued for federalism little more than a decade previously, regionalist in focus. But its concern with the lack of economies of scale led it to conclude that many traditional areas were unsuitable as the physical spaces for newly constructed local government units. If the traditional if contested scopes of individual chieftaincies, traditional states, were not to match the ambit of new councils, the position of chiefs could not be restored. Although they were to recommend that new councils should again have one-third of their membership appointed by traditional councils, they were not to recommend that chiefs were to regain direct access to stool revenues. The new district councils were, the commissioners recommended, to continue to make a financial contribution to traditional authorities while having responsibility for 'the management of stool lands'. The NLM's earlier commitment to an Upper House for chiefs and the UP's later manifesto undertaking 'to uphold and maintain the institution of chieftaincy ... and to ensure that the chiefs play a democratic and effective part in the development of Ghana' were quietly sidelined. The CPP had left the NLC and later governments with a battered chieftaincy from which national politicians had little to fear. Chiefs were no longer a force on the national stage.

Although the commissioners heard arguments for an enhanced role for chiefs, their conclusions adopted the modernizing language of both the later colonial regime and the CPP: 'the complexity and stress of modern life make it difficult to apply the customary procedures associated with the deliberations of chiefs to the urgent tasks of local government ... it would be a retrograde step to accord them

[41] That marked a significant reduction in the earlier number of just less than 300 such units which ranged in size from 1,000 to nearly 400,000 persons for the largest of the district councils.

the majority of seats on ... councils'.[42] Although chiefs had every reason to regard the NLC government as well disposed towards them in contrast with the deposed CPP regime, it and its successors were never to restore to chiefs serious access to wealth or power.

In its most general respects, this remained the position until relatively recently. But, as suggested in earlier parts of this book, materialist accounts of chieftaincy provide us with only some of the clues about what chieftaincy can mean. Although it would be stretching the evidence to agree wholeheartedly with A.S.Y. Andoh when, close as he was to these later events, he claimed that 'community feeling engendered by traditional states and chiefs was overpoweringly strong',[43] chiefs meant and still mean something more than can be expressed by materialist arguments.

It is immensely hard to capture quite what such meanings might be. They differ greatly from place to place just as they have been immensely varied over time. They are also quite frequently internally contradictory, as are most of our deeper feelings. Generations of Ghanaian lawyers, politicians and scholars have tried to specify what 'the position of the chief' might be; most of them implicitly signal just how difficult such specification proves to be. Chiefs, as we have seen, could be at once the object of populist scorn whilst becoming rallying-points in circumstances where regional well-being or pride was being challenged.[44] They have at one time or another been seen as the epitome of the most negative aspects of the past whilst acting in more than merely symbolic fashion as living embodiments of a more obviously African system of governance than the local adaptations of Western forms. They have been viewed as arcane obstacles to progress and then as defensive bastions when 'progress' threatened local and personal liberty. Chieftaincy has historically been seen as an inept provider of local administration but, as in more recent years, when the capacity of central government to provide such administration beyond the city limits has withered, chiefs have again been turned to as arbitrators and as allocators of values.[45]

The wider perception of chiefs as significant figures in the Ghanaian landscape was given formal recognition in the 1992 constitution. The constitutional committee which drew up the draft, eventually approved by popular referendum, had the courage to break with 40 years of history. The constitution removed the right of government to recognize or refuse to recognize newly appointed chiefs. That right reverts to communities and is now regulated by traditional law and custom. Chiefs

---

[42] Report of the Commission of Enquiry into Electoral and Local Government Affairs, Accra, 1968, para. 92, NAG ADM 5/3/174.

[43] 'The structure of local government 1951–1966', paper given to the Institute of African Studies, Legon, in March 1967 (in the IAS Library, Legon). Andoh had served as secretary to the Asantehene as well as enjoying a distinguished academic career at Legon.

[44] As was clearly the case in mid-1983 when Asante opposition to Flight-Lieutenant Rawlings's PNDC regime looked to the Asantehene for leadership; in order to reduce serious tension, he very wisely refused this poisoned chalice.

[45] Nii Lamptey, the great Ghanaian footballer well-known to British fans as a mid-fielder for Coventry City, was reported to have been offered one of the Ga stools. Explaining his rejection of high office he said 'When you are chief you have to sort out many problems – you can imagine how many there are when we have three million people.' *Independent* (London), 21 October 1995.

163

Conclusions

may now hold public office. Chieftaincy has consequently become a more enticing prospect and more candidates for high office are now drawn from the educated and professional elite, people who in recent years would have made every effort to escape selection in order to get on with their careers. The more permissive nature of the 1992 constitution is not, however, a total explanation of why becoming a chief has become the ambition of many successful businessmen and professionals. It is possible that in some cases chieftaincy provides a culturally legitimate avenue which falls short of outright boasting for those who wish to signal their material success. Whatever we might conclude, a major Ghanaian scholar and a member of that constitutional committee writes: 'My supposition is that by virtue of the 1992 Constitution Chieftaincy has become a state agency somewhat on the lines of ... the colonial period.'[46] Chiefs, however, seem unlikely to regain their access to revenue or the relative autonomy they enjoyed in the interwar period.

It would take a more subtle scholar than myself and a very different research project to begin to unravel the deeper meanings that chieftaincy has for some Ghanaians. Some of these have been alluded to earlier. Chiefs continue to symbolize place and Ghanaians can be deeply attached to their physical origins, the physical space of their families and their families' ancestors. Place is more than space; it brings together history, including the investment of generations in making that space habitable and economically viable, and the local deities who have smiled or frowned on all of that effort and invention. As for many of us, such spaces are home even if we are pressed by circumstance to live away from home. Chiefs sitting in state, bejewelled and magnificent, sum up pride in locality and history even if their authority is extremely limited. Chiefs through their intermediary role with the past are also tangible and comforting figures who link place with its spiritual meanings and with ancestors. While chiefs share with us all the weaknesses as well as the strengths involved in being human, they inhabit a particular niche in long chains of history. That complex conjuncture, which is only partially spelled out here, is of unusual importance when the material history of localities and families has been one of suffering and struggle; this has been the sad lot of all too many Ghanaians in recent history. It is entirely possible that some Ghanaians, who share with much of the world a deep cynicism born of bitter experience about politicians and their promises, find in chieftaincy something that is reassuring rather precisely because of its ambivalent position in what has become the disturbing discourse of failing modernity. Whatever answers future researchers uncover to questions about the essence of Ghanaian chieftaincy, that chieftaincy in Ghana survived at all in the light of the rough processes I have tried to describe is something of a miracle. For those who enjoyed and understood the meanings of that wonderful ceremony in Kumase in 1995 with which this book began, that miracle is worthy of celebration.

[46] Personal communication from Nana Arhin Brempong, June 1998. He was chairman of Ghana's National Commission on Culture and is the author of some of the most important and authoritative scholarly work on the Akan.

Bibliography

This is a select bibliography and includes the secondary material I have footnoted as well the published material which has most influenced my thinking. For those eager to follow up the archival and press material I have used, all of the necessary finding data is fully cited in footnotes. The national archives consulted were the Public Record Office, Kew, and the National Archives of Ghana in both Accra and Koforidua. In addition I used the Akyem Abuakwa State Archives located in the Ofori Panin Fie in Kyebi. Most of the ephemera consulted were located in the Africana section of the Balme Library and the library of the Institute of African Studies at the University of Ghana, Legon. The newspaper research was carried out in the National Archives of Ghana in Accra, the library of the IAS, Legon, and the British Library's newspaper holdings at Colindale.

Adamafio, T. *By Nkrumah's side; the labour and the wounds.* Westcoat in association with Rex Collings, Accra, 1982.

Addo-Fening, R. *Akyem Abuakwa 1700-1943; from Ofori Panin to Sir Ofori Atta.* Norwegian University of Science and Technology, African Series, No. 1. Trondheim, 1997.

— 'Customary land tenure system in Akyem Abuakwa', *Universitas,* 9, November, 1987.

Adu, A.L. *The civil service in Commonwealth Africa.* Allen & Unwin, London, 1969.

Akoto, B.O. *Struggle against dictatorship in Ghana.* Payless Publishers, Kumase, 1992.

Akyeampong, H.K, *The Akim Abuakwa crisis.* Accra, 1958.

— *Journey to independence and after* [edited letters of J.B.Danquah], Vol. III (1952–7). George Boakie, Accra, 1972.

— *The doyen speaks: some of the historic speeches of Dr. J.B. Danquah.* George Boakie, Accra, 1976.

Allman, J.M. *The quills of the porcupine; Asante nationalism in an emergent Ghana.* University of Wisconsin press, Madison, 1993.

Allott,A. *Essays in African law.* Butterworth, London, 1980.

Amonoo, B. *Ghana 1957-1966; politics of institutional dualism.* Allen & Unwin, London, 1981.

Andoh, A.S.Y. 'Local government and local development in Ghana', *Insight* 2, 1, February 1967.

Bibliography

— 'The Asante National Liberation Movement of the 1950s in retrospect' in E. Schild-krout (ed.), *The Golden Stool, op cit.*

Appiah, J. *The man J.B. Danquah.* Academy of Arts and Sciences, Accra, 1974.

— *Joe Appiah; the autobiography of an African patriot.* Praeger, New York, 1990.

Apter, D. *The Gold Coast in transition.* Princeton University Press, Princeton, 1955.

— 'The role of traditionalism in the political modernization of Ghana and Uganda', *World Politics* 13, 1960.

— 'Some reflections on the role of a political opposition in new nations', *Comparative studies in society and history* 4, 1962.

— 'Ghana' in James S. Coleman and Carl G. Rosberg (eds), *Political parties and national integration in tropical Africa.* University of California Press, Berkeley, 1964.

Arhin, K. *A profile of Brong Kyempim.* Afram Publishers, Accra, 1979.

— *Traditional rule in Ghana past and present.* Sedco, Accra, 1985.

— 'The search for "constitutional chieftaincy"' in K.Arhin (ed.), *The life and work of Kwame Nkrumah.* Sedco, Accra, 1991.

Armah, K. *Ghana; Nkrumah's legacy.* Rex Collings, London, 1974.

Attobrah, K. *The kings of Akyem Abuakwa and the ninety-nine years war against Asante.* Ghana Publishing Corporation, Accra, 1976.

Austin, D. *Politics in Ghana, 1946–60.* OUP, London, 1964.

— 'Opposition in Ghana, 1947-1967', *Government and Opposition* 2,4, 1967.

Beckman, B. *Organizing the farmers: cocoa politics and national development in Ghana.* SIAS, Uppsala, 1976.

Bediako, K.A. *The downfall of Kwame Nkrumah,* the author, Accra, n.d. but 1967.

Bennion, F.A.F. *The constitutional law of Ghana.* Butterworth, London, 1962.

Bing, G. *Reap the whirlwind; an account of Kwame Nkrumah's Ghana from 1950 to 1966.* Macgibbon & Kee, London, 1968.

Boahen, A. Adu. *African perspectives on colonialism.* Johns Hopkins Press, Baltimore, 1987.

— *The Ghanaian sphinx; reflections on the contemporary history of Ghana, 1972-1987.* Ghana Academy of Arts and Sciences, Accra, 1989.

Bowdich, T. *Mission from Cape Coast Castle to Ashantee,* John Murray, London, 1819.

Busia, K.A. *The position of the chief in the modern political system of Ashanti.* OUP, London, 1951.

Casely-Hayford, J.E. *Gold Coast native institutions.* Frank Cass, London (reprint), 1970.

Crook, R.C. 'Local elites and national politics in Ghana; a case study of political centraliza-tion and local politics in Offinso (Ashanti) 1945-66'. PhD, University of London, 1978.

— 'Decolonization, the colonial state and chieftaincy in the Gold Coast', *African Affairs* 85, 338, 1986.

Danquah, J.B. *Akim Abuakwa Handbook.* Forster Groom, London, 1928.

— *Cases in Akan Law.* Routledge, London, 1928.

— *Akan laws and customs.* Routledge, London, 1928.

— *The voice of prophecy; Dr. J.B. Danquah's historical speech on bi-cameral legislature* (with an introduction by Yaw Twumasi). George Boakie, Accra, 1969.

— *The Ghanaian establishment.* Ghana Universities Press, Accra, 1997.

Danso-Boafo, K. *Political biography of Dr. Kofi Busia.* Ghana Universities Press, Accra, 1996.

Davidson, B. *Black Star.* Allen Lane, London, 1973.

Dei-Anang, M. *Ghana resurgent.* Waterville, Accra, 1964.

Drah, F.K. 'The Brong political movement' in K. Arhin (ed.), *A profile of Brong Kyempim, op. cit.*

Bibliography

Dunn, John and Robertson, A.F. *Dependence and opportunity; political change in Ahafo.* Cambridge University Press, Cambridge, 1973.

Du-Sautoy, P. *Community development in Ghana.* OUP, London, 1962.

Edsman, B. *Lawyers in Gold Coast politics, c. 1900–1945.* SIAS, Uppsala, 1979.

Frimpong, J.H. 'The Ghana parliament, 1957–66; a critical analysis'. PhD thesis, University of Exeter, 1970.

Frimpong, K. 'The Joint Provincial Council of Chiefs and the politics of independence, 1946–1958', in *Transactions of the Historical Society of Ghana,* Vol. XIV, 1973.

Genoud, R. *Nationalism and economic development in Ghana.* Praeger, New York, 1969.

Greenwood, A.F.'Ten years of local government in Ghana', *Journal of local administration overseas* 1,1, 1962.

Hailey, Lord, *An African Survey.* Clarendon Press, Oxford, 1938.

— *Native Administration in the British African territories.* HMSO, London, 1951.

Harvey, W.B. *Law and social change in Ghana.* Princeton University Press, Princeton, 1966.

Hinden, R. *Local government in the colonies.* The Fabian Society, London, 1950.

James, C.L.R. *Nkrumah and the Ghana revolution.* Allison & Busby, London, 1977.

Kesse-Adu, K. *The politics of political detention.* Ghana Publishing Corporation, Tema, 1971.

Kraus, J. 'On the politics of nationalism and social change in Ghana', *Journal of Modern African Studies* 7, 1, 1969.

— 'Cleavages, crises, parties and state power in Ghana'. PhD thesis, Johns Hopkins University, 1970.

Kyerematen, A.A.Y. *Daasebre Osei Tutu Agyeman Prempeh II, Asantehene; a distinguished traditional ruler of contemporary Ghana.* The University Press, Kumase, 1970.

Ladouceur, P. *Chiefs and politicians; the politics of regionalism in Northern Ghana.* Longman, Harlow, 1979.

Ninsin, K.A. and Drah, F.K. *In search for democracy in Ghana.* Asempa Publishers, Accra, 1987.

Nkrumah, K. *Ghana; the autobiography of Kwame Nkrumah.* Thomas Nelson, Edinburgh, 1957.

— *I speak of freedom.* Heinemann, London, 1961.

— *Dark days in Ghana.* Lawrence & Wishart, London, 1968.

Nsarkoh, J.K. *Local government in Ghana.* Ghana Universities Press, Accra, 1964.

Nti, J. 'Local administration in Ghana; a survey of administrative reform efforts in Ghana 1950–1971'. PhD thesis, University of London, 1972.

Nugent, P. 'An abandoned project? The nuances of chieftaincy, development and history in Ghana's Volta region', *Journal of Legal Pluralism and Unofficial Law.* 37–8, 1996.

Ofori Atta, W. *Ghana: a nation in crisis.* Ghana Academy of Arts and Sciences, Accra, 1988.

Ofosu-Appiah, L.H. *The life and times of Dr. J.B. Danquah.* Waterville, Accra, 1974.

Owusu, M. *Uses and abuses of political power: a case study of continuity and change in the politics of Ghana.* University of Chicago Press, Chicago, 1970.

— 'Kingship in contemporary Asante society', in E. Schildkrout (ed.), *The Golden Stool, op. cit.*

Padmore, G. *The Gold Coast revolution.* Dennis Dobson, London, 1953.

Peasah, J.A. 'The civil service of Ghana 1945-1960; a study in bureaucracy, politics and anti-colonial nationalism', PhD thesis, University of London, 1973.

Pobee, J.S. *Kwame Nkrumah and the church in Ghana, 1949-1966.* Asempa Publishers, Accra, 1988.

Price, J.H.O. 'Analysis of legislators' backgrounds', *West Africa,* 2041, 21 May, 1956.

Rathbone, R. (ed.) *Ghana; British documents on the end of Empire.* HMSO, London, 1992.

Bibliography

— *Murder and politics in colonial Ghana*. Yale University Press, New Haven, 1993.

— *Nana Sir Ofori Atta and the conservative nationalist tradition in Ghana*. Boston University African Studies Working Paper No. 183, Boston, MA, 1994.

— 'Police intelligence in Ghana in the late 1940s and 1950s', in R. F. Holland (ed.), *Emergencies and disorders in European empires after 1945*, Frank Cass, London, 1994.

— 'Defining Akyemfo; the construction of citizenship in Akyem Abuakwa, Ghana, 1700-1939.' in *Africa* 66, 4 ,1996.

Rattray, R.S. *Ashanti law and constitution*. OUP, Oxford, 1929.

Rubin, L. and Murray, P. *The constitution and government of Ghana*. Sweet & Maxwell, London, 1964 (2nd edn).

Sarbah, J.M. *Fante customary laws*. London, 1897.

Schiffer, H.B. 'Local administration and national development; fragmentation and centralisation in Ghana', *Canadian Journal of African Studies*, 4, 1, 1970.

Schildkrout, E. (ed.). *The Golden Stool; studies of the Asante centre and periphery*. American Museum of Natural History, New York, 1987.

Tiger, L. 'Bureaucracy and charisma in Ghana', *Journal of Asian and African Studies*, 1, 1, 1966/7.

Tordoff, W. *Ashanti under the Prempehs; 1888-1935*. OUP, London, 1965.

Twumasi, Y. 'Prelude to the rise of mass nationalism in Ghana, 1920–1949', *Ghana Social Science Journal* 3, 1976.

Wallis, C.A.G. 'Reorganisation of local government in Ghana', *Journal of African Administration*, 11, 1, 1959.

Index

169

Index

Index

Builders' Brigade 149
Busia, Kofi 45n, 102, 120n, 128, 151-2, 162

Cabinet *see* Convention Peoples' Party
Cape Coast 11, 25, 154
Casely-Hayford, J. E. 34
censuses 94
Central Province 57
Chapman, C. H. 154
Chichiwere 156
chief regional officers 100-1
chiefs and chieftaincy 2-8, 14, 16, 19-31, 33,
    45-6, 59-61, 64, 67-8, 70-1, 77, 80-3, 85,
    99, 107-10, 135, 137, 142-3, 150-1, 155,
    162-4; courts of law 11, 13, 15, 17-18,
    34, 47-55, 57; hierarchy 144-5, 160;
    paramount 32, 35, 84, 119, 145, 156,
    159-61; succession 35, 93 *see also* Houses
    of Chiefs *and* name or title
Chiefs (Recognition) Bill (1959) 142-3
citizenship 104-5
civil service 133
class, social 34, 77
Clegg, E. L. 41
Cobblah, Daniel 138n
cocoa 38, 67-8, 102-3, 139
Cocoa Marketing Board 102, 135
Cocoa Purchasing Company 61n
Codjoe, Samuel 152
colonialism *see* Britain; France; Ghana
Colony Region 19, 31, 33, 48, 64, 84, 86-9,
    94, 97
Comintern 24
commissioners *see* appeals commissioners;
    district commissioners; political
    commissioners; provincial
    commissioners; regional commissioners
Committee on Youth Organizations 24n
commoners 23-5, 53, 64, 97
concert parties 37
Constitution (Repeal of Restrictions) Bill
    142
constitutions 19-20, 59, 63, 66, 70-1, 86, 91,
    96, 101, 104, 114, 118, 130-2, 136-7, 141,
    151, 157, 163-4 *see also* Bing, Geoffrey;
    Bourne, Frederick; Coussey Committee;
    local constitutional commission
Convention Peoples' Party 6-8, 21-33, 35-
    44, 47, 59-75, 77-87, 89-92, 94-8, 104,

108, 111-12, 119-29, 132-6, 140-1, 143,
    146-8, 150-2, 157, 159n, 161-3; Action
    Troopers 103n, 123; Cabinet 29, 43-4,
    46, 51-7, 60-1, 66-8, 72, 81-3, 85-6, 95,
    98-107, 109-10, 114-16, 124-5, 129-32,
    137, 142, 144, 152-6, 159-60; Central
    Committee 158
corporatism 3
Côte d'Ivoire 9n
councils *see* district councils; local councils;
    municipal councils; provincial councils;
    regional councils; state councils;
    territorial councils; traditional councils
    and name
courts *see* local courts; native courts
Coussey Committee 20-1, 26, 29-30, 43, 46-
    7, 50, 54, 60-1, 82, 87
Coussey, Henley 56
custom 16, 18, 20, 87, 122, 127-8, 142, 144,
    146-7, 156, 163 *see also* law; tradition

Daily Graphic 59, 107, 140, 152
Dangbe 55
Danquah, J. B. 15, 26n, 34, 38-40, 62, 72,
    79-80, 90, 96-7, 100, 121-3, 126, 149,
    152n
dashing *see* bribery
decentralization 31
democracy 3, 16, 31, 47, 73, 95, 116
Denkyira 54-5, 62
Denyase 44, 69, 125
Denyasehene 44
deportation 103-6, 129, 137, 152-4 *see also*
    exile, internal
Deportation Indemnity Act (1958) 137
depression, economic 15
Derikikyi, Musa 104-5
destoolment 13, 18, 24, 27, 33, 36-7, 40-1,
    44, 69, 73-5, 97, 120n, 126-30, 132-3,
    141-4, 146-8, 154, 156, 159n, 161
development, economic 3, 17, 74, 77, 80, 94,
    102, 132-5, 148, 150, 158 *see also* village
    development committees
devolution 136
diamonds 31, 43
Dickson, C. de Graft 133, 154
district commissioners 32, 37, 101, 154-6
district councils 30, 162
Djebian 53

171

Index

Index

Jackson, John 98n, 114, 123
Jamasehene 158-9
Jibowu Commission of Enquiry 61n
Johnson, J. C. de Graft 77
Joint Provincial Council 19, 23, 28, 39-40, 59-63, 68, 72, 79, 87-8, 96, 102, 110, 114-17, 127-8, 131, 148
Joint Territorial Council 26
Juaben 144
Juaben Serwah II, Nana 144n
Juaso Stool 27
justice *see* law

kalabule see bribery
Kaleo, Jateo 142
Kessie, Cobina 97
Keta 53
Kibi *see* Kyebi
Kofi Dei, Nana 141n
Koforidua 154
Kojo Odei II, Nana 62
Kojo Tah 156
Kokofu 69
Kole, Nene Azzu Mate 28
Korbo, E. H. T. 154
Korsah, Arku 105n
Korsah Commission 50-1, 54, 56
Kotoku State Council 120
Kpandu 81
Krobo people 44
Krobos 57
Krontihene 124, 127n
Kukurantumi 39, 62, 73, 97, 126-7
Kumase 1, 26-7, 62, 69, 84, 97, 106, 118, 120, 128, 154, 164; Municipal Council 100, 120; State Council 118, 120, 128, 141
Kumasehene 120
Kumawu 75
Kumawuhene 75
Kwabena Kena II, Nana 72-3, 79, 97, 121, 126
Kwadjo Darko, Nana 152
Kwahu *see* Kwawu
Kwama Gyebi Ababio, Nana 28
Kwawu 27, 57, 94
Kyebi 38-9, 72-3, 79, 89-90, 97, 114-15, 127, 148

labour 10, 13

Lagos, Salami 106
Lamptey, Kwesi 27
Lamptey, Nii 163n
land 10, 13, 15, 31, 34, 45-6, 81, 85, 92, 98, 122, 127-8, 134, 145, 155-6, 162
law 11-12, 18, 21, 34, 48, 52, 58, 83-4, 87, 89, 92, 97, 101, 122-4, 138, 142-3, 149, 151, 153-4 *see also* custom; tradition
lawyers 49-50, 55-6
Lebanese 104
Legislative Assembly 21, 28, 32, 40, 52, 61, 63, 67, 69-70, 72, 80, 85, 96, 98, 100, 118, 127, 131, 137-8, 142, 151; Upper House 30, 60, 87, 162
Legislative Council 18-21, 30, 39, 44, 49, 50
Legon 56
licensing 13, 15, 49
lineage 35
local constitutional committee 68, 83
local councils 21, 30-2, 36-7, 42-7, 65-6, 72-3, 80-1, 84-5, 89-91, 95, 98, 120, 122-4, 134-5, 154-7, 162
local courts 50-2, 55-8, 68, 79, 85, 124-5, 154 *see also* native courts
Local Courts Act (1958) 52
local government 8, 10-11, 16-18, 21, 29-30, 40-1, 49, 57-8, 68-9, 95, 123-5, 130, 134-5, 162-3 *see also* Ministry of Local Government
Local Government Councils (Extension of Tenure in Office) Ordinance 85, 95n
Local Government Ordinance (1951) 30, 32, 43, 80-1, 85, 124, 154
Lyttleton, Oliver 45n

Mallalieu, E. L. 121n
Mampong 69, 145
Mamponghene 145
Mandela, Nelson 6
Mankrado 39
Manso Akroso 54
Manso Nkwanta 156
Manya Krobo 44, 53, 123
Marxism-Leninism 22
men 93
Mensah, Kwabena 40
Ministry of Justice 56-7, 129
Ministry of Local Government 31-2, 42-7, 51-6, 60-2, 68, 72, 81, 85-6, 89-91, 100,

173

Index

Index

political commissioners 129-30
Political Committee 161
politics 6, 24, 26, 45-6, 58, 69-70, 73-4, 76, 89-92, 94-5, 99, 101, 104, 107, 155; and chieftaincy 2, 7-8, 11, 15, 19, 34-8, 40, 60-3, 79, 82-3, 93, 98, 109, 111, 116-17, 120-2, 132-3, 146-7, 157-60
Pomase 42
Positive Action 22, 25, 27, 41
press 107, 129 *see also* name of newspaper
Prevention of Discrimination Act (1957) *see* Avoidance of Discrimination Act
Preventive Detention Act 103, 125, 138, 151-2, 158
provincial commissioners 101
provincial councils 131n
Public Meetings and Processions Regulations 90, 109

Quist, C. W. 107

rates *see* taxation
Rattray, R. S. 34
Rawlings, J. J. 163n
regional assemblies 86-7, 98-9, 102, 109-10, 118, 124, 130, 136
regional commissioners 32, 100-2, 110, 114, 116, 119-20, 123-4, 126-7, 129-30, 133-5, 144, 153-9
regional councils 30, 114
rioting 19, 41-2, 74, 88
ritual 17, 24
roads 13
royalties 31, 43
royalty 23-4
rural areas 93, 101-2
Russell, Colin 101, 144

Sakyi, Baffuor Kwesi Dua 79n
Sampson, Magnus 128
Sarbah, John Mensah 34, 48n
Sarko Addo Commission 118, 128
schools *see* education
Scott, G. L. 121n
Sedition Bill 152
Sefwi 9
Sekondi Takoradi 52, 89
Senchere, E. K. 84n
Shama 53, 89

slavery 15n
socialism 71, 72n
South Africa 6
Southern Togoland Council 28
Special Delegates' Conference 26
Staff (Local Government Council) Regulations (1955) 91
state 123
state councils 17, 21, 60, 85, 90, 97-8, 130, 132, 136, 144, 147, 156-7, 160 *see also* name
State Councils (Amendment) Bill (1956) 88, 160
State Councils (Amendment) Ordinance 84
State Councils Ordinance 84, 98
State Councils Regulations (1954) 127
Statutory Instruments Bill 154
stool lands *see* land
Stool Lands Act (1958) 128
Stool Lands (Amendment) Act (1960) 156
Stool Property (Recovery and Validation) Bill 142n
stools 13, 21, 26-7, 35, 37, 71, 84n, 92-3, 157, 163n *see also* destoolment; enstoolment
strikes 22, 27
Suisi 53
Sunyani 154
Supreme Court 52, 131, 142

Tafo 39, 72-3
Tafohene 27n, 97
Tamale 25, 154
Tampuri, M. 133
taxation 10, 17, 31, 34, 42, 55, 80, 95, 134, 155
Taylor, E. Kurankyi 77
Tekyiman 144
Tekyimanhene 69
Tema port 136
territorial councils 26, 29-30, 59-60, 63n, 65, 68
Tetremhene 156
thrones *see* stools
Timothy, Bankole 89, 107
Togoland Congress 107, 152-3
Tolon Na 65, 148
Towns Ordinance 13
trade 10, 104

Index